Music on the Internet

(and where to find it)

Ian Waugh

PC Publishing

PC Publishing
Export House
130 Vale Road
Kent TN9 1SP
UK

Tel 01732 770893
Fax 01732 770268
email info@pc-pubs.demon.co.uk
website http://www.pc-pubs.demon.co.uk

First published 1998
© PC Publishing

ISBN 1 870775 58 9

British Library Cataloguing in Publication Data
A catalogue record for this book is available from the British Library

Printed in Great Britain by Bell and Bain, Glasgow

Contents

Introduction

You're connected! You're on-line! You're wired!

You're also in a hurry.

Surfing is great fun but your time vanishes faster than a politician's promise.

There is so much information out there that finding it can be like looking for a needle in a haystack. Even the Search Engines don't have all the answers – and sometimes they can be so-o-o-o-o-o slow...

This book is designed to help you find things on the Net fast. One of its most important sections is the list of Web addresses. These cover a wide variety of sites which will interest everyone involved in the playing, performing, creation and enjoyment of music. They are categorised and indexed to help you find what you want quickly.

There is also a section on searching the Web with hints and tips on how to do it faster and more efficiently. This includes making better use of the on-line search engines and using search applications which can search further, wider and faster.

This is not a techy tome and although it contains some information about the Web and the Internet it does assume that you already have access to the Net. If you want a 'What is the Internet?' book, you'll find them two shelves along on the left. Even better, pick up one of the dozens of magazines about the Net at your local newsagent and they'll tell you what you need and how to get connected.

Once you are on-line, prepare for the greatest info-fest you can imagine. No book, no magazine, no newspaper, no library could possibly contain as much up-to-date information as the Net. Someone releases a software update, some new sounds for a synthesiser, a new musical instrument, some editing software – you can find out about it within hours on the Net. You don't have to wait six weeks to read about it in a magazine – or even 24 hours to read about it in a newspaper.

The Net also gives you access to some of the most knowledgeable people in the music business – developers, manufacturers and experienced users! If you have a problem, the chances are someone out there knows how to fix it.

Welcome to the information age. Welcome, literally, to the world of music.

Dedication

To Julia, my wife

...without whose understanding and encouragement this book would never have been written and with whom life simply gets better and better and better...

With much love

Welcome to the Web

The terms 'the Web' and 'the Internet' are generally used interchangeably but they are not quite the same thing. For the sake of splitting a few hairs, let's look at what they are.

The Internet

Ask a number of different people what the Internet is and the chances are you'll get a range of answers. Even so-called experts may describe it in different ways but the Internet is really quite easy to understand. It's its vastness which can sometimes make it seem awesome!

Let's say you work in an office and use a computer to write letters, plan production schedules and play games (it's okay, I won't tell). You get an assistant to help with the planning and it would be useful if he could share the production data, so the company links – or networks – the two machines. He can now access the production data stored on your computer and you can access the data on his.

The office expands, there are more and more people, each with a computer. Many share tasks and need to share information so the company networks all the computers. You can now access information from many computers and send messages to other people in the office.

This is a miniature Internet. Such inter-office connections were usually simply called a Network but recently the term Intranet is being used.

Now, imagine your office being linked to a similar office down the street and to one across town and imagine those offices being linked to other offices in other towns and even in other countries. This is a little like the Internet. Stretch your imagination to include millions of computers and you have an idea of its size.

The Internet has been aptly described as a network of networks. At its heart is a collection of high speed host computers, many situated in government departments, education, large corporations and so on. No one is really sure how many computers are on the Internet but the figure must be over 10 million. But that's just a guesstimate – it could be more, perhaps even 20 million. Yes, it's big!

When you log on or connect to the Internet, your computer dials into the host computer of your ISP (Internet Service Provider) which is permanently connected to the Internet. Once you are 'in' or logged on you can access any of the millions of computers connected to the Net.

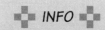

INFO

Rightly or wrongly, I bow to popular usage and you'll often find the terms Web and Net used in this book to mean more or less the same thing. However, as the book is mainly about the Web, there should be no confusion.

INFO

An Intranet is an office network which uses Web-type tools such as a browser, email, Web sites and so on for communication.

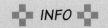

*T*he Internet was originally developed in 1969 by a department of the Defence Organisation in the USA. Its purpose was to allow information to be transferred between strategic sites using several different routes so if one line of communication was destroyed during a war, for example, the information could still be sent along other lines.

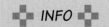

*F*TP – File Transfer Protocol, a system which allows files to be transferred between computers. There's more about this a few pages on.

What is the Web?

The Web – or the World Wide Web to give it its full title – is a way of accessing the Internet. It's highly graphic, easy to use and adopts a system of Hyperlinks which you click on with the mouse to take you from one site to another.

Without doubt, the advent of the Web played the most important part in the popularisation of the Internet. Before the Web, you had to access the computers, files and information on the Internet by typing in often arcane instructions or using some pretty obscure software.

For the vast majority of people, the Web is by far the easiest way to use the Net and most people will never need or want – or know! – any other kind of access. Indeed, such is the popularity of the Web that the other forms of access have all but been forgotten, certainly for popular use.

However, you may still see terms such as Gopher, Archie, Telnet, WAIS and FTP, to name but a few, in magazines and books about the Net. These are all ways of connecting to, searching and communicating with the computers on the Net.

No apologies at all for ignoring them all with the exception of one – FTP – although some Net users, particularly those on CiX, find Telnet useful for certain types of communication. (CiX is the Compulink Information eXchange, a UK-based conferencing system which also offers connection to the Internet. There's more about CiX in Chapter 5.)

To be slightly technical, an Internet computer (commonly called a server) must be compatible with the Web in order to allow users to access it via a Web browser. The Web, therefore, can be regarded as a subset of the entire Internet but the Web is so popular and so powerful that virtually all popular sites now support it.

All of which leads us neatly into...

Browsers

For the vast majority of Internet users, the browser is the Internet. It is certainly the Web. It is a window on the world through which you travel, see Web sites, search for information and download files. Most also include an email facility.

The main browsers in use today have been developed by Microsoft and Netscape. Microsoft's browser is Internet Explorer, Figure 1.1. Netscape's browser is Netscape Navigator but the company has also produced a range of associated and ancillary software such as Netscape Communicator which incorporates Navigator and includes several additional features.

In the main, any extra features you may find in a browser offer additional functionality rather than enhancing your browsing of the Web. Netscape's Collabra, for example, provides discussion forums that make it easy to share information and create a 'knowledge base'. Netscape Composer helps you to create on-line documents, and Netscape

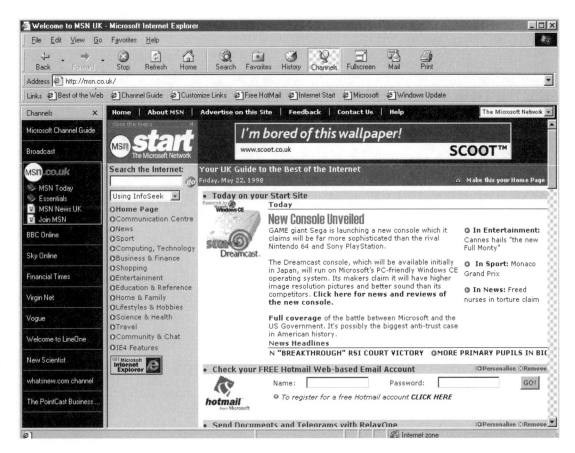

Figure 1.1 Internet Explorer

Conference supports audio/video conferencing. Netscape Netcaster, Figure 1.2, enables you to subscribe to and schedule automatic delivery of information instead of manually downloading and searching for information.

But the basic browsing functions of all browsers are more or less the same. By definition, they must allow you to view Web pages and to move from one to the other via Hyperlinks. However, as the Web has developed, so has the system used to create and view Web pages so you may need to keep updating your browser in order to keep up to date with all the new goodies the Web developers keep producing. There's a bit more about these later in this chapter.

Although Internet Explorer (IE) and Netscape probably account for well over 90 percent of browsers in common use, they are not the only ones available by any means. However, as the developers have added more and more facilities, some people say they have become bloated and look for trimmer solutions.

Unless you have a particular reason for using an alternative browser, there seems to be little to be gained by forsaking the most popular ones. After all, when designing Web pages, developers make sure they work with IE and Netscape. But if you wish to experiment – a desire not in any way to be denied – you will find copious references to other browsers if you do a search on the Web – see Chapter 4.

✛ *INFO* ✛

The Web was developed in 1989 for the European Laboratory for Particle Physics (commonly referred to as CERN – Conseil Européen pour la Recherche Nucléaire) by Timothy Berners-Lee.

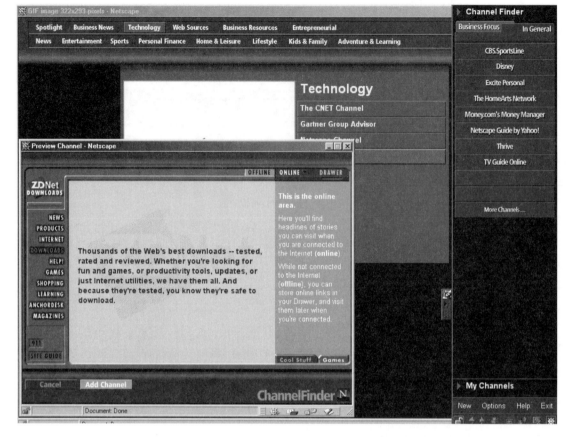

Figure 1.2 Netscape
Netcaster

Browsers are in a continuous state of change so there's little point in going into detail about any of them but do please read the rest of this chapter. The main feature of a browser – that which enables them to be used with the Web – is common to them all and that is...

Hyperlinks

Hyperlinks are what make the Web so easy to use. Essentially, they 'point' to a Web page on a site on a computer linked to the Internet. By clicking on the 'link' you can jump from one page to another and from one computer to another even though they may be on opposite sides of the world.

In most Web pages, hyperlinks appear as underlined text, often in blue as in Figure 1.3. You can't see the colour but you can see the underlines.

However, pictures can also contain hyperlinks. You can tell if they do because when you move the mouse pointer around the page in a Web browser, if it moves over a hyperlink, the pointer will change into a pointing finger as in Figure 1.4. Click here to win lots of money. Not.

If you look at the bottom of the browser, Figure 1.5, it will tell you where the link is pointing. It could be a different place on the same page, a different page on the same Web or a page on a Web half way across the

Figure 1.3 Each line of underlined text is a hyperlink, and clicking on one will take you to a new page containing information about the book

Figure 1.4 If you move the cursor over a picture and the cursor turns into a pointing finger, you know the image contains a hyperlink

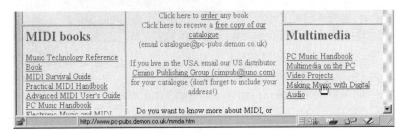

Figure 1.5 When you rest the cursor on a hyperlink, the URL appears at the foot of the browser

world. Technically, the address is known as the URL (coming up in the next chapter) and clicking on the link will take you there.

That's really all there is to hyperlinks and to surfing the Web! You look, you browse, you point, you click, you surf...

You can now dive off into the other chapters of this book. If you want to hang around here you'll find a bit more information about how the Web works. It's not essential, but you might find it interesting and it may help you understand some of the problems and error messages you may encounter during your time in cyberspace.

Frames

Many modern sites uses frames which is simply a way of dividing the page into two or more sections which can each contain different documents. It sounds like a good idea but when frames were first introduced a few years ago they caused havoc. Many browsers didn't support them so users had to upgrade to a browser which did. The time taken to display frame-based pages seemed longer and there were many badly-designed sites with frames which made them far more difficult to navigate than they should have been.

Figure 1.6 Many framed
pages use one frame to show
the contents of the site

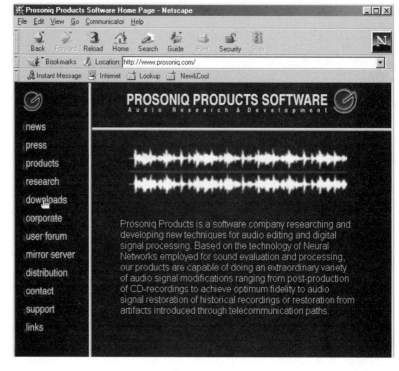

Most of these problems have now been solved and some of the more thoughtful sites offer the user a choice of a frames or no frames display. The widespread use of faster modems has cut down the display time and most site designers – but not all – are using frames sensibly.

The most common use of frames is to create a strip down one side to hold a menu or contents list with the currently-selected page displayed in the body of the browser. This allows you to see what's on offer at all times while still being able to move from page to page. Figure 1.6 shows the Prosoniq site which has a banner frame along the top and a contents frame down the left.

HTML – the language of the Web

The pages that you see when you surf the Web have to be designed and constructed in some way. A simple method called HTML was devised to do it.

HTML stands for HyperText Markup Language. It's based around a series of tags which are used to tell Web browsers how to display text and graphics and how to react when a user clicks on a hyperlink. It's not a programming language as such, more a system of 'marking up' normal text to tell the browser how it should be displayed. If you're old enough to remember DOS-based wordprocessors such as WordPerfect, you may recall that they had a 'reveal codes' option which did a similar thing.

HTML is not terribly complicated to learn although, as with all new things, it may seem strange at first. The good news is, you really need know nothing at all about HTML in order to surf the Web. However, if you're just a tad curious, read on.

Basic HTML instructions set a font size, say whether it should appear in bold or italics and where it should be positioned. As Web designers became more ambitious, HTML has developed to accommodate all sorts of other functions such as tables, forms, and multimedia objects.

Here's a very short and simple example of HTML:

```
<HTML>
<HEAD>
<TITLE>Gigs Galore!</TITLE>
</HEAD>
<BODY>
If you're looking for a gig, you've come to the right place.
Greg's Gig Room lists all the venues in all the towns in the South East
of England.
</BODY>
</HTML>
```

The tags are the instructions inbetween the angled brackets < >. Many browsers allow you to see the native HTML text used to create the page you are currently viewing. In Netscape, for example, it's accessed from the View/Page Source menu.

HTML has undergone several enhancements over the years and the latest browsers often support 'unofficial' HTML features which may – or may not – be ratified by the W3C in who-knows-how-many month's time?

You don't need a special editor to produce HTML documents – they can be created in any wordprocessor and saved as straightforward text. In fact, some Web professionals create their Web pages almost entirely in a text editor.

Web design software

But for us mere mortals, there are many alternatives, graphic-based HTML editors – Web page designers – which help you to create Web pages by dragging and dropping images, selecting text attributes from a menu or toolbox as you do in a wordprocessor and you may never even see a line of HTML.

Programs to look out for include: Microsoft's FrontPage 98 (www.microsoft.com), Macromedia's Dreamweaver (www.dreamweaver.com), Corel's WebMaster Suite (www.corel.com), SoftQuad's HoTMetal Pro (www.softquad.co.uk), Claris Home Page (www.claris.com), Adobe Page Mill (www.adobe.co.uk), Allaire Home Site (www.allaire.com), Asymetric Web Publisher (www.asymetrix.com), Netscape Composer (www.netscape.com), and MicroVision's WebExpress (www.mvd.com).

There are also many books about Web page design, and the Internet and computer magazines regularly run features on the subject. Let's get back to our subject which is seeing what makes the Web work.

Java

Again, with Java, we touch on a programming aspect of the Web and, again, you don't have to get involved with it but you will undoubtedly come across it on the Web, even if it's just in an error message!

There are two sides to Java and although it may seem a bit like splitting hairs, it's as well to note the difference. Java is an object-oriented programming language, similar to C++ but smaller. It was designed to be platform-independent so it can run on any computer which makes it ideal for use on the Web.

JavaScript is a scripting language that is related to Java but more like AppleScript or VisualBasic scripting. It's not as powerful as Java but it's easier to write and it can be included directly in HTML pages.

The most popular use of Java on the Web is for applets which may perform a variety of functions such as producing animations and special effects. JavaScript can also be used for animation and it is commonly used for validating forms, and for other types of interaction with the user.

There are lots of books on Java and JavaScript should you want to get involved and, of course, the Web is littered with Java sites including many with applets you can use or buy.

As the Web has developed, so additions have been made to HTML, and other goodies, like Java, have appeared on the scene. If you want to take advantage of all the latest developments it's important that you use a recent browser. If you don't, your browser may well throw up error messages as it encounters new stuff which it doesn't recognise as in Figure 1.7. You can usually download browser updates from most sites including

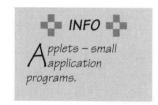

Figure 1.7 JavaScript error – rare is the surfer who never sees one of these

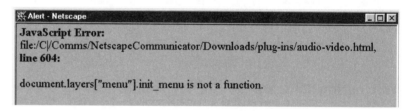

those of Netscape and Microsoft. The downside is that in order to accommodate all the new goodies, the browsers invariably increase in size and operation can sometimes be sluggish. However, if you don't have a browser which runs the latest adornments you may be plagued with error messages…

Plug-ins

One of the really neat features which we're starting to see more and more in music software is the ability to add additional features to a program through plug-ins. These are small programs which integrate with the main program to offer additional functionality. Plug-ins have been around for a while and are well-known to users of Adobe Premier and Photoshop.

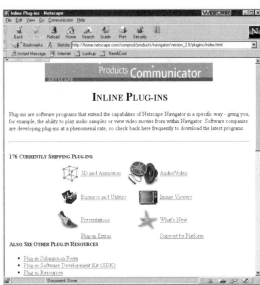

One of the most popular types of plug-in is for digital effects and the most popular format is DirectX-compatible plug-ins for the PC which most of the major digital audio software supports. Now plug-ins are appearing for Web browsers and you simply wouldn't believe the number or variety of ways in which you can enhance your surfing experience.

Netscape currently has a Plug-ins menu (Help>About Plug-ins) which lists the plug-ins currently installed, Figure 1.8. From here you can go to the Netscape site which lists most of the major – and many of the minor – plug-ins, Figure 1.9. The address is currently:

Figure 1.8 Plug-ins currently installed on your saystem and Figure 1.9 Plug-ins available from Netscape

http://www.home.netscape.com/comprod/products/navigator/version_2.0/plugins/index.html

The plug-ins are divided into categories such as 3D and Animation, Business and Utilities, Image Viewers and Audio/Video. There's little point in trying to create a definitive list as new plug-ins are added at a phenomenal rate. However, it's worth mentioning a few of the audio plug-ins which you may like to seek out and try. Actually, most of the plug-ins which support audio also support video and other multimedia data. Many were developed more for multimedia and interactivity than for audio but sometimes the two go together.

QuickTime by Apple
This plays QuickTime animation, music, MIDI, audio, video and VR objects directly in a Web page. The 'fast start' feature allows it to play QuickTime content while it's downloading.

Bamba by IBM (PC only)
Supports high quality audio and video streaming for low-bandwidth con-

 **INFO**

*C*ontent – spindoctor, hypermedia, PR speak! A general cover-all for data such as audio, video or textual data which is played or displayed by a program. Hence, '...deliver multimedia content across the Web'.

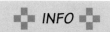

nections. It contains algorithms that determine the connection speed and file size and then it makes adjustments accordingly to maximise the transmission speed.

Beatnik by Headspace
Plays Rich Music Format (RMF) files and others including MIDI, MOD, WAV, AIFF, and AU within Web browsers. It has high-fidelity sound quality comparable to high-end soundcards. It can also create music that is highly interactive, due to a comprehensive set of JavaScript functions.

Cineweb by Digigami (PC only)
Brings real-time streaming audio and video to the Web using standard movie (AVI, MOV and MPG) and audio (WAV, MID and MP2) files.

Crescendo by LiveUpdate
The second generation of Crescendo delivers high-quality stereo MIDI music to the Web and uses a CD-like control panel and digital counter. The Crescendo Plus plug-in adds live real-time streaming.

Digital Sound and Music Interface for OS/2 by Julien Pierre (OS/2 only)
Plays 32-channel digital music module files.

InterVU Player by InterVU
Lets you play any industry-standard MPEG audio-video file without special MPEG hardware decoders. It provides a view of the first frame of the video in the Web page, streams the video while downloading, and provides full-speed cached playback from your computer's hard drive.

IP/TV by Precept (PC only)
Broadcasts high quality, real-time audio and video. Typical applications include corporate communication, employee training, distance learning, and dissemination of video news to the desktop.

Koan by SSEYO (PC only)
Creates generative, continuously changing music in a variety of styles from ambient and chill-out to rock and techno on your PC. Files may be only a few K in size but they can play for up to eight hours. Playback is via MIDI but the system also supports SoundFonts.

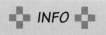

Liquid Music Player by Liquid Audio
Allows users to listen to and purchase CD-quality music tracks and CDs over the Internet. Exclusive Dolby Digital technology provides superior sound while you view album graphics, lyrics, and liner notes. Additional features include personal music library management and the ability to record an actual audio CD from music purchased on-line.

MacZilla by Knowledge Engineering (Mac only).
This is a Navigator Macintosh plug-in that does (almost) everything (it

says here!): QuickTime; ambient MIDI background sounds; WAV, AU, and AIFF audio; MPEG; and AVI. It has its own plug-in component architecture and can extend and update itself over the Net with the click of a button.

MIDIPLug by Yamaha
Features a built-in Soft Synthesiser with 128 GM-compatible voices, 8 drum kits, and reverb. External MIDI playback equipment such as an XG sound module or daughter card can be connected if required.

MODPlug by Olivier Lapicque (PC only)
Allows you to play high quality Mod/s3m/xm/it files over the Internet.

MusicGenie by SuperPlanet (PC only)
A MIDI player plug-in which allows users to control volume, balance, treble, and bass, as well as fast forward and rewind controls. It catalogues and saves MIDI files for off-line listening.

Net Toob Stream by Duplexx Software (PC only)
Delivers high quality, real-time streaming audio and video to the Web using standard MPEG audio and video files and standard MPEG audio-only files. It also plays all the standard file formats like AVI, MOV, MPG, FLC/FLI, WAV and MIDI. It can also play embedded links from within Internet email readers.

Netscape Media Player by Netscape
Brings high-quality streaming audio and synchronised multimedia to your desktop even with 14.4 Kbps modem connections. It uses automatic bandwidth-optimised streaming for the best possible audio quality at various connection speeds. Audio can be synchronised with HTML documents, Java applets, and JavaScript.

RapidTransit by Fastman
Decompresses and plays music that has been compressed up to 40:1 but still sounds good. It provides full 16-bit, 44.1kHz, CD-quality sound at compression rates of 10:1 or better.

RealPlayer by RealNetworks
Provides live and on-demand real-time RealAudio and RealVideo streaming content on the Web. RealAudio offers broadcast-quality stereo with 28.8 Kbps modems, AM-quality at 14.4 Kbps, and near-CD-quality audio at ISDN and faster connections. RealVideo delivers newscast-quality video at 28.8 Kbps and full-motion at faster connections.

Shockwave by Macromedia
A set of plug-ins designed to play interactive multimedia on the Web. They support two types of movies – those created by Director and those created by Flash.

T.A.G. Player by Digital Renaissance (PC only)

Provides a complete development and delivery system for hyperlinking time-based media (audio, video and animation), allowing Web site visitors to interact with the media through a series of hyperlinks. T.A.G. supports a wide range of media formats including ActiveMovie, NetShow, RealAudio, RealVideo, Oracle VideoServer and Macromedia Flash.

TrueStream Player by Motorola (PC only)

Lets you see and hear streaming video and audio content on the Web at all connection speeds from 28.8 Kbps up to LAN speeds without having to wait for lengthy downloads.

ViewMovie QuickTime by Ivan Cavero Belaunde (Mac only)

A Netscape Navigator 2.0 plug-in that supports the viewing and embedding of Apple QuickTime movies in Web pages. The movies can be used as link anchors and image maps.

WebTracks by Wildcat Canyon Software

WebTracks uses a proprietary music format to compress music files and begin playing them immediately when you reach a web page with music on it and it plays all standard MIDI files. The WebTrack Internet Music Kit includes everything you need to put WebTracks music on your page in a variety of styles and formats without requiring any knowledge of HTML.

FTP

Earlier in this chapter we mentioned a load of techy-sounding Net terms and promised to come back to this one. So here we are. FTP stands for File Transfer Protocol. Its a protocol used for copying files between remote computers on the Internet. Before the Web, FTP was one of the most popular ways of transferring data and it's still in popular use today.

There are dedicated FTP programs which let you use FTP with a reasonable degree of automation – that is, point, click and drag – and if you are creating Web pages, you may well have to FTP them from your computer to your Web site on your ISP's server. But the good news is, most modern Web browsers handle and display FTP files virtually automatically so if you're simply surfing, you don't have to learn anything new.

However, it's useful to know a bit about FTP because sometimes you will see a site address with a ftp rather than a www (World Wide Web) address and often FTP transfers can be quicker and more efficient than using the Web.

The main difference you'll notice in your browser is the way files on an FTP site are shown, Figure 1.10. They are displayed the way Windows or the Mac would display a list of files or folders and you navigate your way through them by pointing and clicking in exactly the same way as you do on your computer. You will notice that the files and folders are underlined which means they are hyperlinked so you can open a folder or access a document by clicking on it.

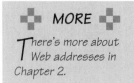

MORE

There's more about Web addresses in Chapter 2.

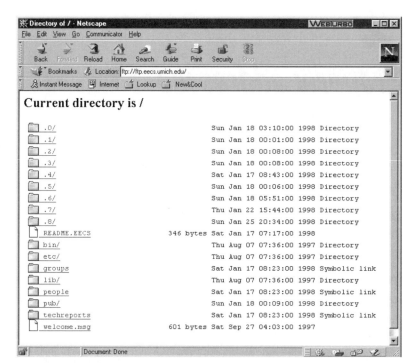

Figure 1.10 FTP sites show files and documents in a directory format

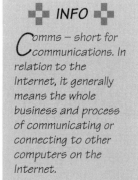

INFO

*C*omms – short for communications. In relation to the Internet, it generally means the whole business and process of communicating or connecting to other computers on the Internet.

PCs and Macs

One of the nice things about the Internet is that you can access it using virtually any kind of computer. However, the vast majority of people, certainly individuals, use a PC or a Mac.

Another nice thing about the Web is that much of the comms software for the PC and Mac is very similar. There are versions of Internet Explorer and Netscape browsers for both machines, for example, and they work and you use them in almost identical ways.

All the information in this book is equally applicable to users of both Macs and PCs – and, indeed, to users of any other computer or system which allows them to access the Web. Some of the software mentioned may only be available for one machine or the other and there is undoubtedly more software on the Web for the PC than for the Mac but that's the way it is in the commercial software field, too. Interestingly, according to statistics, 70 percent of Web sites are supposed to have been designed on the Mac...

However, any information you may be looking for is accessible using any computer – all the graphics, text, information and so on can be read by any machine. Standard MIDI files and sound files can also be read by most computers although some may need a conversion utility – and there are lots of those on the Web!

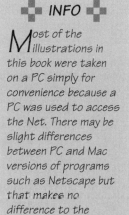

INFO

*M*ost of the illustrations in this book were taken on a PC simply for convenience because a PC was used to access the Net. There may be slight differences between PC and Mac versions of programs such as Netscape but that makes no difference to the content of most of the illustrations.

Properly addressed

Hyperlinks (see Chapter 1) make it very easy to move from one Web site to another. You don't need to know where the sites are, which country they are in or which computer they are on. All you do is point and click.

Domain names

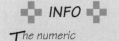

INFO

The numeric addresses are known as IP – Internet Protocol – addresses.

However, the Web has to know where the sites are and, because it's computer-based, it does this numbers. Sometimes you'll see these pop up in the Address or Location line of a browser. Fortunately for us mere humans, the addresses can also be represented as names and the Internet uses a system called DNS (Domain Name System) to convert between the two. So, the numeric address of a site may be something like 158.152.1.43 while its more human equivalent might be mysite.mycomputer.co.uk.

DNS allows the Net to support millions of different sites. The naming system makes it easy (or easier!) for us to remember the addresses and if you look at the end of the address of a site (technically, the first or top-level domain name), you can tell a little bit about the site and the company or organisation which owns or runs it. Here are some of the major ones:

.com	Used by commercial companies.
.edu	Used by educational establishments.
.ac	Used by academic sites, mainly in the UK.
.int	For organisations established by international treaties or international databases.
.net	Used for the computers of network providers.
.org	Organisations – intended as a miscellaneous category for organisations which don't comfortably fit elsewhere.
.mil	Used by the US military.
.gov	Originally intended for any kind of US government office or agency but more recently it was decided to register only agencies of the US Federal government.

There are also country domains which indicate where the site is situated. Here are some:

.uk	UK	.es	Spain
.us	USA (although this is often omitted from a URL)	.fr	France
.au	Australia	.it	Itraly
.be	Belgium	.jp	Japan
.ca	Canada	.nl	The Netherlands
.de	Germany	.nz	New Zealand

The country codes can be used with other codes – ac.uk, for example, which indicates an academic site in the UK.

URLs

The address of a site or a page on the Web is called a URL which stands for Uniform Resource Locator. Bit of a mouthful, isn't it? A common analogy is with a street address which tells you the country, the county (or state if you're in the good ol' USA), the street, the house number and the name of the person the message is to be delivered to. The URL can point to the exact location of a document or file on the Web and if you know its address you can jump straight to it.

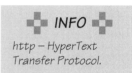

http – HyperText Transfer Protocol.

The first part of the URL indicates the protocol to be used to access the resource. The most common ones are http and ftp, although occasionally you may see an address which starts with another type of transfer such as gopher, telnet or news (which points to a newsgroup – more about which in the next chapter).

This is followed by a colon (:) and it's usually (but not always) followed by two forward slashes (//).

So, the first part of an address on the Web will usually be:

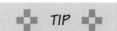

If you've used DOS, you'll be more familiar with the backslash (\) than the forward slash (/) which is used in URLs. Make sure you use the correct slash otherwise the URL will not work.

http://www.

The next part is the host name which is a specific Internet server. It could be something like microsoft.com, macromedia.com or leeds.ac.uk.

Conventionally, Web addresses are written in lower-case but most URLs are case-sensitive and site developers may use both upper- and lower-case letters in a URL. If you develop a site, use lower-case letters only for the URL. If you don't, it will make the site less easily accessible to users. If someone dictates a URL to you, assume it's in lower-case – it usually will be. Most of the URLs in this book are in lower-case but watch out for the odd ones which aren't!

Any following information points to a specific area of the site. It's like a directory structure (for those who remember DOS) with the sub directories separated by forward slashes. The URL can even point to a section of a page in which case you may see the hash (#) character. You will see lots – and lots! – of addresses later in the book.

The naming of the parts

It's useful to know how to pronounce the address if you want to describe it to someone over the phone, for example.

Most Web address start with 'http' but as most people use the Web exclusively, it's fast becoming common practice to omit the 'http' and simply start with 'www'. If you're giving the address to a Net Newbie, you may prefer to start with 'http' and don't forget the 'colon, forward slash, forward slash' (://).

Again, many people simply say 'slash' rather than 'forward slash' and as it's a Web address we all know which sort of slash they mean. Some people say 'double slash'. The full-stops are pronounced 'dot'.

A few addresses contain a tilde (~) which some people call 'the squiggly character' but everyone seems to know what they mean. Its position on the keyboard varies. Once upon a time you could say it was the character over the hash on a PC keyboard or to the right of the Command key on a Mac keyboard but new designs and layouts keep moving it around.

So, let's look at an address:

> **http://www.compulink.co.uk/~route66/**

The full name would be pronounced as follows:

> **http, colon, forward slash, forward slash, www, dot, compulink, dot, co, dot, uk, forward slash, tilde, route66, forward slash.**

BIG TIP

Most Web browsers acknowledge the fact that most of the address you'll be entering are to be fount on the Web and accessed via http, so if you omit the http:// part of the address, the browser puts it in for you automatically.

Email addresses

The same naming system is used with email addresses although these all have an additional character – @ – which most people know as the 'at sign' and it is, indeed, called 'at' in email addresses. As in: the c@ s@ on the m@. If you want to send an email to the boss man at PC Publishing, his address is: phil@pc-pubs.demon.co.uk.

htm and html

If you look at the URL of a page in the Location area of your browser you will often see that the last entry ends with .htm or .html. This is the name of the document which you are viewing in your browser. Some browsers don't show this but if you save the page or the frame the browser will usually offer the name with a .htm or .html extension in the Save As... dialogue box.

.html seems an obvious extension as the pages are written in HTML and most site designers who use Macs seem to favour this. However, prior to Windows 95, PCs could only recognise extensions with up to three letters so .htm was used.

It used to be that you could tell if a page was created on a Mac or a PC by the extension. Nowadays, with virtually all systems capable of handling long filenames, it's no longer so easy. Not that it really matters because all pages can be viewed on all systems.

After installing a browser on a Mac or a PC, it will usually automatically associate .htm and .html files with itself. Double-clicking on such a file will open the browser and load the file.

Note, however, that associated images will probably not be loaded as the Save function does not automatically save any images in the page. Also, the page expects to find the images at a certain place on the host machine, not your PC. You can see the locations if you look at the HTML source of the page (View/Page Source in Netscape). You can also load a HTML file directly into a wordprocessor or text editor and you'll see exactly the same layout and information.

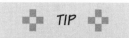

TIP

If you're at a site containing a lot of information which you'd like to study, save the page or the frame and look at it later off-line. If there are any images you need, you'll have to save them separately.

TIP

Home page – the first page on a Web site, the starting point and usually the first page visitors see. Internet Explorer calls it a start page.

Default and index files

The home page on a Web site is usually called index.htm or index.html. Sometimes, it is called default.htm or default.html. Most browsers automatically look for and load this page so you don't usually have to specify it in the URL. However, there can be many other pages in the 'root' directory of a site and a URL may point to another page such as:

www.mysite.co.uk/home.htm
or
www.mysite.co.uk/songs.htm

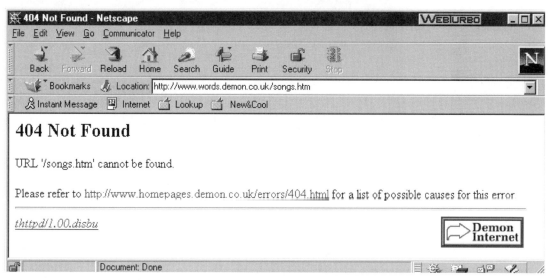

Figure 2.1 Not Found error

If you're struggling to access a site and the system reports a Not Found error as in Figure 2.1, try putting one of the four index or default files at the end of the site address. For example:

INFO

Webmaster – the person or organisation responsible for maintaining the Web site. Most sites have a Webmaster email address which you can usually find at the bottom of the home page.

www.mysite.co.uk/index.htm
www.mysite.co.uk/index.html
www.mysite.co.uk/default.htm
www.mysite.co.uk/default.html

If that doesn't work, get in touch with the Webmaster and ask if there's a problem. There probably is.

Newsgroups and mailing lists

Newsgroups (and Mailing lists, which we'll look at in a moment) are an incredibly useful source of information. They provide a forum for the discussion of a wide variety of subjects and there are newsgroups for virtually every kind of topic you can think of – and many you can't! In newsgroups, people pass on news and information, ask questions, give answers, exude opinions and so on.

Newsgroups work a little like email but instead of sending messages to individuals, messages are posted to the newsgroup as a whole and anyone who is a member of the newsgroup can read them and post their own messages in reply to them.

Newsgroups are distributed over a computer network known as Usenet and when you post a message it goes to the group rather than to an individual.

Newsreaders

In order to access newsgroups you need a newsreader program. Most browsers have one built-in but there are several separate ones, each with their own features, which you may prefer to use. You can seek out newsreaders on the Web by doing a search for 'newsreaders' – of course! There's more about searching the Net in the next chapter.

Many on-line services such as AOL, CompuServe and CiX – see Chapter 5 – have built-in facilities to help you access newsgroups.

Internet Explorer incorporates a newsreader and Netscape Communicator currently has a Message Centre called Collabra which is a newsreader. These work fine but you may also like to check out this page:

http://cws.avalon.nf.ca/32news-reviews.html

which contains reviews of many other popular PC newsreaders. The site also contains information about lots of useful Internet programs and points to areas where they can be found and downloaded.

Here are a few newsreaders to investigate:

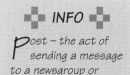

INFO

Post – the act of sending a message to a newsgroup or mailing list.

INFO

Usenet or UseNet – short for User Network, a world-wide network of computers which handle the messages posted to newsgroups.

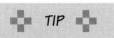

TIP

If any of these addresses report a File Not Found error, refer to the File not found section in Chapter 8 for help.

Free Agent
ftp://papa.indstate.edu/winsock-l/Windows95/News/fa32-111.exe
One of the best free newsreaders available.

Agent
ftp://ftp.forteinc.com/pub/agent/a32-15.exe
A commercial version of Free Agent with more features.

News Xpress
ftp://ftp.malch.com/nx201.zip
Another excellent freeware newsreader.

WinVN
ftp://ftp.ksc.nasa.gov/pub/winvn/win95/wv32i999.zip
One of the first newsreaders and still very popular.

NewsFerret
ftp://ferret.aitcom.net/pub/ferret/NFT111.exe
A useful tool for finding articles on Usenet.

Anawave Gravity
ftp://ftp02.anawave.com/pub/gravity.exe
A rules-based newsreader.

Outlook Express
http://www.microsoft.com/ie/ie40/oe/
Microsoft's heavyweight do-it-all Internet mail and communications software.

Mac newsreaders

There's a little less choice for Mac users but check these out:

NewsWatcher and MT-NewsWatcher
http://www.santafe.edu/~smfr/mtnw/mtnewswatcher.html
Highly regarded by many Mac users. MT-NewsWatcher includes additional features such as spell checking, speech recognition and filtering.

InterNews
http://www.dartmouth.edu/~moonrise/
Read news by selecting articles from tiled windows.

MacSOUP
http://www.snafu.de/~stk/macsoup/
An off-line reader which handles news and mail which can optionally interface with Eudora or Claris Emailer if you use them for email.

Outlook Express
As of writing, being ported to the Mac from the PC.

If your browser doesn't have a newsreader or you want to see what the others have to offer, a consensus of opinion would suggest trying Free Agent for the PC and a version of NewsWatcher for the Mac.

How newsgroups work

Newsgroups are distributed over Usenet. Your ISP or on-line service provider will subscribe to a range of newsgroups and store them on its server. The newsreader software allows you to list the newsgroups, subscribe to them, read the messages and post your own to the newsgroup.

Not every ISP carries every newsgroup, particularly some of the adult groups and groups with a perceived minority interest. Each newsgroup requires storage space and system administrators may decide the space could be better used for other data. Many systems can also take a while to add a new newsgroup to their system. If you know a newsgroup exists but your server isn't carrying it, send a request to them asking for it to be added to their list.

Newsreaders differ slightly in the way they work although most have a set of common functions. Generally, when you open one, it will show you a list of newsgroups available on the server. You may have to access a menu to request a list. If this is the first time you have opened the newsreader it will have to collect the list from the server which could take several minutes.

Clicking on the Newsgroups List window in Free Agent, for example, Figure 3.1 lists all the available newsgroups on the server.

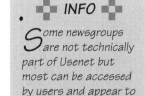

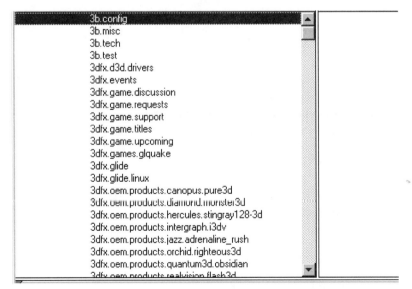

Figure 3.1 Newsgroups List window in Free Agent

Members of CiX who use the Ameol OLR can easily download a list of newsgroups and select ones to subscribe to, Figure 3.2.

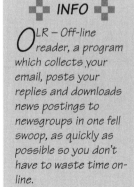

Figure 3.2 *Some of the newsgroups available on CiX with 'music' in their title*

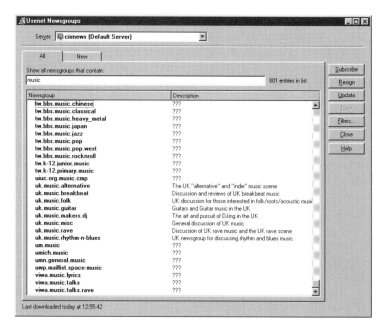

Newsgroup names

Newsgroups are named according to a hierarchy which divides them into categories. The further to the right of the name you go, the more specific and specialised the category. Here are the nine most common categories and you will see these at the start of the newsgroup name:

alt	Alternative groups
biz	Business groups
comp	Computer-related groups
misc	Miscellaneous groups
news	News and information about Usenet
rec	Recreational topics
sci	Scientific discussions
soc	Social issues
talk	Discussion/debate-oriented groups

There are many other groups including:

microsoft	Microsoft newsgroups
clari	News items originating from Clarinet, a commercial news service
uk	Newsgroups originating from the UK

Finding suitable newsgroups

One of the problems with newsgroups is that there are so many of them. There are certainly over 30,000 and some sources say there are 50,000 or more! Others are added every day.

Because newsgroups produce a high volume of data they can quickly accumulate many hundreds of megabytes of messages. Many service providers only keep messages on their system for a certain length of time. This may be a week or, if the newsgroup has a very high volume of traffic, it may only be for a few days. If you join a busy, active newsgroup, you may have to log on every few days in order to keep track of the discussions.

As of writing there are over 400 newsgroups with 'music' in their name – and there are many more whose name includes MIDI, sounds, synth, audio and so on. Other newsgroups are devoted to specific types of music and to individual artists.

Not to put too fine a point on it – most newsgroups are utter garbage! Perhaps, once upon a time, someone had a germ of a good idea but the majority of newsgroups seem to fall quickly into neglect or end up as a rubbish bin for spammers and bulk emailers.

The best way to see if a newsgroup is what you're looking for is to try it. Most newsreaders will collect a sample of the headers in a newsgroup so you can see the topics under discussion. You can then download the body of the articles of any headers which look interesting. Figure 3.3 shows a collection of headers in the comp.music.midi newsgroup.

INFO

Spammers – People or organisations who send the same email message to multiple newsgroups. Named after the Monty Python Spam sketch!

INFO

Header – the title or subject in a newsgroup posting which should give you an indication of what the message is about.

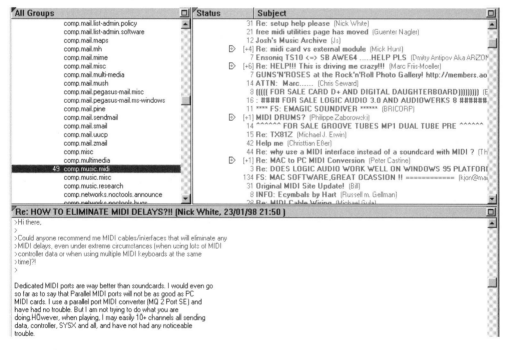

Figure 3.3 A collection of headers in the comp.music.midi newsgroup.

If you are looking for specific information about a program, a piece of equipment, an artist, or a particular type of music, there are dedicated Web pages to help you look for it. There's more about searching the Web in Chapter 4.

DejaNews http://w2.dejanews.com/

DejaNews, Figure 3.4, is a search engine which specifically searches newsgroups as opposed to Web pages which most other search engines concentrate on. You could, for example, see who had been posting messages about Yamaha's AN1x virtual analogue synthesiser. Figure 3.5 (dejanews2) reveals that there were 57 comments at the time, which it lists along with the name of the newsgroup the comments were posted in and you can see the entire posting by double-clicking on the subject.

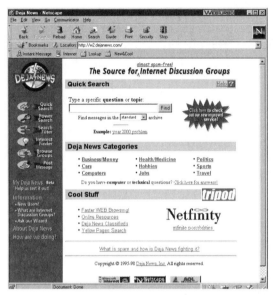

Figure 3.4 (above) DejaNews searches newsgroups rather than web pages

Figure 3.5 (above right) There were 57 comments at the time

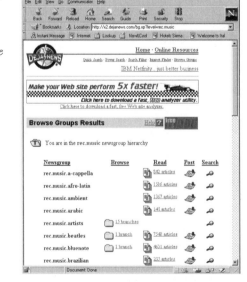

Figure 3.6 (right) DejaNews lets you browse the newsgroups list by category

DejaNews also has an Interest Search which finds groups where people are talking about a specific topic.

Liszt of Newsgroups http://www.liszt.com/

This is another newsgroup searcher which lets you search by keyword or browse by topic. You can home in on specific types of newsgroup and there's even a list of uk.music groups, Figure 3.7.

Figure 3.7 List of uk.music groups returned by Liszt

Subscribing to a newsgroup

Joining a newsgroup is called subscribing and you can do this very easily from a newsreader by clicking on a Subscribe button. In Free Agent, for example, if you right-click on a newsgroup a menu pops up containing several options including Subscribe, Figure 3.8.

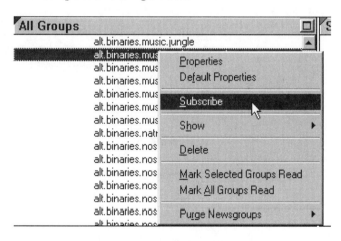

Figure 3.8 You cna join a Newsgroup in Free Agent by the Subscribe option

Each time you log on, there could be dozens of new messages in each newsgroup so most newsreaders wait for you to tell them to get the latest batch before they start downloading. Free Agent again, lets you get all the new messages or simply sample a certain number of the most recent ones, Figure 3.9.

You can then move through the headers deciding which ones sound

Figure 3.9 Sampling recent messages in Free Agent

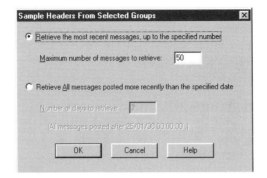

interesting and retrieve the full postings. You'll soon get the hang of this through necessity if nothing else, because downloading unwanted messages takes forever and you'll notice the effect of your curiosity in three-month's time on your phone bill.

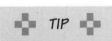
TIP

When you first start to investigate newsgroups, don't be over-enthusiastic. There are hundreds of potential interest and retrieving the body of the messages of even a half dozen could take hours! Be selective. Scan the headers. Retrieve only those messages of interest. And do it at a weekend when local calls are cheap!

Netiquette

As with most things in life, there's a right way and a wrong way to do things and there are 'rules' for interaction with newsgroups. Many people don't bother with the niceties as can be seen from the postings but if you want to enlist the help of the members of a group or engage them in conversation, it's a good idea to follow a few rules.

Yes, netiquette is etiquette for Net users and it's simply a few dos and don'ts which help make life easier for everyone. They apply equally to email and mailing lists as well as to newsgroup postings.

1 Be polite and courteous. This should be obvious but it's surprising how many people aren't. Because of the sense of distance on-line communication gives you, many people tend to be far more rude, argumentative and disagreeable than they would in face-to-face discussions. But not everyone.

2 Don't spam! If you want to ask a question, don't post it in dozens of newsgroups. Select the one which you think is most appropriate and post is there. Post to two if you must. Many subscribers will be members of related newsgroups and if they see the same message in several groups they could retaliate.

3 Use meaningful headings. As most users download headings first, if it doesn't tell them what the message is about they may not retrieve the body of it.

4 DON'T SHOUT! Some people, particularly newbies, think that writing in capitals makes their message more important. It doesn't! It makes it more difficult to read and it annoys everyone. Some people put a word in caps if they want to emphasise it – the equivalent of italics – but a better and more popular way is to use the underscore like _this_ or asterisks like *this* or slashes like /this/. But DON'T USE CAPS!

5 Do not post ads unless you're sure this is acceptable to the newsgroup. Newsgroups are easy prey for spammers and bulk-emailers although many are now taking steps to minimise this type of posting. Just because you see ads in a list, it doesn't mean they are welcome. If you're an active member of a newsgroup and have just released your first CD, for example, most members would probably not object to you mentioning this fact. However, commercial ads are usually frowned on and posting them is a sure fire way of making yourself unpopular.

MAKE $1 MILLION IN A WEEK!!!

Many of the bulk-emails you'll see in newsgroups are of the 'get rich quick' kind. Other than ignore them, the next best thing you can do is to become an active member of the anti-spam lobby and work with your ISP and group administrators to minimise this sort of thing.

Before posting to a newsgroup it's a good idea to lurk for a while. This allows you to see who the most active participants are, what sort of subjects are discussed, which ones have been discussed and how subscribers react to newbies.

Newbies are sometimes worried that they'll make a faux pas with their posts but most netizens are helpful souls who will make allowances and gently steer them in the right direction. Of course, there are exceptions, and you'll find ignorant, arrogant and aggressive people in cyberspace just as you find them in all walks of life.

Be deferential and courteous, as you might approach a group of people talking things over at a party, and you'll get on fine.

Net revenge
Netizens have their own way of dealing with those who transgress the rules of netiquette.

Flaming
This is the most common form of retribution. It's an abusive or insulting message about a person, usually posted to a newsgroup or mailing list but sometimes sent directly to the person in an email. If you annoy an entire newsgroup you may get flamed by all its members – which could be many hundreds or even thousands of people!

It's quite easy to get het up in an on-line discussion and it's very easy for people to take offence. Lurk a little in almost any newsgroup and you'll soon see examples of flaming. Sometimes it can be amusing but generally it's a waste of cyberspace, it adds to your phone bill as you have to spend time downloading it and you waste time reading it.

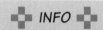 **INFO**

Lurker – someone who reads newsgroup postings but doesn't post any messages to the group.

Netizen – a citizen of the Net, someone who communicates on-line especially through newsgroups and mailing lists.

Bozo filter

Many email programs and newsreaders have a facility which enables users to filter out messages arriving from specified individuals. You may also be able to ignore a particular thread. Human nature being what it is, most people don't find this as satisfying as flaming, as the bozo being filtered remains unaware of your action but it can at least save you from his or her rants.

Mailing lists

Another method of mass communication on the Net is the mailing list. The principle is the same as a newsgroup – members post messages, information, add comments and so on – but there are a few noticeable differences.

Newsgroups and mailing lists – what's the difference?

As its name suggests, a mailing list is a list of email addresses of people who are interested in a specific subject. All messages posted to the list are sent on to subscribers via email. They aren't stored on a Usenet system that anyone can access – although most mailing lists are freely available to anyone who wants to subscribe.

If you don't want to read a message or a thread in a newsgroup you can skip over it and opt not to retrieve the message body. If you're on a mailing list, however, every messages drops onto your email doormat and if you don't want to read one your only recourse is the Delete button.

There are a few other differences, too, which you'll notice as we move through the rest of this section.

Moderated and unmoderated lists

Most mailing lists are handled automatically by a computer program. You send it a request to subscribe to a list and the program then automatically sends you a copy of all the messages posted to it, as they are posted. There is, therefore, no human intervention in the activities of the members of the list – it's unmoderated – and it's basically up to the members to keep order among themselves.

Some mailing lists, however, are moderated and a human sits between the senders and the recipients, filtering out messages which he or she considers to be unsuitable. This sounds like a nice idea but it can be incredibly time-consuming and few people have the time or inclination to moderate a list. Therefore, most lists are unmoderated.

Moderated lists also mean an inevitable delay between posting a message and it arriving at the subscribers' mailboxes. This could be anything from a few hours to a few weeks if the moderator is on holiday!

And moderating a list can be a thankless task because decisions about 'suitability' are made by one person and other members of the list may

INFO

A thread is a string of messages relating to the same topic. If you post a message and someone adds a comment to it, someone else comments on that and so on, this is a thread. Most newsreaders have an option to group or link messages by thread so it's easy to see which ones are related.

INFO

Mailing lists are also called discussion groups, email discussion groups or sometimes simply lists.

INFO

Newsgroups use less of the Internet's resources because a single message is only stored once whereas with a mailing list it may be sent to several hundred or thousand people.

disagree with decisions they make. But, if it's their ball, they're entitled to pick it up and go home whenever they like and the other members can start another list if they like. And it wouldn't be the first time that this has happened.

However, the moderator can remove anyone from the lists who is being a nuisance, step in to tell people to cool down if the flaming gets too hot, and otherwise keep order and see things run smoothly. So a conscientious moderator can be an enviable boon.

Joining a mailing list

It can often seem more difficult to use a mailing list than a newsgroup. Many newcomers get confused over where to send postings intended for the list and where to send instructions to the list administrator. It will help if you know a little about how lists work.

Mailing lists are managed by a computer program known as a list server or mailing list manager. There are three main mail manager programs – Listserv, Majordomo and Listproc – which work in a similar way. Listserv was the earliest and some people still refer to mailing lists as listservs but it's better to use the term 'mailing lists' to avoid any possible confusion.

The programs run on computers at a specific Web addresses and will probably be responsible for controlling a number of mailing lists. For the sake of example, let's use the Majordomo program running on the server at Manchester University. Its address is:

Majordomo@mcc.ac.uk

You interact with the programs by sending them instructions or commands and, as you're talking to a computer, you these have to be exact. If you want to know which mailing lists the Majordomo program at Manchester supports, send an email to the above address containing the word 'lists' in the body of the message. That's all.

The program will chunk away and send you a list of its, er, lists. At the time of writing, you would receive the following reply:

```
>> lists
Majordomo@mcc.ac.uk serves the following lists:
analysis-l              Analytical Science mailing list
aua99                   Association of University Administrators 1999
cave-biology            Cave-biology (biospeleology) email discussion list
cubase-users            Cubase Users Mailing List
cubase-users-digest     Cubase Users Mailing List (Digestified Version)
```

Many mailing lists are open to the public but many are also started as a private platform for discussion of a common topic. In such cases you need to ask the moderator if you can join and in some cases you may be asked to prove your eligibility. If you want to join a list set up for the benefit of studio engineers, for example, you may be asked for your engineering credentials.

Majordomo – From the Latin 'major domus' meaning 'master of the house' – a person who speaks, makes arrangements or takes charge for another. Literary lot some of these Net folk.

iam-digest	
interface-l	The Laboratory Equipment Interfacing Discussion Group
jstor-staff	MC and contract staff working on JSTOR service
logic-users	Logic Users List
logic-users-digest	Logic Users List (digestified version)
ma-itmanagement	Tutorial group for MA in IT Management
perl-moderation-panel	Potential moderators for the comp.lang.perl re-org
process-l	The Process Analysis Discussion Group
protool3	List for parties involved in the Protool project
scoutnet-uk	ScoutNet UK staff mailing list
sounddiver-users	SoundDiver Users Mailing List
sounddiver-users-digest	SoundDiver Users Mailing List (Digestified Version)

Use the 'info <list>' command to get more information about a specific list.

There are two or three music-related lists here which could be of interest to you. Let's say you want to subscribe to the cubase-users list. You would send another message to Majordomo with the following in the body of the message:

subscribe cubase-users myname@myemail.co.uk

In this case you will get a message back saying:

Someone (possibly you) has requested that your email address be added to or deleted from the mailing list 'cubase-users@mcc.ac.uk'.

The message will then give you an authorisation code which you have to send back to confirm that you really do want to perform the action suggested – in this case, join the list. This is to prevent mischievous persons joining other people to a multitude of mailing lists. If you ignore the message and don't send the authorisation code, you will not be joined to the list.

Actually, in this case you will get another message saying your request has been forwarded to the owner of the list for approval. As mentioned earlier, many lists are 'closed' and this serves as an extra check and helps keep the riff-raff out. But unless you're a known bozo of the highest order, it's very unlikely you'd be refused entry to the Cubase list.

When you are joined, you will get a welcome message.

KEEP THIS MESSAGE!

Sorry for shouting but you could get into a heckuva mess and annoy lots of people if you don't. This message contains a list of commands telling you how to post messages to the list, how to get files related to the list, find out who is on the list and how to unsubscribe. To do all these things, you send an email to the Majordomo address containing specific commands.

However, to post a message to the list, you don't send it to Majordomo but to: cubase-users@mcc.ac.uk. It's important that you remember this. In a busy list you will see lots of 'unsubscribe' messages sent to the list rather than to the list manager.

Common list manager commands
Most lists respond to a 'help' command in the body of the message as well as subscribe and unsubscribe commands but the syntax sometimes varies. That's why it's important that you keep the welcome email. Here are some common commands used by the three main list managers.

Listerver. This is popular with University-based lists.

Subscribe	subscribe listname firstname lastname
Unsubscribe	unsubscribe listname
Digest	set listname digest
List subscribers	review listname

Listproc.

Subscribe	subscribe listname firstname lastname
Unsubscribe	unsubscribe listname
Digest	set listname digest
List subscribers	recipients listname

Majordomo. The most common manager used by commercial Internet providers.

Subscribe	subscribe listname email-address
Unsubscribe	unsubscribe listname
Digest	set listname digest
List subscribers	who listname

Finding suitable mailing lists
Trying to track down all the mailing lists in existence is not quite as easy as getting a list of newsgroups. While most newsgroups live in Usenet, mailing lists can live anywhere. However, as ever on the Net, there are ways of finding out these things.

In particular, there are several Web sites containing lists of mailing lists – commonly called lists of lists or LOL for short. Here's a collection of useful links to help you investigate the wonderful world of mailing lists:

Email Discussion Groups
http://alabanza.com/kabacoff/Inter-Links/listserv.html
Information, help topics and lists of lists, Figure 3.10.

Figure 3.10 E-Mail Discussion Groups

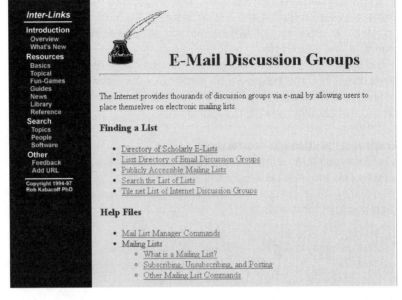

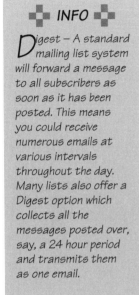

Mary Houten-Kemps' Everything E-Mail
http://everythingemail.net/
As it says, a site which discusses all issues relating to email and it includes a section on email discussion groups.

Find Mail
http://www.findmail.com/index.html
Lots of public mailing lists divided into categories with search facilities.

Tile Net
http://www.tile.net/tile/
A search engine which lets you search mailing lists, newsgroups and other areas of the Net.

Figure 3.11 Tile Net searches mailing lists, newsgroups and other areas of the Net.

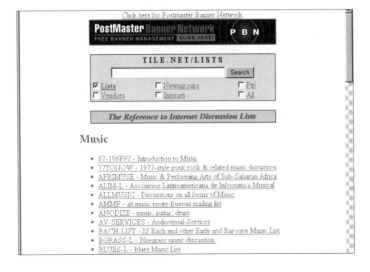

E-Mail Discussion Groups/Lists – Resources
http://webcom.com/impulse/list.html

Intended as a one-stop information resource about email discussion groups, it has four sections: background information about the software that supports the groups; an introduction to listserver commands; links to other Web sites where you can search for discussion groups; and a selected list relating to advertising, public relations and marketing.

Majordomo FAQ
http://www.cis.ohio-state.edu/~barr/majordomo-faq.html

Everything you ever wanted to know about Majordomo. For users who want to run their own mailing lists.

LoMML – Lists of Music Mailing Lists
http://www.shadow.net/~mwaas/lomml.html

A very good place to start if you're looking for music-related lists. This is a comprehensive project dedicated to cataloguing all email-based music-related resources in the world, including mailing lists, magazines, periodicals and newsletters.

Figure 3.12 LOMML

There are also three sub-branches of LoMML:

IMML (International Music Mailing Lists) covers all 'traditional' musical genres, including classical, jazz, blues, fusion, country, bluegrass, reggae, new age and world music. It also encompasses musical composition and the discussion of actual musical instruments including electronic instruments.

PMML (Popular Music Mailing Lists) covers all popular music genres – virtually any style that shows up on Billboard's Hot-100 list with any regularity – including rock, pop, alternative, progressive, metal, folk, R&B, rap, hip-hop, dance, grunge, and all similar, reasonably-popular styles.

UMML (Underground Music Mailing Lists) supports all less well-known musical genres, including Acid Jazz, Ambient, BritPop, College Radio, Dark Alternative, DiY, Electro, 'Electronica', Ethereal, Funk, Gothic, Hardcore, IDM, Indie, Industrial, Jungle, New Wave, Punk, Rave, Ska, Synthpop, Techno, Trance, Trip-Hop, and related offshoots. It also contains lists for unknown artists who would normally be included within PMML. A very useful list for promoting unsigned, unusual and non-commercial musical styles.

PAML – Publicly Accessible Mailing Lists
http://www.neosoft.com/internet/paml/
A list of lists arranged alphabetically and by category with search facilities. The site also includes an Answers sections which aims to answer all your questions about mailing lists.

Figure 3.13 PAML – Publicly Accessible Mailing Lists

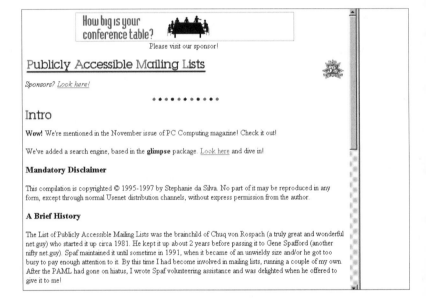

The List of lists
http://catalog.com/vivian/interest-group-search.html
Search a database of mailing lists. Includes a wry description of the life cycle of a mailing list from conception to death – or maturity! Read this before you start your own.

Best mailing lists on the Net
http://www.lucifer.com/~sasha/lists.html
One man's view of the top 100 lists. Not a music list in sight – but we don't live by notes alone and there are some interesting lists here...

Liszt's lists
http://www.liszt.com/
This site, which also keeps track of newsgroups, has a mailing list spider which trawls the Net looking for mailing lists and compiles the results into

a single directory which you can search. It lists the, er, lists by topic and the site also contains lots of information about mailing lists.

CTI Music: A List of Musical Discussion Lists
http://www.lancs.ac.uk/users/music/research/musicallists.html
A long list of mailing lists about various areas of music.

CTI Music: A List of Musical Discussion Lists (Instruments)
http://www.lancs.ac.uk/users/music/research/instrumentlists.html
A list of musical instrument lists, everything from the accordion to MIDI wind controllers.

Music mailing lists
There are far too many lists to list, but here are a few which you may like to investigate.

majordomo@darkwing.uoregon.edu
ddesign: Digidesign digital audio products.
sursound: Surround sound discussion.

majordomo@oak.oakland.edu
dp4, eps: Ensoniq products.

listproc@u.washington.edu
prophet: Sequential Prophet 2000 and 3000 samplers.

listproc@mcfeeley.cc.texas.edu
bass: Bass and DIY loudspeakers.

listserv@amaerican.edu
emusic-l: Electronic music discussion.
synth-l: Electronic music 'gearhead' list.

listserv@unseen.aztec.co.za
trax-weekly: TraxWeekly newsletter for the discussion of the less-esoteric aspects of synthesis.

majordomo@infopro.com
mixmasters: Constructive criticism of members' audio productions.

majordomo@frisbee.net.au
amarok-daily: The official Mike Oldfield mailing list.

majordomo@lists.xmission.com
jarre: Jean-Michel Jarre.
orb: The Orb.
Kraftwerk: Kraftwerk.

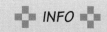

LISTSERV@HOME.EASE.LSOFT.COM
CLASSICAL: The Moderated Classical Music List, a place where classical music enthusiasts can discuss music, musicians, composers, composition, instruments, performance, music history, recordings and all topics even remotely related to classical music from all periods.

LISTSERV@MANA.LANDOFHAZE.COM
GUITARIST-L: A discussion area for both amateur and professional guitarists. Topics can include instruments, amps, mixing, effects, or anything else related to the art of playing the guitar.

majordomo@cs.uwp.edu
tadream: Tangerine Dream and related artists.

listserv@sunsite.univie.ac.at
cakewalk-l: For users of Cakewalk sequencers.

majordomo@mcc.ac.uk
cubase-users: Discussions, suggestions and moaning about Cubase on Atari, PC and Mac platforms. Several of the programmers are members of the list. The mailing list is copied to the newsgroup alt.steinberg.cubase but postings to that group are not sent to the list.

listserv@dis.ulpgc.es
multimedia: All about multimedia, from authoring to sound card configuration problems including user interfaces, marketing strategies, products reviews, and so on.

http://www.ghp.net/indynet/mailinglist.htm
The Web site of the IndyNet Mailing List where you can sign up for is an approximately-monthly newsletter that contains tips, featured bands, web resources, and educational articles of use to the Indie musician. The list strives to offer the best free new information and to feature the best tips and resources found during the month.

INFO
DAW – Digital Audio Workstation.

http://www.missionrec.com/pcdaw.html
Web site of the PC-DAW Mailing List which discusses digital audio workstations as they relate to the IBM PC and clones. Members include many knowledgeable end users as well as manufacturers.

http://www.yellowdog.com/jpl/
Home of the Jazz Programmers Mailing List, a free service to all Jazz Programmers, announcers and other jazz industry personnel who are invited to join in and participate.

http://www.mooncafe.com/lists/vs880.html
A Web site, home of the Roland VS-880 Mailing List.

majordomo@horus.sara.nl

synth-diy: The synth-diy list is for discussions about synthesiser electronics and the building of (mostly analogue) synthesisers. Expect discussions on modulars and their various modules like voltage controlled oscillators, filters, ring modulators and the like. Topics like heated dual transistors for the ultimate exp converter are certainly not shunned here.

Newsletters

As well as the interactive mailing lists described, many companies send out email newsletters to interested parties. You'll find details of these on the Web and to receive them you often have to do little more than click on a hyperlink although you may be asked to enter your email address and perhaps give a few more details about yourself or your interests.

These newsletters are one-way only and you can't strike up a conversation with the sender – although if it's a small list the person or company responsible may well respond to email.

Newsletters are useful for keeping up to date with what's happening in a certain area of interest or to hear about new products or services which companies are offering. The email newsletter is a cheap and easy way to keep people informed compared with the snail mail alternative of creating a paper newsletter with a DTP program, printing it and posting it to customers.

INFO

Snail mail – a common on-line term for messages delivered by the postal service.

FAQs

FAQs – Frequently Asked Questions – are very important on the Net. Most newsgroups and mailing lists, and many Web sites have one. They contain a list of the – yes, you guessed – questions most frequently asked by members of the list or visitors to the Web site.

Before you post a message or send an email, you ought to read the FAQ. If you're a newbie, the chances are the FAQ may answer the question you were going to ask. It may also contain a list of dos and don'ts and suggested behaviour for members of the list or newsgroup, such as the group's attitude to members posting adverts.

INFO

It's considered very bad form to ask a question which has been answered in a FAQ. If you do, you may well be flamed.

4

Searching the Web

Although this book contains a lot of URLs and address information to help you find what you want fast, at some time you will almost certainly want to search the Web to look for a piece of software, an update, news on a recent music show, information on a product, or to track down the solution to a problem.

Performing a search on the Web is dead easy. Finding exactly what you want among millions of Web sites, newsgroups and mailing lists is not always so easy. As with many things on the Web, there is an overkill of possibilities.

The most obvious thing to try first, is to contact some of the major search engines and you can do this directly from most browsers simply by selecting the Search option. Netscape has a Search icon and when you click on it you may well get a page which looks something like the one in Figure 4.1.

Figure 4.1 Netscape's Search Page offers you a list of popular search engines to search from

The page currently lets you connect to one of nine major search engines. It's a useful shortcut provided by Netscape, so thank the boys for that. The check box below the text entry area in Netscape's Net Search (Figure 4.1) lets you select your favourite search engine which will automatically be selected each time you go to this page.

How search engines work

You don't have to know how search engines work in order to use them but if you do, it will help explain some terms you may come across such as Meta Tag and Keywords. It will also help explain how some sites seem to appear so many times, often with strange descriptions and without necessarily containing what you want!

A search engine is basically a directory or database of information pulled from the millions of pages on the Web. When you perform a search, you are searching the database – your query does not go out on the Web 'live' – so the success you have with a search engine depends on how up-to-date and thorough its information is, how well organised it is and how easy and flexible it is in allowing you to refine specific search queries.

Strictly, a search directory has been organised by people so you know the sites you are likely to hit will be relevant to your query. The data in a search engine has been compiled by software and although there may be more of it, because it hasn't been sifted, some hits may produce results which are not relevant to the query. This is a common occurrence.

It can also be important to take into account how the engine ranks its finds. Some rank them by Web site which is not always very helpful if you have a few hundred to wade through. However, many engines rank them according to how relevant they think the site is to your query. There's more about this in a moment.

Let's see how the search engines get their information. With so many sites out there, it's impossible to catalogue the Web by hand so most engines use programs called spiders, robots (sometimes called Web bots) or crawlers. These zoom along the cyberspace highway, basically following hyperlinks from one site to another, and when they discover a new site they send back information to the parent search engine database for it to be indexed.

Web sites change very rapidly so spiders also update sites which have been changed. How often they do this depends on the search engine. Historically, search engines have been divided into two types according to the way they organise and allow you to access their data. One indexes the information by subject, enabling you to home in on a topic or category. The other looks up specific words or phrases which may occur not only in sites devoted to a particular subject but also in sites in other subject areas.

Both systems have their strengths and weaknesses. The main problem with doing a search for a word is that you could get thousands of hits which could take an age to sift through. Most engines have advanced search facilities to help you narrow your search and we'll see how to use these to advantage in a moment.

INFO

New search engines seem to appear almost daily but a few have been around for a while. Some of the most popular ones include: Yahoo, AltaVista, Infoseek, Excite, Lycos, HotBot, WebCrawler, Magellan, Search.Com, AOL NetFind and LookSmart.

The distinction between search engines is rapidly blurring and no matter how they organise their data, virtually every one allows you to enter a search query which can be run through all its data.

Where spider data comes from

When a spider finds a new site, what information does it send back? This depends on the search engine but there are two common methods of data retrieval.

One uses the first 100 or 200 words on the Web site. Let's say it finds a site is called 'Bill's Music Page'. It's essentially about creating original music but after the header the site has a long list of MIDI files Bill has composed. If the spider only sends back the first couple of hundred words, very little about music, MIDI or original compositions will be stored in the database.

Some spiders return every word in a site for indexing. However, this can be a mixed blessing as a site could mention something in passing which could show up in a search but which is not a major part of the site and not at all what you are looking for.

Some spiders concentrate their searches on popular sites, ones which are visited regularly or whose contents change regularly. The assumption is that such sites contain more popular and up-to-date information but this could be at the expense of more static sites and ones which cater for more minority interests.

Many search engines allow you to register a Web site with them by giving them its URL and it will then send out a spider to index the site. It can, however, take up to eight weeks for a site registered with a search engine to appear in its database. Obviously, this is of no use whatsoever if you are looking for news and up-to-date information.

Meta Tags

Site creators can influence the information some spiders take by putting key features in Meta Tags. Tags are used in HTML to tell the browser how to display the text. A Tag would be used to make text bold or italic, for example (see Chapter 1 for more about HTML).

Meta Tags are used in the head of the document and don't appear on the screen. A Description Tag is used to describe the site and the spider will pick up information from this rather than from the site itself. There is also a Keyword Tag in which you can include words which people may use when searching for the site.

If a site doesn't contain keywords in a Keyword Tag, it's up to the search engine to decide what they could be. To do this, it makes Keywords from words which are near the top of the page and from words which appear in the document several times.

Now, site designers have discovered this and know that they can make their site appear more 'relevant' to a search engine by including the same word several times. So, if Bill wanted to entice surfers looking for 'MIDI files' or 'free software' to his site, he could increase the number of times his site would appear in a hit list by including those words in the Meta Tags. In fact, if the Keyword content read 'MIDI MIDI MIDI MIDI MIDI MIDI MIDI MIDI MIDI MIDI MIDI MIDI' Bill could expect his site to appear highly ranked in a search conducted by someone looking for MIDI information.

Having said that, the search engines know that site designers get up to these sort of tricks and some ignore any words which are repeated more than four or five times. Can't win, can you? However, this helps explain why some searches produce sites which are irrelevant to your query and why searches with correct keywords may not find relevant sites.

Basic searches

The most common form of search is called a Basic Search. It's conducted on a word which the search engine looks for in its database, returning the URLs of the sites containing that word.

But try doing that with 'MIDI' or 'music' and you'll be swamped with hits. At the time of writing, WebCrawler found 4524 entries for 'MIDI', Excite found 31,907 relevant pages, Infoseek reported over 144,000 pages containing the word while HotBot found over 447,000 matches!

Clearly, we need a way to fine tune the search. And, of course, there is not just one way, but several.

Advanced search techniques

Before you start a search, it helps if you can define exactly what it is you're looking for. Do you want information about a record released in 1968, are you looking for a software update for one of your music applications, do you want to know if there's a piece of software which will convert between two audio file formats, or are you simply surfing to see how many MIDI files are out there waiting to be downloaded?

Search engines which are organised into categories and sub-categories such as Yahoo are very useful if you can work your way down through the levels to home in on your target. This is fairly easy to do because music is not a such a massive category on the Web but topics are generally not created with the musician in mind so you may want to look in categories such as computing, audio, multimedia, media and so on.

However, using an indexed approach like this, particularly in the field of music, is often limited because engines which adopt this method tend not to have such large databases. Their benefit is that all the topics and subcategories will be relevant to the main category but they often omit relevant sites because they are considered too minority to be included in the database.

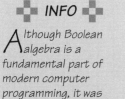

❖ INFO ❖

*A*lthough Boolean
algebra is a
fundamental part of
modern computer
programming, it was
developed in the mid-
nineteenth century by
mathematician George
Boole.

Using Boolean operators to refine a search

You will often need to refine your query in order to produce fewer but more relevant hits. Most search engines let you do this using Boolean operators. If you don't have a computing background this may seem a bit techy but the basic stuff is easy enough.

Let's say you want to see if there's any information on the Web about MIDI files and notation. You could enter either subject into a search engine but you would get many MIDI hits and many notation hits which have nothing to do with each other. WebCrawler returned over 4500 MIDI hits, see Figure 4.2 and over 2800 notation hits, see Figure 4.3.

Figure 4.2 WebCrawler
returned over 4500 MIDI
hits ...

Figure 4.3 ... and over 2800
notation hits

Using Boolean operators you could enter 'notation AND MIDI' and the search would look for occurrences of both words. WebCrawler returned just over 200 hits, which is a lot less to wade through.

If you want to find references to notation but not in relation to MIDI, you could enter 'notation NOT MIDI'.

The logic functions in different search engines are often implemented in different ways. Some, such as Excite and Northern Light, let you add a + to a word to make sure it's included in a search and a – to one to make sure it isn't.

You'll be pleased to know that many search engines have wised-up to the fact that dabbling with Boolean logic is not everyone's favourite pastime and an increasing number use pop-up menus which express Boolean logic in plain English. So, you might select a menu which tells the engine to look for all the words, any of the words, the exact phrase and so on as in HotBot, Figure 4.4.

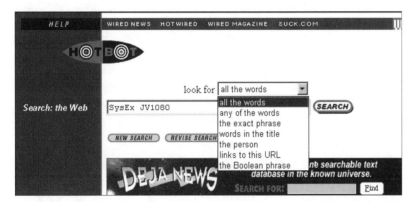

Figure 4.4 More user-friendly searching in HotBot

Let's say you have a Roland JV1080 and want to know if there is any information on the Web about its use of System Exclusive data. You could do a search on JV1080 (HotBot returns over 880 matches) or on SysEx (over 2332) but by searching for them both, the number is reduced to a far more manageable 50.

A rather nice feature which is finding its way into several search engines such as Excite, for example, is a list of suggested words which you may like to include in your search. To add them, you simply click on the check box next to them, Figure 4.5.

Figure 4.5 Excite includes a list of suggested words which you click on to add to the search

Some search engines produce a list of associated topics which they think may be useful. AltaVista's advanced search facilities offer you a list of associated words which you can include in the search, and Lycos' advanced search options has several menus and ticky boxes to help you fine tune your search.

All these facilities are designed to help you refine your search to get closer matches to the subject you are looking for.

Concept-based searches

One or two search engines are concept-based which means they try to find out exactly what you're searching for rather than simply doing a search on the words you enter. Excite is probably the best-known example and on a good day it will find sites which are 'about' the subject your query suggests you are interested in.

Rather than use artificial intelligence or a linguistic approach to discover what a site is about, Excite counts the number of times certain words appear and if they occur in the same document, it 'deduces' by statistical analysis that the site is about a particular subject.

If a site contained words such as hi fi, CD, songs, playback and speakers the software might deduce that it was about music and return the site as a hit if you entered 'music' as a query even though the site did not contain that actual word. Sometimes, of course, it gets it wrong and there's an example of how this works coming up next.

When using a concept-based engine like Excite, you'll get better results if you enter as many related words as possible.

Ranking and relevance

Most search engines present the hits in order of relevance. Many engines put a percentage figure next to each hit – the higher the percentage, the more the engine thinks the result will provide what you're looking for.

Doing a search using only one word will generally not give a very high percentage rating as it's almost impossible to know what 'subject' you are searching for.

For example, the highest rating when doing a search on the word 'audio' using Excite was 67 percent. Doing a search with 'digital audio' produced an 80 percent rating. 'digital audio effects' got this up to 85 percent. 'PC-based digital audio effects' returned several results over 90 percent.

Some of these hits were the same as the ones produced by the searches with fewer words, the difference being that the search engine is more confident that the results will match your needs.

One of the results returned by Excite on this search – and given an 86 percent rating – was for a company which specialises in signs and graphic design so it doesn't get it right all the time. However, the majority of the results were highly relevant.

Which search engine?

Needless to say, because search engines collect data in different ways, organise it in different ways, and let you search for it in different ways, there is no one overall winner in the search engine stakes. If different engines are given the same query then, of course, you can compare them but that's not to say that the winner – however you choose to judge them – will be best if given a different query.

And with so many search engines to choose from, it's almost as difficult deciding which one to use for a search as it is to find what you're looking for.

Search engine technology has been developing rapidly. Individual engines have had extra features added and new engines appear with monotonous regularity. It's hardly surprising, therefore, to discover that many computer magazines and even individuals have tried them, tested them, and analysed the results, some of which are shown below.

Best:	AltaVista	*Ratings out of 5:*	
Most comprehensive results:	Excite	AltaVista	5
Most usable:	Infoseek	HotBot	5
Most relevant results:	AltaVista	Lycos	5
Most likely to find a hit:	AltaVista	WebCrawler	5
		Yahoo!	5
Fastest:		Excite	4
AltaVista		Infoseek	4
Excite		LookSmart	4
HotBot		Search.com	4
Infoseek		AOL NetFind	3
Lycos		Open Text	3
Top 3 in order:		*More ratings out of 5:*	
HotBot		AltaVista	5
AltaVista		HotBot	4
Infoseek		Infoseek	4
		Open Text	4
Top 8 in order:		Excite	3
Lycos		Lycos	3
Infoseek		WebCrawler	3
OpenText		Yahoo	3
AltaVista		*Another set of ratings:*	
Magellan		AltaVista	A
Excite		Infoseek	A
HotBot		Yahoo	A
Yahoo!		Excite	B
		HotBot	B
		Lycos	B
		WebCrawler	B

One American magazine even organised a contest to see which search engine was best. It involved the designers of the engines themselves and they had to find the answers to several questions which resided somewhere on the Web. It was a contest not only of speed but also of knowing which questions to ask. The tasks were marked out of 30 and this is the result:

> HotBot 13
> Excite 12
> AltaVista 6
> Infoseek 4

Check out the details yourself at:

> http://www.zdnet.com/pccomp/srchoff/srchoff.html

There's also a link to the questions they asked – ooo! some hard ones here, too – if you want to try it yourself.

Several things are apparent from these ratings. The most interesting thing to note is that no two tests, reviewers or ratings agree with each other although some search engines do appear in the lists time and again.

Currently, AltaVista seems to be performing very well and HotBot is strongly fancied but other than that it's difficult to draw any firm conclusions. Will these engines still figure highly in the ratings in six month's time? Who knows?

And are such tests useful in the real world, anyway? It's worth bearing in mind that most of the tests tend to be performed with either the business user or general information seeker in mind and they may not accurately reflect searches in other areas such as in the music field.

Search engines change and develop, others come along offering additional facilities and many of the developers are working on improved user-interfaces. A Top Ten list is bound to change rapidly.

As with many walks of life, searches are often a compromise and, depending on what you're looking for, it will usually pay to use more than one search engine. Needless to say, there are way of using several at the same time and we'll look at this in the Metasearching section.

Try some of the engines, pick a few which suit your way of working and add others to your list if your regulars get stuck on a search. Do use the advanced features as this really does help you home in more accurately on the information you're looking for.

Search engine sites

There are dozens of search engines. Here are some of the most popular ones – and some less well-known ones, too.

AltaVista
http://www.altavista.digital.com/
Currently one of the top search engines in most categories. It has a vast database of information and if it's on the Net, AltaVista ought to find it. Must be one of the first engines you try when doing a search.

Figure 4.6 Alta Vista – one of the best, and
Figure 4.7 AOL

AOL.com
http://www.aol.com/
A Web guide consisting of a collection of subjects pointing to sites catering for a wide range of interests. A good place to start if you fancy a spot of non-directional surfing. There's new stuff up here every day.

Britannica Internet Guide
http://www.ebig.com/
A directory from the Encyclopedia people with topics and search facilities.

INFO

Web guides are organised like directories – you search through a series of topics and subjects, a little like using a library index system. Many sites incorporate a guide or a directory system as well as a search facility.

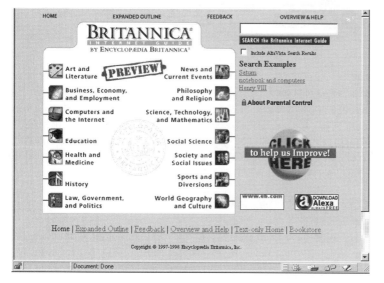

Figure 4.8 Britannica Internet Guide

Directory Guide
http://directoryguide/com/
A comprehensive catalogue and directory of over 400 sites.

Disinformation
http://www.disinfo.com/
A sort of alternative, counter-revolutionary, sub-culture search engine... Awe, go check it out, anyway.

Euroseek
http://www.euroseek.net
A European-based search engine but which can search in any country in the world and in any language.

Figure 4.9 Euroseek can search in any language

Excite
http://www.excite.com/
Excite's concept-based searches can narrow down a search to a few relevant sites. It can occasionally be a bit hit or miss if your collection of search words isn't quite right but it's often spot on and can home in on information very quickly. There's an Excite site in the UK (http://excite.co.uk) which can search UK and European sites.

GOD (Global On-line Directory)
http://god.co.uk
They must have been glad to get this domain name! A directory based in the UK but which nevertheless can search globally. No apparent religious affiliation.

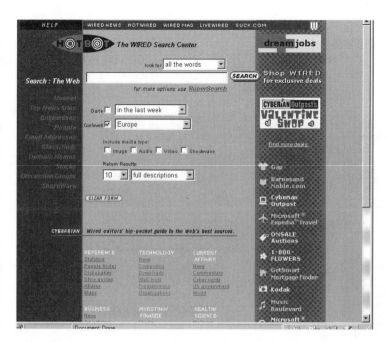

Figure 4.10 HotBot is one of the top-ranked search engines

HotBot
http://www.hotbot.com/
Another very popular engine, fast and powerful with lots of categories to search in. Particularly good at news items, albeit with a US slant. No UK-based site but it can do a search of sites in Europe.

HumanSearch
http://www.humansearch.com/
Enter a search query and select one of 15 topics to search in. If you don't find what you're looking for, you can pass your query to a set of human searchers who will do their best to track down the information you seek and email it to you. Now there's a novel idea!

Infoseek
http://www.infoseek.com/
Another powerful and comprehensive search engine with a large database. Includes Web guides and it also searches newsgroups and other Net sources. You can enter search keywords, phrases and even questions but the questions tend not to be as reliable a search method as traditional searches. Also has a UK site. Try the Ultra site, too (http://ultra.infoseek.com) which searches the Web, news, companies and Usenet data.

Infospace
http://www.infospace.com/
It calls itself the ultimate directory. Lots of categories to search plus Yellow Pages, White Pages, business listings, and personal email address-es including addresses of the famous. The UK site has a business finder and a people finder.

Lycos
http://www.lycos.com/
One of the longest-established search engines, large, fast and an effective search tool. It's also available in the UK (http://www.lycosuk.co.uk), Figure 4.11, with the option of searching UK and Ireland sites.

Figure 4.11 Lycos UK has the option of searching UK and Ireland sites

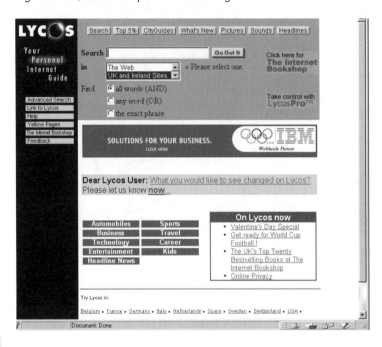

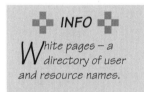

LookSmart
http://www.looksmart.com/
The user-friendly search engine, backed by Reader's Digest, with search topics divided into over 17,000 categories. Check out the UK site at (http://www.looksmart.co.uk) which can search UK or world-wide sites.

Magellan
http://mckinley.com/
Once one of the prime search engines but it recently seems to have fallen out of favour somewhat. Strictly a directory like Yahoo, it has a list of topics for easy browsing and you can do a search on the Web. Search Voyeur lets you see what other people have been searching for and it has access to Yellow Pages, a People Finder and other areas.

The Mining Company
http://home.miningco.com/
Another list of categories covering over 500 topics. The main thrust of the site is that the topics each have their own areas run by Mining Company Guides, individuals from across the world who are experts and enthusiasts in a particular subject.

Check out the MIDI Music site (http://midimusic.miningco.com/index) which has wads of information, MIDI files, book lists, newsgroup lists, discussions and links to associated sites.

Also, check out the Music Technology site (http://musictech. miningco.com/) which has lots of information about instruments, software, synthesisers, artists, manufacturers and so on. You'll also find links to around two dozen music-related sites at the Co. It's very American but it has a lorra lorra information and regular updates.

Northern Light
http://www.northernlight.com/

This site has a few interesting features such as search folders which organise the results into folders to help narrow your search. It also includes information from over 2900 journals, books, magazines and databases which it claims are not available on any other search engine.

Open Text
http://opentext.com/

Powerful and worth using but it currently has lots of graphics which slow it down and lots of Me Me Me Aren't I Great promotional stuff which you don't really want to see.

PlanetSearch
http://www.planetsearch.com/

A relatively new search engine with news, finance and wealth links – US-based, of course. Likely to return lots and lots of hits. If you search using several words, it uses a colour-coded bar system to indicate the rating of the sites by each word, as in Figure 4.12.

TIP

Many sites, including The Mining Company, have links to other sites but in browsers such as Netscape, the URL seems to suggest that they are part of The Mining Company site. Linking to the North American Steinberg page, for example, still shows The Mining Company URL in Netscape's Location area. Apart from being downright deceptive, it means you can't bookmark the URL for future reference. To get around this, right-click on the link you want to explore and select 'Open in New Window' from the menu. The link will open in a new browser window with the correct URL.

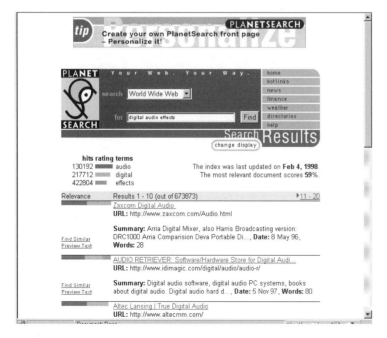

Figure 4.12 Planet UK uses a colour coded bar system to indicate the relevance of the sites

Search.Com
http://www.search.com/
Here you can search in a range of categories and the list of topics makes for easy browsing. There are over 100 speciality searches listed alphabetically including several music entries.

UK Index
http://www.ukindex.co.uk
This contains a list of UK sites which you can search by category although you can't browse the list.

WebCrawler
http://www.webcrawler.com/
You can search by topic and create personalised search pages. Currently its UK site link takes you to Excite UK.

Webtaxi
http://webtaxi.com/
Allows you to select from a large list of directories and search engines using a range of search criteria.

Wired Cybrarian
http://www.wired.com/cybrarian/
What else would you call a library in cyberspace? There are currently nine main categories – Reference, Technology, Current Affairs, Business, Recreation, Investing and Finance, Media, Culture, and Health and Science – each with several sub-categories. It contains links to several sites with hosts of freeware and shareware.

Figure 4.12 Yahoo is one of the longest-established and most well-known search engines

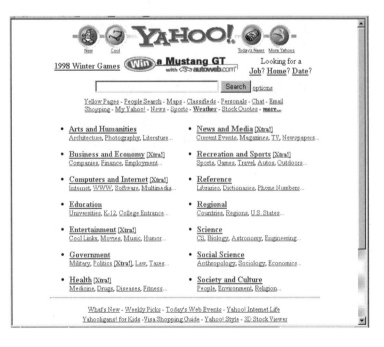

Yahoo
http://www.yahoo.com/
The first and probably the most well-known search engine and directory on the Net. Browse through a list of categories or use one of a number of search methods. Maybe not as comprehensive as some of the other engines but still a good jump-off point. Try http://www.yahoo.co.uk to search UK and Ireland sites.

Other search vehicles

Although perhaps not totally in keeping with the book's music brief, it's worth pointing out that there is a large number of specialist search engines designed to find all sorts of sites and information. They can find people's email and street address, unearth business statistics, report news, financial and political information, and some simply list cool sites. Here's a few.

100 Hottest Sites
http://www.100hot.com/
A directory of cool and popular sites in ten categories – Tech, Entertainment, Business, Buzz, Life Style, Shopping, Games, Sports, News and World. If you're a Mac user, check out the Mac sites listed here – a veritable cornucopia of Mac news, information and software. The music sites are well worth browsing, too, along with the audio and CD listings.

Bigfoot
http://www.bigfoot.com/
With Bigfoot you can search for someone's email address, track down the Web address of a company and search through a Yellow Pages directory of companies – albeit in America. But the first two searches work on a global scale and can track down some buried references.

The Free Encyclopedia
http://www.encyclopedia.com
As its name says, this is a free encyclopedia containing over 17,000 articles from The Concise Columbia Electronic Encyclopedia. You never know when it may come in useful.

News from Yahoo
http://www.yahoo.com/headlines/international/
World headlines and stories provided by Reuters divided into categories such as new, world, biz, tech, sport, politics, entertainment and health.

People Search
http://www.yahoo.four11.com/cgi-bin/Four11Main?yahooe&template=yahoo.t
The URL is a bit of a mouthful but this is easily accessed from Yahoo's site. As its name suggests, it's a search engine for people and it does a reasonable job of tracking down anyone you think may have an email

address. It can also try to come up with a phone number but this relies on the respondent putting that up on the Web somewhere and it may not always be very successful at discovering the numbers of UK residents.

Search engine information

Needless to say there are lots of sites devoted to telling you what a search engine is, how it works, how to get the best out of one and so on. Here's a few to check out. For a more complete list do a search on 'search engines'…

CNet
http://cnet.com/Content/Features/Dlife/Search/
Can you trust your search engine? This is a feature, now a few years old, but it contains lots of information about search engines, how they work and how to use them. It includes a comparative search so you can check the results returned by two search engines on the same search data.

Search Engine Watch
http://searchenginewatch.com/
Bags and bags of information about search engines, links to the major search engines and to many, many others. Information on how to use them and how to get the most out of them. An essential visit.

Figure 4.13 Search Engine Watch contains a wealth of information about search engines

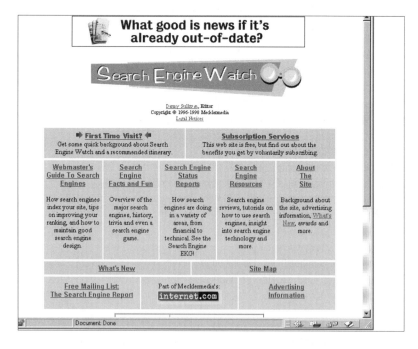

Searching the Web
http://www.hypernews.org/HyperNews/get/www/searching.html
A plethora of information about search engines, searching services, direc-

tories, search software and articles about searching. Currently, too many links had expired for comfort but it's still an essential visit for anyone wanting to get more out of the Web and squeeze the last amount of information from it.

The Spider's Apprentice
http://www.monash.com/spidap.htm
A set of pages devoted to search engines and how to use them. Good content and recommended reading.

The Web Robots Page
http://info.webcrawler.com/mak/projects/robots/robots.html
Not strictly about search engines but about the software bots and spiders which engines use to gather their information. Interesting background info and a site techies and programmers in particular will enjoy.

Metasearching

If you can refine your queries in a standard search engine to find exactly what you're looking for then you're good, but you know you've achieved Mega Search Master status when you start using several search engines at the same time. This enables you to use the best features from a number of engines and so maximise the search results.

Fortunately, you don't have to use the engines individually because – as may have already guessed – there are utilities which allow you to use search several engines at once. They are known as metasearch engines and there are sites which can do this for you along with stand-alone programs.

The problem with searches on the Web is generally not that they don't find what you're looking for – although if it's not in a engine's database, obviously, it won't return a result – but that you get far too many hits.

The advantage of metasearches is that they can look for information in lots of places at the same time, dramatically reducing the search time and as you're using more engines you can usually be more specific with your search query which, hopefully, will produce more accurate results. The following is a representative but by no means an exhaustive list of metasearch sites.

All-In-One
http://www.albany.net/allinone/
This is a compilation of various forms-based search tools available on the Net, collected under one roof for ease and speed of access.

Ask Jeeves
http://www.askjeeves.com/
This is a very interesting site where you can ask 'Jeeves' a question in English and it will reply with a list of answers about where you can find (hopefully) related material. As with many interpretative engines of this type, it doesn't always get it exactly right and sometimes it misses the

thrust of the question entirely but it can be fun and its searches for software include Mac as well as PC. Worth asking...

CUSI – Configurable Unified Search Engine.
http://www.nexor.com/public/cusi/

Offers a wide range of customised searches with a range of engines including WWW indexes, robot-generated indexes, software searches, people searches and dictionaries. Currently includes searches based on 'older' protocols such as Archie, Veronica and WAIS – great for the techies and old Net hands but anyone can use it. Also includes lots of information.

Dogpile
http://www.dogpile.com/

What names must they have rejected as unsuitable before they settled on this one, you may wonder? Anyway, this is a multi-search engine search engine – IYSWIM – which interrogates a customisable list of up to 24 search engines and allows you to specify the order in which they will be searched. Wads of results, ideal for heavy searchers.

Husky Search
http://www.huskysearch.cs.washington.edu

What is it with dogs, eh? Written by the author of MetaCrawler, this lets you specify how long the engines perform the search. There are several search options such as searching by region, target site or category and a recently-added Java interface lets you see the results as they come in.

Inference Find
http://www.inference.com/infind

'An Internet search tool that calls out in parallel all the best search engines, merges the results, removes redundancies, clusters the hits into neat understandable groupings, and returns it all to you faster than you can say 'Nothing but Net'.' It says here. It lists results by subject and by site. This is an interesting site with powerful multi-search capabilities although the query must be phrased carefully in order to get accurate hits.

The Internet Sleuth
http://www.isleuth.com/

An excellent starting point for a search – lets you select up to six databases in a variety of areas such as news, business, software, and Web directories. Its list of 21 categories can be expanded to include sub-categories to make it easier to home in on a topic of interest.

Metasearch
http://metasearch.com/

Enter a word or two or a phrase and this site pops up half a dozen search engines you can send your query through. It's not parallel processing but with most engines you can select terse, standard or verbose output which can be very helpful.

Savvy Search
http://guaraldi.cs.colostate.edu:2000/
This is an experimental search engine designed to query multiple search engines simultaneously. You decide whether to search for all or any of the query terms and indicate the number of results you'd like from each engine. When you submit a query, a Search Plan is created which ranks the 19 search engines and divides them into groups of anticipated useful-ness. Very interesting and well worth trying.

W3 Search Engines
http://cuiwww.unige.ch/meta-index.html
Created by the University of Geneva, this site lists some of the most use-ful search engines on the Web. You can search in list-based catalogues, spider-based catalogues, people databases, and a whole variety of search engines.

Metasearch software

The advantage of using software rather than a Web site-based search engine is that it can be more flexible, perhaps store the information so you can organise it and view it off-line, and it is often much more cus-tomisable. Against this, you need to weigh up the amount of disk space it will use if it is storing complete Web pages. However, if you search the Web regularly and like to keep tabs on the results, you'll find some of these programs here very interesting.

There is a lot of software out there so here, again, what follows is just a sample. The URLs are where we found the programs but if you do a search you may discover several alternative sites.

Copernic for Windows 95
http://www.download.com/PC/Result/TitleDetail/0,4,203-27560-g,501000.html
Lets you search simultaneously using many of the major search engines

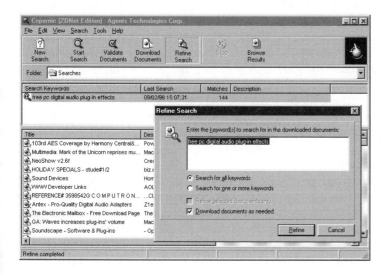

Figure 4.14 Copernic for Windows 95 lets you search many of the major search engines simultaneously

using any or all of the words in the query. Duplicates are automatically removed, the results stored in folders for easy retrieval and the program ranks the results. You can further refine the search, look for certain words in the results and open the results as Web pages. Searches are stored for later reference. It's a topping search tool, an indisputable Must Try after which it will probably turn into a Must Have.

Data Grabber for the PC
http://www.wildcowpublishing.com/datagrab.html

A small utility which resides in the task bar until required. You simply type in a search query, select a search engine from the drop down menu and click on Go. The results are presented in your browser window. The program gets its list of search engines and their URLs from a text file and you are invited to edit this to add your own favourites and to update outdated links. You can also arrange them to create different categories for different searches – one for news, one for MIDI files, one for phrase

Figure 4.15 Data Grabber for the PC is cheap and cheerful but works wonderfully well

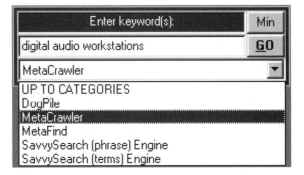

searches and so on. The editing looks a bit techy but you can copy the examples in the file. It's a bit cheap and cheerful, DIY and dirty but it's dead easy to use and it works wonderfully well.

Go-Get-It for Windows 95
http://www.jla.com/htms/gogetit/ourdwnld.htm

You can search up to ten search engines using keywords and phrases and store them in folders for easy reference. Results are displayed as soon as they are found and you can view them in the program or transfer them to a browser. The program can also download Web pages and complete Web sites for off-line viewing and you can set up a personal information service that retrieves customised information. Certainly one to try.

WebTurbo for PC, Java version for Mac
http://www.webturbo.com/

Installation puts an icon on the header bar of the browser (some other software does the same and they may interfere with each other) for quick access. It includes an on-screen video tutorial but it's fairly easy to use, anyway. Activation opens the program in the browser itself. It queries many popular search engines and it can search on multiple topics. The Web Preview section creates summaries of the pages so you can rapidly see their contents. WebTurbo is free — the company makes money selling advertising through a window on the program. Definitely one to try.

SearchWolf
http://www.msw.com.au/search/
'Don't search the Net — Hunt it!' says the blurb. SearchWolf is an expert system which lets you search several selectable engines via a simple easy-to-use interface. MSW has developed several other Wolves including FTP Wolf which can search most of the FTP search engines for a given file. WebWolf is a Web page crawler which compiles lists of files, FTP sites and links. Of prime interest to musicians is MP3 Wolf which scans the Net for MP3, MIDI, Wave and other music files and links.

Internet FastFind for Windows
One of a growing number of commercial search programs. This one comes from Symantec, best-known for the indispensable Norton Utilities. Essentially, it queries a combination of on-line resources such as search engines and Usenet, summarises and organises the results, updates the information and finds new information at regular intervals. It's a powerful and flexible program and generates some excellent hits as well as storing past searches. The ability to update information automatically lets you keep tabs on sites of interest. The main WebFind function searches using many of the major search engines, removes duplicates and prioritises the

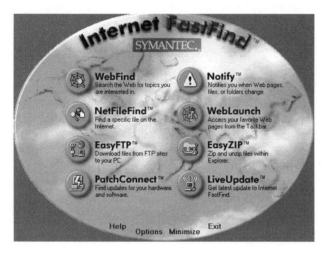

Figure 4.16 Internet FastFind for Windows searches a combination of on-line resources

results. NetFileFind searches for a specific file, Notify tells you if your favourite Web pages have changed. PatchConnect helps track down new patches and drivers for your system although this can be a tad involved.

WebWhacker For Windows and the Mac
http://www.bluesquirrel.com/
This is a commercial program although there are demo versions for Windows 3.1, Win 95 and the Mac. It allows you to download entire sites for speedy off-line viewing. Blue Squirrel has several other Web utilities of

interest including WebSeeker which utilises up to 120 search engines; TechSeeker which combines the results of over 90 on-line technical resources to perform searches for drivers, software, technical solutions and product information; and Grab-a-Site, an 'industrial strength' off-line browser which can download an entire Web site! One for the ISDN users – or those with a free connection, perhaps.

Web Compass
http://www.quarterdeck.com/
Here's another commercial program, this time from Quarterdeck and a demo is available from the above address. It can query up to 35 search engines at one time and more can be added. It ranks for relevancy on a scale of 1 to 100, it builds summaries from the results and automatically organises results by topic. It even includes a thesaurus to assist in searching. Now there's thoughtful for you. An excellent and comprehensive tool, well worth trying.

Net Utilities

Once you get hooked on surfing the Net, you'll discover lots of interesting utilities designed to make your life easier. A wade through some of the software sites such as those specialising in Net-related shareware will reveal a host of utilities you think you can't live without.

With your new-found search power, you should be able to track down the following programs with ease – but the addresses where they were found have also been included.

NearSite for the PC
http://www.nearsite.com/
NearSite collects and stores Web pages for off-line browsing. You can set up any number of pages or sites and the program will automatically download them while you're on-line browsing, saving wads of time. The schedule facility can automatically update the sites at predetermined

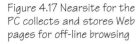
Figure 4.17 Nearsite for the PC collects and stores Web pages for off-line browsing

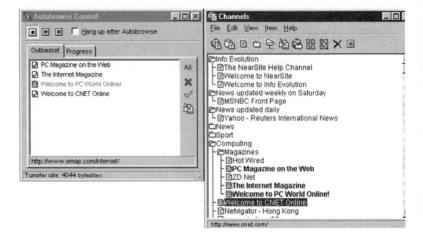

times. It's ideal for keeping tabs on magazine updates and news information. Well worth downloading.

NetAttache Lite for Windows 95 and 3.1
http://www.tympani.com/ftp/download/NetAttache/na32v25e.exe
This program retrieves Web pages for off-line reading. You organise Web entries in 'briefs', maybe importing addresses from a Bookmark file. NetAttache logs on, retrieves the pages and stores the text and images. You can read the pages off-line using your regular browser, complete with interactive linking on-line if you wish. Bit of a naughty installation routine, though, which requires you to enter personal details. Tell lies, I say! It also has an annoying advert bar which you can't close. No such thing as a free lunch, eh?

Tierra Highlights 2 for Windows 95
http://www.tierra.com/products2/highlights2.html
You select sites and Tierra Highlights monitors them for changes. You can ignore image changes so you aren't notified when adverts are changed. The program is configured through a toolbar which you can hide and then a task tray icon tells you when changes have been detected. It works with Netscape and Internet Explorer.

Bookmarks

As you surf you will discover dozens, probably hundreds, of interesting sites which you may well want to return to. You can store the URL of a site using a browser's bookmark facility. This is usually easily done by selecting Add Bookmark from a menu although different browsers work in different ways and have different facilities.

In Netscape, for example, you can drag the Page Proxy icon in the Location tool bar to the Bookmark icon. Internet Explorer uses a Favourites list which has a similar function.

One particularly useful feature is the ability to create folders to organise the bookmarks and favourites list. You probably organise your applications and utilities into folders and it makes sense to do the same with bookmarks otherwise you will end up with a totally unmanageable list scrolling off the page when you start looking for one.

In most browsers, you can change the name of the bookmark and it's often useful to do this. The browser picks up the name of the page from the site but sometimes it can appear as the URL or even as 'Untitled'. Not very informative.

Another very useful feature is Netscape's Update Bookmarks and Internet Explorer's Subscribe feature. They both scan the bookmarked pages to see if they have been updated since your last visit.

Bookmark – a link to a Web site or page saved as a file to a hard disk to enable the user to return to the Web page quickly at a later time.

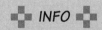

Some sites will send you email to notify you when they have been updated, but few music-related sites seem to have included this facility yet.

5

Commercial on-line services

INFO

ISP – Internet Service Provider.

There are several ways of accessing the Internet. Most people use an ISP or one of the growing number of commercial on-line services. With an ISP you usually get the software required to connect you to the Net – a browser, email software and perhaps some utilities. You go on-line, launch the browser and start surfing. That's as much as many people need.

On-line services give you a little bit extra. Sometimes a lot extra. They generally host an on-line community which offers all the main facilities most people want from the Web. These include email, news, financial information, sport, games, travel, extracts from news-stand magazines and, of course, they all have a computing section.

Most on-line services charge for content. In other words, if you want to browse around the financial section you may well have to pay so-much per hour for the privilege. This is often offset by the lower monthly fees which most service providers charge. You have balance the amount of time you expect to spend on-line against the cost of accessing the areas you're particularly interested in.

INFO

Other ways to access the Internet include via a business, through an educational establishment and at your local friendly Cyber Cafe.

On-line service providers

There are currently over 200 ISPs but only a handful of on-line service providers. The most well-known are probably AOL, CompuServe and MSN (Microsoft Network) but others include LineOne, Which? On-line and CiX.

Some of these services are massive and have an amazing number of sections. They often offer on-line technical support, chat rooms where you can talk – or type! – to other users on-line in real-time, search tools, access to a wide range of software, and you can usually access the wide world of the Internet through them, too.

You may think that you don't need this if you have the Web but there are advantages. Most services have dedicated software which offers a consistent interface which many users appreciate. Many have news and features which are updated daily and each time you sign on you could be presented with a What's New list.

For newcomers, there is usually copious amounts of on-line help and even chat rooms with resident technical support staff. The various areas make it easy to find what you're interested in and keep up to date with it and you're not troubled with spam as you are in newsgroups and mailing lists (see Chapter 3). It all helps to create a sense of community and offer easier access to certain topics and areas of interest.

The number of ISPs and on-line services seems to change continuously. Any list would be out of date before it was printed so if you want to know what's current, check out some of the many Internet magazines.

But to give you a flavour of what's available, we'll have a look at three popular on-line service providers...

CiX

CiX – pronounced 'kicks' – is a UK-based service. It has no fancy graphics and uses an OLR called Ameol. It is essentially a development of the older BBS (Bulletin Board System) which has all but died out thanks to the ease of access to and sheer scope of the Internet.

So, amid the glitz and glamour and animated icons of the Web, what has CiX got to offer? Actually, quite a lot. Apart from the fact that it uses an OLR, the system is not full of fancy graphics so it's much faster than dedicated on-line services which do use graphics. Also, you generally dial directly into the system and so don't have to wait while your connection routes through several servers. If you log-on at 33.6K, for example, you will access the system at that speed except for exceptionally busy periods. So, benefit number one – it's fast.

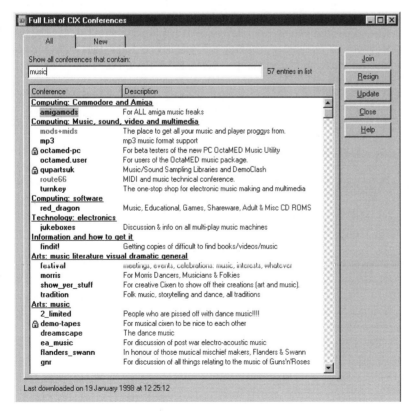

Figure 5.1 Some of the music conferences on CiX

INFO

BBS – Originally a one-computer – and usually a one-man – system, often with one modem.

INFO

OLR – Off-Line Reader, a program which logs onto a site, uploads and downloads files and messages and logs off automatically. You spend the minimum amount of time on-line, saving phone bills, and you can deal with the messages in your own time.

INFO

There's more about modem speeds in the next chapter.

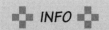

INFO

In case you're too young to 'geddit', the reference is to a song called 'Get Your Kicks on Route 66' which was a hit for various artists including Nat 'King' Cole in the early 40s and later on for Chuck Berry whose version, recorded in 1961, is probably the best known.

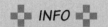

INFO

NRPNs – Non-Registered Parameter Numbers, used to perform functions such as adjusting a voice's vibrato, filter, envelope generator and so on, particularly in GS and XG instruments.

But perhaps its main attractions is its Conferencing system. There are over 4500 different conferences covering every kind of interest and activity imaginable. Conferences are akin to newsgroups but as they are run in a closed system you aren't bombarded with spam. They are quick and easy to use and there is a definite sense of community among the members.

CiX has a very high number of knowledgeable members in many subject areas – including music – and most cixen (CiX citizens) are friendly and helpful, make newcomers welcome and are happy to help out if you have a problem.

As CiX is a UK-based system, the vast majority of members are in the UK and although it make be nice to think of ourselves as part of a Worldwide Global Village, there are definite advantages in being able to chat to people who are in the same locality – not least of all when buying and selling items (CiX is an excellent medium for buying second-hand gear and disposing of your old stuff) and comparing notes on good shops, gig venues and so on.

CiX has several music-related conferences, Figure 5.1. The most popular one is route66 (where you get your kicks – geddit?), Figure 5.2, which is frequented by a wide range of people from experienced gigging and studio musicians to newcomers just dipping their toes in the musical water. Help flows copiously and there is a lot of interesting discussion on all music-related matters from copyright to NRPNs.

There are other conferences devoted to soundcards, Cubase, Mods, multimedia, composition software, MIDI files, samples – all sorts of musical things. Most conferences have a files list which contain files you can download. In the music conferences you'll find MIDI files, Wave files, music software utilities, demo programs and software drivers.

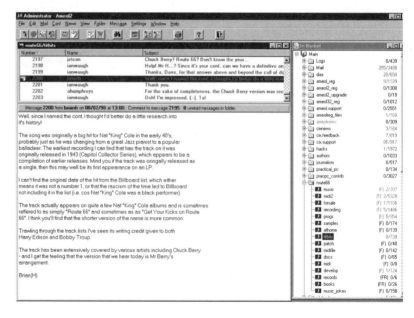

Figure 5.2 The Route 66 conference on CiX is the most popular music conference

You can also access the Internet from CiX so you can leap out into the Global Village. Access its not quite as straightforward as using an ISP, however, and many CiX users also have a separate Internet account.

AOL

AOL – America On-Line – Figure 5.3, is one of a number of on-line services which offer an all-in-one package, a community which some users may feel they never have the need to leave. It was one of the first with the concept and it is one of the largest providers in the world, currently with a UK-base of over 400,000 and a claimed world-wide base of 15 million or more.

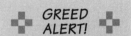

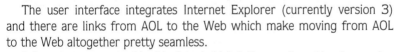

Figure 5.3 AOL's main menu

The user interface integrates Internet Explorer (currently version 3) and there are links from AOL to the Web which make moving from AOL to the Web altogether pretty seamless.

It has chat rooms and buddy lists (which tell you when friends are also on-line) which are useful if you like chatting – or tapping – on-line. Although the chats generally take place around 9 PM when phone calls are cheaper in the UK, this facility is generally more popular in the USA where local calls are virtually free.

Although all areas can be accessed by any subscriber, AOL has a number of UK-based areas. Music areas include ones about UK-based rock and pop music, the charts and music news.

The main area for computer-based musicians is the PC Music and Sound Forum, Figure 5.4, which contains lots of help documents and information, a message area (Figure 5.5 (aol3)), information on music companies and a list of music-related Web sites. There is also a software area, of course, and the Music forum has a healthy selection of music files

INFO

Mods – Short for *Modules* and often abbreviated in capitalised form to MODs. These are self-contained sample-based pieces of music which contain the samples within the file itself.

GREED ALERT!

Until BT and the new crop of telecomm companies start offering local calls on the same basis as US companies, the full potential of the Net will never be realised in the UK. It's not just about on-line chat but about making Web access more affordable and bringing the Web and its facilities to more people. The high cost of UK telephone calls is probably the major reason why the UK lags behind the US in Internet access.

Figure 5.4 AOL's PC Music and Sound Forum

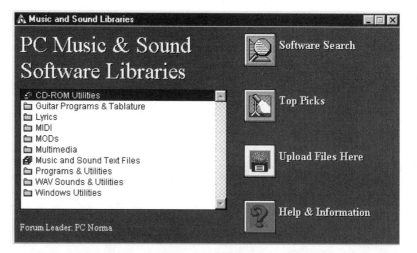

Figure 5.5 The message area on AOL

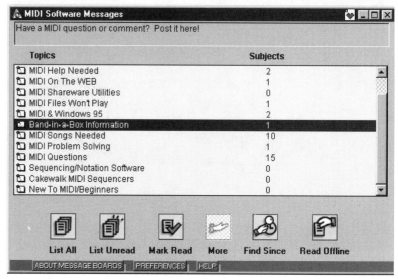

for Mac and PC users, including MIDI files, Mods, Wave files and utilities.

It also hosts on-line conferences covering a range of subjects such as MIDI, Wave sounds and utilities and individual software programs.

And the lovely Joanna Lumley (well, her voice, at least), welcomes you to AOL, tells you when you have new post and says goodbye.

CompuServe

CompuServe, Figure 5.6, has also been around for a long time. It, too, integrates its own user-interface, on-line forums and communities with access to the Net. It's international although it also has some UK-based areas and it currently has over 1000 public forums. A list is available for anyone who wants to browse through it.

Figure 5.6 Compuserve's main menu

CompuServe uses a series of forums and communities, areas which contain information dedicated to specific subjects. You access these by typing 'GO' followed by the name of a forum although you can navigate your way to them via menus. You can store your favourite places in a list for quick access, do searches, access your email at the Mail Centre, chat to other users, read the news and so on.

The main music area is the MIDI/Music forum, Figure 5.7, which includes a message board for posting messages and requesting information, and a files library which contains a good range of files – shareware, demos, updates and so on. It caters for all computers including the Amiga and ST (although the most recent updates here were in mid-1997) but most programs are for the PC, followed by the Mac.

Message Sections		22 Sections
Section Name	Topics	Messages
General [1]	35	196
Synths/Samplers [2]	42	208
New to MIDI [3]	12	56
MIDI Interfacing [4]	35	129
Macintosh [5]	20	70
Amiga/Atari ST [6]	1	1
IBM/PC Compatible [7]	45	378
Pre-Owned Equipment [8]	93	149
Composing/Sequences [9]	17	66
Live MIDI Perform. [10]	3	23
Windows Media Sound [11]	4	9
MIDI Controllers [12]	5	17
Music Discussions [13]	7	27
Acoustic Instr. [14]	1	2
Sound Cards [15]	36	158
Recording/Audio [16]	197	2290
Surround/DVD Audio [17]	0	0
Effects Gear [18]	10	31
DAWs/HD Recording [19]	57	597
Guitars/Amps/MIDI [20]	23	254
Internet MIDI/Audio [21]	8	30
Jam Session [23]	17	132

Figure 5.7 The Compuserve MIDI music forum

Much of the wealth of CompuServe seems to be hidden beneath its surface and you need to dig below its glossy graphics to get at the good

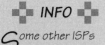 **INFO**

Some other ISPs also produce magazines for subscribers. Demon is one and although it's strictly an ISP, the magazine is excellent, very informative and often contains new software. Demon was bought by Scottish Power in early 1998.

bits. Access, however, can seem slow and some of its functionality is not quite on a par with that of other ISPs. Users don't seem to mind, however, and there is a wealth of information here although you will probably need to venture forth on the Web to access much of the music information you may require.

Members also receive a magazine called GO... Online which contains information about new developments at CompuServe, new community areas, new and interesting Web sites, and features on a range of Web and electronic communication topics. It may include a CD containing the latest versions of the CompuServe software and some utilities. In general, the magazine explains how to get more out of your membership and it's a nice extra, adding to the feeling of belonging to a community.

In 1998 CompuServe was acquired by AOL and Bertelsmann although it continues to operate as an independent service.

Choosing a service

If you don't already have a service provider, it's worth weighing up the benefits of an on-line service provider or even using two providers as many of the more dedicated surfers do. If there's a problem with one – and rare indeed is the service which is totally fault-free – you can always use the other one and some are more adept than others at certain functions. You may choose CiX, for example, for email and its conferencing and an ISP for Web access.

Speed is king

In the land of the blind, the one-eyed man is king. In the realm of cyberspace, the man – or woman – with the fastest Internet connection gets the goodies more quickly and with lower phone bills.

We can't let a book about the Internet go by without a chapter on speed. As the amount of information on the Internet continues to proliferate and as software continues to increase in size, it is becoming increasingly important to be able to get what you want without having to spend forever on the phone. Especially with the exorbitant cost of calls in the UK.

As high-speed access is such an essential part of the surfing process, this chapter looks at ways of connecting to the Net and at the issues involved in transferring data.

 QUOTE

'Speed isn't everything – it's the only thing'. Seymour Cray, father of the supercomputer.

Modem basics

We're not going to get too technical but it's worth looking at some of the issues surrounding modems and how they work so you can make a sensible choice when looking to buy or upgrade. This will also help you understand some of the problems you will inevitably experience when connecting to the Net.

Let's get some terminology out of the way first of all. A modem allows data to be transmitted between computers via a standard telephone line. The word 'modem' is derived from two words – 'modulator' and 'demodulator'. During transmission, a modem converts the 0s and 1s of digital data into analogue signals by modulating an analogue carrier wave. A receiving modem converts or demodulates the frequencies back into digital data.

As you'll be aware, modems come in different speeds which often form part of the modem's name. Common speeds are 2,400, 9,600, 14,400, 28,800, 33,600 and 56,000. These figures are bps or bits per second. They refer to the number of bits of data a modem can transmit or receive each second. This is often shortened to kbps – kilo bits per second or 1000 bits/sec. Some people prefer to write 28.8 kbps rather than 28,800 bps and it does look a little neater. However, an even more common shorthand is simply to use K instead of kbps as in 28.8K and 33.6K. There are only a few speeds in common use so it doesn't get confusing and that's what we'll use from now on.

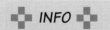
Baud stiff

Sometimes you may see a speed expressed in baud. Technically, this is
how often a modem's frequency changes each second. With each change
of frequency the modem would transmit a single bit of data. In older
modems, the baud rate was the same as the data rate but modern
modems use encoding and compression techniques which increase their
data transfer rate. A bps rating, therefore, is a far more accurate description of a modem's capabilities. For example, a 9.6K modem operates at
2.4K baud but uses encoding to achieve a transmission rate of 9.6K. As a
rule of thumb, divide the bps rating by 10 to discover how many cps
(characters per second) your system can transfer.

The 56K modem

It's not so long ago that the 28.8K modem was the master of all it logged
onto but, the 33.6K modem replaced that in 1997 and now you need a
56K modem or an ISDN connection if you don't want to sit twiddling your
thumbs every time you log onto a new Web page. At least, so the pundits
would have you believe. We'll look at the reality of the situation a little
closer over the next few pages.

Once upon a time – well, just a couple of years ago, in fact – it was
thought that the highest possible speed you could achieve over an analogue telephone line was 33.6K. You see, there is a physical limit to how
much information you can chuck down a telephone line before it turns to
slush and 33.6K seemed to be it. But then some boffins had an idea. As
ISPs use digital connections, they ought to be able to send data faster
than 33.6K. And so, it transpired, they could which led to the 56K standard. As most users are still hooked into analogue lines, they can still only
transmit at 33.6K but as most people receive more from the Net than
they send, this is not seen as a major problem.

As far back as 1996 – which is a very long time in Net terms – modem
manufacturers announced 56K modems and they became available – and
affordable – in 1997. However, two separate developers had been working on the same idea and, wouldn't you know it, they released two separate and incompatible standards – the X2 and K56Flex.

Needless to say, few buyers where keen to commit to one in case the
other won out – a replay of the VHS and Betamax video recorder wars.
Even fewer ISPs were keen to splash out on the technology for the same
reason. However, reason – and commercial sense – prevailed and a new
56K standard was agreed. If you already have one of the X2 or Flex
modems you may be able to upgrade it to the new standard. Or you may
not. If you're thinking of buying a new 56K modem, make sure it supports V.90 or that it can be easily upgraded to the standard for no or
minimal cost. Check with the modem supplier. Most have a Web site and
usually post details of new modems and upgrade possibilities.

Although some ISPs supported one of the 56 standards in advance of a
settlement – and some even supported them both! – many have been playing a waiting game. Inevitably, however, any ISP worthy of its name will
have to support V.90. It will take some a lot longer than others to come
'up to speed' so if you're looking for an ISP, check their V.90 support.

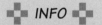

Cable modems

Your TV will eventually become the centre of your communications universe. With it you will be able to check your bank statement, do your shopping, see Aunt Lil on videophone and access the Internet. One day. However, for a few people living in selected test areas of the world this is already becoming a reality.

As you might expect, if you want to know how cable modems work there's a bit of techno-babble to get to grips with but here's an abridged version. They key word is 'broadband'. Essentially, broadband modems work on similar lines to a standard modem but they have more bandwidth to play with and so are able to transfer much more data.

You know how a voice sounds thin and filtered down a telephone line? That's because the line only supports a limited frequency range or bandwidth. Cable TV, on the other hand, supports a much greater frequency range so you not only get excellent speech quality but also hi fi music and video images on your TV.

Using this greater bandwidth, a broadband modem is theoretically capable of data transfer rates several magnitudes greater than current systems.

Imagine connection rates of 8 Mbps (yes megabits!) or even 30 Mbps! Currently, that's considered to be the top speed and the reality may be a rather more sober 1-5 Mbps. Still, most of us could live with that. For the moment...

As and when this does come on board, we'll still have the same Internet bottlenecks faced by current users such as slow servers and heavy demand causing slow access. However, many cable suppliers are investing very heavily in the technology and Internet by cable could be the major communications developments of the future.

At the moment, the technology is still in its infancy. There are many problems to overcome and, of course, there is more than one system in use and under development so the smart money is sitting tight until the factions get their act together. Industry sources claim that we could see a serious cable modem system appearing within three years in the USA. Forecasts for the UK range up to ten years.

>   *TIP*
>
> *It's probably good advice to suggest that you do not buy a modem from a manufacturer which does not have a Web site. Apart from the fact that it looks a little suspicious – a bit like a cook who doesn't eat his own food – a Web site lets you access the latest drivers and updates and the better sites are good for technical support.*

ISDN

Although 56K modems are currently the fastest thing on two legs, if you really want to lord it over your neighbours you need an ISDN connection. Integrated Services Digital Network is currently being touted as the best thing for comms users since the telephone itself.

ISDN is essentially a digital telephone connection which works over existing copper telephone wiring and which can operate at speeds of up to 128K. There is more than one system in use but the most appropriate type for individual computer users is the ISDN BRI (Basic Rate Interface) which only supports speeds of up to 64K.

Briefly, BRI divides the telephone line into three digital channels. One takes care of the housekeeping while the other two can be used for data.

One ISDN line, therefore, can handle two sets of data such as a voice line and a modem line each with their own telephone number.

In the UK, BT is trying very hard to promote ISDN but it's shooting itself in the foot with high installation costs and high line rental charges. The mass market for ISDN is the millions of Internet users but you need to be a very dedicated surfer indeed to install an ISDN line.

If the system had only a minor premium over ordinary telephone lines, we would all be tempted but it's currently only an option for companies or the terminally rich. And in any event, access to the Net is still hampered by slow servers and busy routes.

However, being digital, ISDN is inherently more reliable than analogue lines and another good reason for using it would be if your current line causes a lot of dropouts and other data transfer problems.

As competition increases, the price of ISDN will undoubtedly come down and BT seems to have splurges of special offers. If you're in the market for a new line it may be worth considering but don't forget additional costs such as the line rental charge and any additional hardware you may require.

ISDN is being touted as the 'next big thing' after the 56K modem. Its major competitor seems to be cable systems but ISDN is here now and cable, in the UK at least for most people, is several years off.

Modem-to-computer transfers

Here's a bit more techy stuff.

If you look up information about modems and data transfers, you'll probably see references to DTE and DCE. Thank the boffins for that. DTE is an acronym for Data Terminal Equipment which is a device which has the ability to transmit information in digital form over a communications line. In other words, a computer, but why use one word when several will do?

DCE stands for Data Communications Equipment, a device which transforms data from a DTE before sending it to a recipient. Yes, a modem.

However, with these two acronyms we can explain an often-misleading phenomenon. The modem setup screen in many comms packages includes a section where you can specify the connection speed. This usually has settings such as 4800, 9600, 19200, 38400, 57600 and 115200. You are usually advised to select the highest setting and you may wonder why as no modem – yet – can run at 115200.

The answer is that this is the DTE setting. It's the speed at which the computer communicates with the modem via the Com port. Some software actually pops this figure up onto the screen, making you think you're whizzing along. You won't be!

What you ought to check is the DCE speed which is the data transfer speed between your computer and the one you're connected to, taking into account factors such as the on-line traffic, the routing path, line noise, modem settings and so on. This is a more accurate indication of how fast the system is performing.

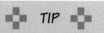
TIP

If you're using a 2400bps or 9600bps modem – get a faster one! If you'd rather not, set the DTE to the same as your modem's speed. If your modem supports V.42bis data compression – check the manual – use the 115200 setting.

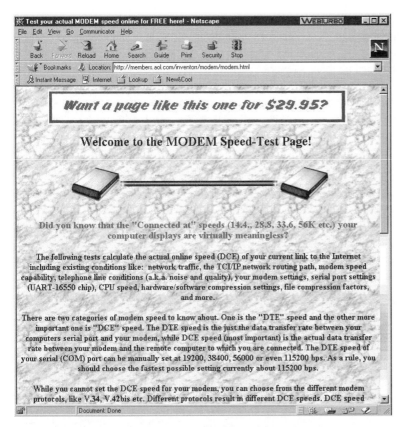

Figure 6.1 The Modem Speed-test Page contains a number of real-time tests which tell you how long your system takes to download text and graphic files.

Some software pops the carrier speed onto the screen. This is the speed at which your computer has connected to the ISP. At the least it will tell you if you're connecting at the optimum speed. If you want to perform a test with your modem, check out the Modem Speed-test Page:

http://members.aol.com/inventorr/modem/modem.html

This contains a number of real-time tests which tell you how long your system takes to download text and graphic files. It can make interesting reading.

Connecting at speed

No matter how fast your modem is, you need a reciprocal connection at the ISP end otherwise you: a) simply won't connect or, b) you'll connect at a slower speed. If you're looking for a modem, an ISP or both, do make sure that the two are compatible. Virtually all ISPs will support the new V.90 standard soon, if they don't do so already, if they want to remain in business.

If you have an ISDN connection your ISP needs to have ISDN access, too, in order to make use of its advantages.

There's something else you need to take into account, too. Just because you can connect to your ISP at 56K, it doesn't mean to say that all your downloads will take place at this speed. In fact, the likelihood is they will be much slower.

If you're already on-line, say with a 28.8K modem, you will undoubtedly have noticed that many of your transfers are much, much slower. Sometimes they can even crawl along at a few K per second. This can be caused by a number of factors:

* Such high speeds from 28.8K upwards are more than analogue lines were designed to handle and a bad connection or line noise can easily lower the data transfer rate, often quite severely. After a packet of data has been sent, a checksum is calculated to make sure the data has arrived correctly. If it has not, the data is sent again. Noisy lines can easily corrupt data making it necessary to resend which, in turn, increases the overall transfer time.
* When you surf the Net, your path to the machine you appear to be connected to will probably be routed through several servers which may be operating at different speeds. This will obviously affect the transfer rate as the overall speed is only as fast as the slowest connection.
* During peak times, if a server is busy it will not be able to devote its full attention to everyone who is connected to it. It has to apportion its time, transmitting data to one person then another and this can often result in very slow transfers. The morale of the story is to log on at off-peak times. If you're logging onto a server in America from the UK and working out peak times, remember there can be up to an eight-hour time difference.

 BT TIPS

If you're having trouble accessing at 28.8K or higher with a modem capable of those speeds, call your local, friendly telecom engineer and ask them to increase the gain on the line. Some may, some may not but this little tweak increases the difference between the modem signal and the background noise making the signal more reliable.

All modern modems incorporate data compression enabling them to compact data during transmission allowing more data to be transferred in a given time. However, this only works with compressible data such as text. Data which has already been compressed such as .zip and .sit files cannot be compressed further. It will, therefore, generally take the same length of time to transfer 100K of compressed data as it will to transfer 200K of uncompressed data.

By now you'll have realised that just because you have a 56K modem, it doesn't mean you'll be able to transfer data at 56K. In fact, after reading all that's gone before you'll probably be expecting a transfer rate of 1K!

It's actually not as bad as that. Practically, with a 56K modem and using a service provider which supports 56K, you should achieve transfer rates of between 40K and 50K. If you can hit 48K you're doing very well and that's currently about the best most people ought to expect. However, that's still a major improvement on 33.6K and a whole wad better than 28.8K.

To put the this into perspective, it's worth noting that poor and slow connections between the servers which make up the Internet can play a greater part in slowing down the transfer rate than a slow modem, especially if you are transferring data from a site half way around the world.

It's also worth noting that you ought to get faster transfers when using an on-line service provider (see Chapter 5) as there is a more direct connection between your computer and the one at the other end. However, even this connection may slow down during peak periods.

Being digital, ISDN ought to be more reliable, less prone to errors and able to maintain higher transfer rates. However, that assumes that both ends of the connection are digital. Even if your ISP has an ISDN connection, as soon as you leap into cyberspace, you could be back to analogue lines. At least with the current state of play.

Mirrors

During your surfing you may have noticed that some sites have addresses of mirror sites. These are copies – mirrors – of the original site situated in different locations. They are there to ease the load on the main site and you will often find that you can access a mirror site which is physically closer to you more quickly than the original.

Of course, the same caveats apply to mirrors as to any Internet site and mirrors which have slow servers, which you hit at local peak times and which bear heavy traffic will be slow.

If you find that downloading from an original site is slow, it's always worth trying a mirror as long as you remember that a mirror can be as slow as any site. It often happens that a site is fast one day and slow the next. If you're trying a download from a site and it slows to a crawl, try a mirror. If that's still slow, try at a later time.

Buying a modem

Let's cut right to the quick here. If you're thinking of buying a new modem or upgrading to a faster one for surfing the Net, it is absolutely pointless to even consider one slower than 56K unless you're not in a hurry and someone else is paying the phone bills.

The current crop of 33.6K and 56K modems are very affordable and becoming more so every day but the price difference between the two continues to get smaller and it won't be long before the 33.6K modem follows the 2400 baud modem into the trashcan of communications history.

If you don't want to surf the Net and simply want to log onto a service to do email, there could be a case for using a slower modem. But even Perry Mason would struggle to make a case for that! Get the tools for the job.

It's a commonly-held belief that if you get a faster modem you will spend less time on-line, so saving on your telephone bill. It ain't true! You'll spend the same amount of time on-line but you'll be able to do much more in that time. And as the Net gets bigger and as software grows larger, you need the fastest connection possible.

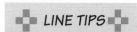

LINE TIPS

The quality of the line is extremely important for high speed transfers. If you're struggling to download at 28.8K or 33.6K because of a poor line, you'll get very little, if any, benefit from a faster modem. If you are getting a new line installed specifically for comms, make sure the provider knows it's for 56K speed communications. The better providers will then not try any shortcuts such as splitting a line (using one set of wires to carry two telephone signals).

Modem links

You won't be surprised to learn that there is a lot of information on the Net about modems, high speed communications, cutting-edge technology and all that. A search will reveal them all. Here's just a handful you may find interesting.

Curt's High Speed Modem Page
http://www.teleport.com/~curt/modems.html
This contains a veritable plethora of modem information, news, FAQs, tips and tricks. It has information about the latest high speed modems, and links to manufacturer's pages. Definitely one to bookmark.

Figure 6.2 Curt's High Speed Modem Page.

Ask Mr Modem Figure 6.3
http://www.spy.net/~dustin/modem/
This lists virtually every modem under the sun – and a few above it, too! Select your modem and it will give you a list of suggested settings which you may need to configure your comms software.

Modem Fault Finder
http://www.airtime.co.uk/users/hal9000/modem/mdm_dead.htm
This is a neat list of 72 questions designed to track down any problems with your modem. Depending on your answer, the list directs you to another question. By the time you reach number 72, your modem ought to be working.

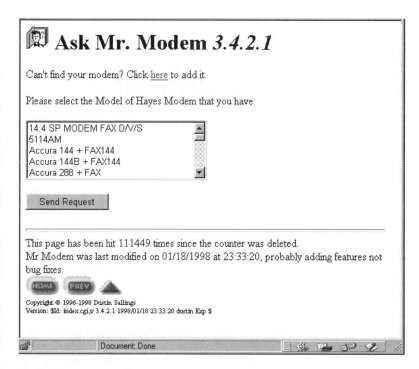

Figure 6.3 Ask Mr Modem contains settings for virtually every modem under the sun.

Optimising your modem
http://www.airtime.co.uk/users/hal9000/modem/mdm_opt.htm
One for the slightly more confident. This runs through a series of AT commands designed to help you set up your modem to establish the best Internet connection it can.

Downloading software

You're on-line, you're surfing, you've discovered some terrific sites containing lots of free software, demos, information about new gear and software updates. How do you get all this from the Web to your computer?

It's not quite as straightforward as copying files from a floppy disk or a CD onto your hard disk but it is generally quite easy. There are two considerations when transferring files from the Net – speed and more speed.

As you will have gathered, the need for speed in comms transfers is driven by the size of the files. If you simply want to download files which are a few K in size, speed is not much of an issue but when the files are measured in hundreds of K and even Megabytes as many are now, then it becomes very important indeed. Obviously, therefore, the smaller the files are in the first place, the faster you can download them. Consequently, most files on the Net are compressed.

Compression

Compression is the process of squeezing a quart into a pint pot. It's not new; it was around before the Net became a household word and it was used to allow users to store more data than normal on floppies (which used to be expensive) and on the rather small hard disks which were the state-of-the-art just a few years ago. And which were also expensive.

Nowadays, storage is not such a problem. There is a range of removable drives at very affordable prices and CD-R has really come into its own. CD-R drives continue to fall in price and CD-R discs can be picked up for well under a pound each. Many manufacturers are producing CD-RW drives at good prices, too.

But until we all have an Internet server under the desk, the relative slowness of data transfers over the Net means that compression is an important part of the process.

Compression methods

Compression can work in a number of ways. One method involves replacing often-repeated patterns of bits with a symbol which represents them. For example, let's say you were compressing a graphics file of an image which contained a lot of blue sky. If you – or the computer – examined

CD-R – Recordable CDs. A CD-R drive contains a low-powered laser which can burn CDs.

CD-RW – Rewritable CDs. CD-RW drives can write CD-R discs like any CD-R drive but, using special CD-RW discs, they can also erase data on them and rewrite it.

the data which contained the blue pixels you might find a repeating pattern of four bits which represented that shade of blue. If each occurrence of this pattern was represented by less than four bits, the file could be reduced in size.

Compression software is required to compress a file and decompression software is needed to restore it to its original form. One important thing to note is that, in the above example at least, the data is restored exactly to its original state. This is termed lossless compression for obvious reasons.

There are other ways of compressing data but further explanation is beyond the scope of this book and, in any event – the good news – you don't need to know how it works in order to use it.

We must, however, mention lossy compression which, as you might imagine doesn't work in quite the same way. The compression program looks for 'redundant' information which it believes will not be missed by the ear or eye and removes it.

Information such as text, numbers and other data files must be compressed using lossless techniques and modern compression software may be able to squeeze such files down to around 40 percent of their original size.

Most graphics, video and sound files, however, contain a lot of information which could be removed without our senses being aware of any reduction in content. In fact, you'd be amazed at just how much information can be removed from this type of data before we become aware of it. Some lossy compression techniques can reduce a file to around five percent of its original size.

Lossy compression is incredibly useful for transferring audio data over the Net and for use in multimedia. However, in spite of the claims, most musos worth their salt, having strived to create high quality, high content 16-bit or 24-bit files will want to retain every bit of their music during any form of conversion. There are, fortunately, commercial and shareware programs which do just that.

But before we look at those let's look at standard file compression software.

PC compressors

For the PC, the most popular compression program by far is PKZIP and its Windows counterpart WinZip, Figure 7.1, which is essentially an easy-to-use front-end for the Zip engine. You can recognise Zip files by their .ZIP extension and it's probably true to say that well over 90 percent of compressed PC files on the Net are in Zip format.

The majority of the other others are probably in ARJ format and can be recognised by their .ARJ extension. You may also come across a few other formats including LHZ, LHA and ARC. When configured correctly, WinZip can handle all these although setting it up to do so is not as straightforward as it could be.

A relative newcomer to the file compression scene is the RAR Archiver

Figure 7.1 WinZip compression
software is available from the
WinZip Web site.

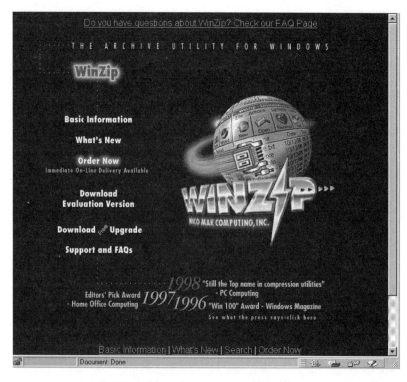

(whose most common manifestation is the WinRAR program) whose compressed files have a .RAR extension. It is widely praised by the cognoscenti and it does, indeed, have many good points and it can handle the
common compression formats, too. However, the vast majority of PC
files continue to be Zipped, so the necessity of having RAR is not immediately urgent.

A lot of software, particularly the larger programs, now has an installation or setup routine and it's becoming increasingly common to find
applications stored on the Web as a single compressed file which automatically extracts its contents and installs the software when double-clicked.
These generally have a .EXE extension and don't need decompressing
after downloading – you simply run them as you would any application.

Mac compressors

There are several compression utilities for the Mac, too, but the most
popular and almost universal one is Stuffit by Aladdin Systems, Figure
7.2. Although Mac files generally don't have an extension, Stuffit files are
often given a .SIT suffix to make them easily recognisable.

Other compression formats include Compact Pro, Mac Binary and there
is a version of PKZIP for the Mac, too. You won't be missing much by not
having these, however, and you can always add them to your collection if
the need arises.

We'll pre-empt the next section a little by mentioning BinHex which

Figure 7.2 Stuffit from Aladdin Systems is the most popular compression software for the Mac.

converts Mac Binary files into 7-bit files with a .HQX extension.

Stuffit Expander, however, can decompress virtually all the compressed file types for the Mac you're likely to come across, plus PC Zip files and it is the main decompressing program you should have on your Mac.

Sending files over the Internet

Now, to add confusion to that which has gone before, we need to consider the way in which data is sent over the Internet. For various technical reasons which are, again, beyond the scope of this book, data is usually transferred in ASCII or Binary format.

The former is often referred to as Text format. It's often used for email and it essentially uses 'printable' characters – the numbers and the letter of the alphabet. It can generally be represented using only 7 bits.

Binary, on the other hand, uses a few non-printable characters and requires 8 bits to be fully represented. It's the standard format of application files, for example.

So what? Well, certain types of data transfer over the Internet are restricted to 7 bits rather than 8 bits and if you try to send an 8-bit file over a system which only supports 7 bits the data tends to get garbaged.

So, to prevent this happening there are utilities to convert Binary 8-bit files into 7-bit files. For the PC, these include Wincode although WinZip can also handle it, and for the Mac the most common one is UUencode although Stuffit can also create and decode BinHex files, too.

Now, in case this compression and transfer lark is seeming to get out of hand – don't worry. These considerations usually only come to the fore

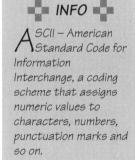

TIP

The quick guide to compression:

PC: Get WinZip
Mac: Get Stuffit Expander

INFO

ASCII – American Standard Code for Information Interchange, a coding scheme that assigns numeric values to characters, numbers, punctuation marks and so on.

Figure 7.3 When you download a file you are usually presented with a standard Save As ... dialogue box.

when sending files to other users via email in which case you may have set up your email program to use MIME or UUE format, for example – another subject beyond our scope.

When accessing the Net with a browser, the vast majority of PC files you'll see will have a .ZIP extension and can be decompressed by WinZip. Virtually all Mac files have a .SIT or .HQX extension, both of which can be decompressed by Stuffit Expander.

Enough of the theory, let's look at some practical examples.

Downloading files

All the files which you can download from the Net are well marked. The people who put them up there want you to have them so they're easy to find. Generally, you can download a file simply by clicking on its name or description in the Web page. A standard dialog box usually appears allowing you to select the filename and the folder into which it is be saved as in Figure 7.3.

The programs or their descriptions usually appear as hyperlinks and when you pass the mouse pointer over this you should see the filename at the bottom of the browser window. Using the XGEdit page as an example, Figures 7.4, 7.5 and 7.6 show what appears at the bottom of the browser when you pass the finger cursor over the names of the three different versions of XGEdit.

Figure 7.4 contains one .EXE file which you can run directly after downloading. It extracts bits from itself to install the XGEdit program. Figure 7.5 contains a .ZIP file which needs to be unzipped into its constituent parts before running. Figure 7.6 is the Mac version of the program and contains a .HQX file which Stuffit Expander will extract into the files shown in Figure 7.7.

If a file doesn't open the file dialog box as you'd expect, or if the box

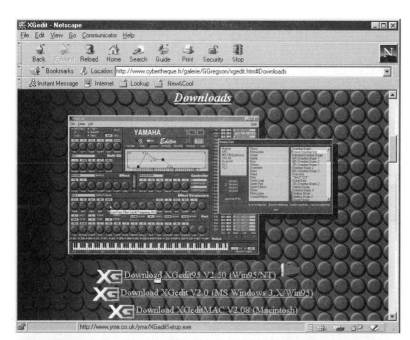

Figure 7.4 Placing the cursor on the name of the file shows the actual filename at the foot of the browser window. This example shows a self-contained .EXE file which, when run, will automatically install the program.

Figure 7.5 This shows the file has been Zipped and the parts need to be extracted with WinZip.

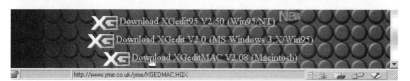

Figure 7.6 The .HQX tells you this is a Mac file which needs decoding with Stuffit Expander

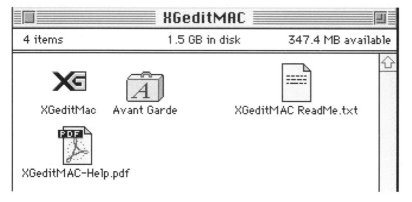

Figure 7.7 After extracting the Mac .HQX file, you will see these files on your hard disk.

doesn't include a filename, click the right mouse button over the filename and select Save Link As...

Holding down Shift and clicking the mouse button opens the file dialog box directly, too.

Downloading files via FTP

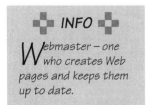

Webmaster – one who creates Web pages and keeps them up to date.

FTP (see Chapter 1 for more about FTP) is one of the forerunners of the Web although it's still used, particularly by Webmasters to transfer files and Web pages between the computer they are created on and the host Web site. It effectively gives you two-way access between your computer and the host machine, allowing you to transfer files between them.

Figure 7.8 shows the FTP program supplied with Turnpike which is commonly used to access the Net via Demon. As with most ISPs, Demon subscribers get free Web space and the FTP program is used to access the homepages, allowing users to put their sites on the Web.

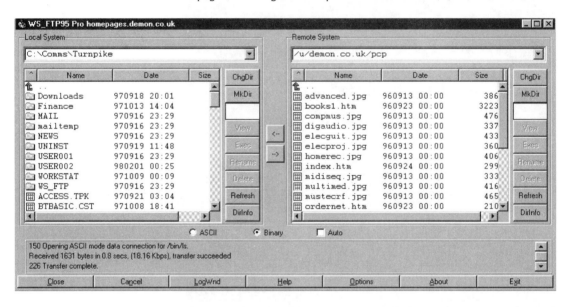

Figure 7.8 Turnpike's FTP program allows users to put their sites on the Web.

Many Internet sites are still set up for FTP and you could use an FTP program to access them. However, most Web browsers support FTP transfers, too, although usually just one way, from the site to your computer. You access FTP sites simply by entering their name into the Location area of your browser such as:

ftp://ftp.cs.ruu.nl/pub/MIDI/PATCHES/

There are other examples in Chapter 9. You can hyperlink to an FTP site and to all intents and purposes, you can access files from an FTP site just as you can from a Web site.

FTP sites are usually short on graphics. They are essentially a collection of files, often arranged in directories as in Figure 7.9. Opening a directory will reveal its contents. Again, moving the cursor over the file names will reveal the full names of the files in the bottom line of the browser as in Figure 7.10. This is useful to remember because most sites only allow a limited number of spaces for the filename and the last part is often missing as you can see in Figure 7.10.

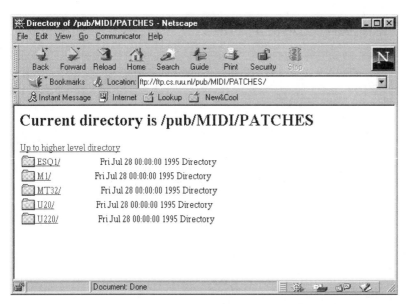

Figure 7.9 Files on FTP sites are usually arranged as a collection of directories

Figure 7.10 Moving the cursor over the file names will reveal the full names of the files in the bottom line of the browser.

FTP sites, as opposed to Web pages, are often used to store or archive large numbers of files. Many FTP sites are supported by educational establishments and some of the contents go back several years.

Because FTP transfers give you access to the files at the other end, you usually need a password to log onto the system. However, files which are for general consumption can usually be accessed through 'anonymous ftp' which means you can log in as 'anonymous' and use your email address as a password.

Accessing FTP sites with a browser requires the same procedure as accessing them via a FTP program but the browser should negotiate logging on for you automatically. Most FTP sites have a 'pub' or 'public' directory which is freely accessible. You will probably be able to see other directories but unless they support anonymous FTP you will not be able to access them and will likely get a message similar to that in Figure 7.11.

Figure 7.11 You will see this login error if the site or directory does not directly support anonymous FTP.

FTP Error

Could not login to FTP server

User anonymous unknown.

What's a virus? A virus is a parasitic program which attaches itself to a file and duplicates itself, spreading to other files and other computer systems. A virus becomes active when a file is run or, if it's stored in the boot sector of a disk, when the boot sector is accessed during startup. Data files cannot transfer a virus but a virus can damage them.

Virus alert – but don't PANIC!

Viruses are a fact of computing life and rare indeed is the surfer who has not picked up a virus on his or her travels. That's not to say they are lurking around every corner – viruses are nowhere as common as some of the more sensationalist press would have us believe – but they do exist and the more downloading you do, the greater your risk of acquiring one.

Some viruses may appear to be harmless and do little but replicate but others can cause varying amount of damage to your system ranging from the annoying to the disastrous. Even the 'harmless' variety eat up your drive space and system resources and should be routed out and removed

Common virus symptoms

* Computer runs slower than usual
* A program takes longer to load than usual
* The drive light flashes when files are not being accessed
* The size of a program file keeps changing
* Files are deleted
* Strange files appear
* The cursor behaves strangely
* Strange messages flash onto the screen
* CHKDSK reports less than 655,360 bytes available

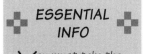

You must take the threat of virus infection seriously.

These symptoms are not necessarily proof that you have a virus – some could be caused by other factors – but if you are experiencing any of the above, it's worth checking your system. In fact, check your system regularly, anyway.

Here are a few virus facts:

* Your computer can only acquire a virus from an infected file. If you never download a file or put a floppy disk or CD into your machine it will remain virus-free.
* A virus cannot run by itself. It becomes active when you run the file it is attached to or access the boot sector of a disk.
* It is possible, although exceedingly rare, to get a virus from a piece of commercial software.
* It is possible and, fortunately, also rare, to get a virus from software on a magazine's cover CD. But it has happened.
* Most viruses are written for the PC. Some sources claim there are over 6000 PC viruses compared with a little over 50 for the Mac.

After downloading a file from the Net, it's certainly worthwhile running a virus checker over it, just in case. Don't keep a virus scanner running in the background – they hog system resources and have been known to cause compatibility problems with other software. Put all your downloads into one folder and let the checker give them the once-over before you use them.

Let's get back to compression and downloading files.

Lossless audio compression software

Regardless of how much data scientists say can be removed from an audio file without our ears being able to tell the difference, most musicians will prefer to keep every byte they've painstakingly crafted. If you need to compress audio data, therefore, the chances are you'll want to get every bit of it back! You can do this with WinZip and Stuffit but there are also a couple of pieces of commercial software designed specifically for the lossless compression of audio files – TrackPac and ZAP.

TrackPac is produced by Waves, a company well-known for its digital audio plug-in effects and it's available in Pro and Lite versions. It's available for Windows and the Mac and uses a simple drag-and-drop interface. It can compress 16-bit files down to 50 percent or more and it can squeeze 8-bit files down to between 20 or 30 percent of the size of the original material.

TrackPac Lite is freely available so you can try before you buy, although it can only perform one compression at a time and is limited to file sizes of 2Mb or less.

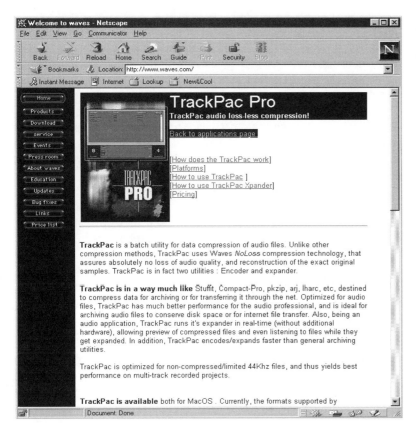

Figure 7.12 Information about TrackPac and a Lite version can be downloaded from the Waves Web site.

Figure 7.13 Emagic's Zero
Loss Audio Packer.

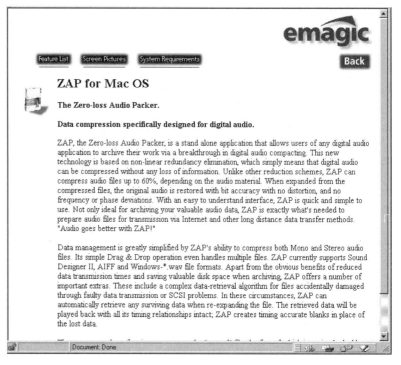

ZAP (Zero Loss Audio Packer), Figure 7.13, comes from Emagic, developer of the famous Logic series of sequencers. It uses a technique called 'non-linear redundancy elimination' and it basically creates a set of instructions for constructing the file based on the material it contains. It's not totally dissimilar to the compression method described at the beginning of the chapter.

Noise does not compress very efficiently because it contains lots of random signals. Silence, on the other hand, compresses extremely well as it contains lots of similar 'material' and it can be described very simply. For the same reason, solo instruments compress more efficiently than vocals and full mixes.

Typical compression rates vary from 20 to 60 percent and it can compress audio files to around half the size Stuffit can manage, for example. It can create self-extracting files which add a few K to the overall file size. It also performs a check on the data and warns you if it has been corrupted.

Lossy audio compression

With the advent of faster modems over the past few years, many Web sites have a lot of 'media-rich content' – which is spin doctor speak for lots of graphics and sound.

As you probably know, audio files tend to be quite large – around 10Mb per minute for stereo CD quality audio. Movie files such as QuickTime and Video For Windows are quite large, too. If you've done much surfing you can't fail but to have noticed the fancy graphics, animated icons and so on, which many designers are incorporating in their sites.

These, too, are larger than plain graphics and so take longer to download.

It's not unusual to have to wait two or three minutes for one of these media rich pages to appear on your computer.

Recent developments, however, allow media such as movies and audio to be 'streamed' to your computer and played on-the-fly as they are being transferred. Streamed files generally use a lossy compression to reduce the transfer time.

This sounds great in theory – instant access, no more waiting to see or hear the file. In practice, however, if there's delay in the transmission, the file will pause and there's often a delay with some streaming systems while it waits for part of the file to download. If you get a fast connection, however, streaming can be very impressive.

So, a good idea but currently hampered a little by unreliable connections and unsustainable throughput. However, streaming technology is useful for 'thumbnail' sketches of audio and video and as there are now services which let you buy audio over the Net, it's a useful way to give you a taster.

The are several streaming technologies in vogue including RealAudio, Shockwave, Beatnik, Audioactive and ASF (ActiveX Streaming Format). Most of these require a software plug-in for your browser which allows them to play the files as they arrive.

Sources of files

Needless to say, there are many sites hosting a range of software and information about compression software, viruses and the downloading process in general. Here are some of the main sites along with a few other sites of interest.

Downloading a Web browser
http://www.guide.net.nz/browsers/
Tips for downloading a Web browser – just in case you don't have one already or fancy a change – plus links to the official instructions for Netscape and Internet Explorer.

Compression

WinZip
http://www.winzip.com/
Lots and lots of information about the world's most popular compression program. Read the FAQs and download the evaluation version.

Wincode
http://snappy-software.com/
http://www.members.global2000.net/snappy/
The first URL is the official Wincode homepage but it is not always available. The second URL is a mirror site and seems to be more reliable. It contains lots of information about the program and the latest versions to download.

WinRAR
http://www.rar.de/
The official WinRAR Web site and it contains lots of information about the program, details of new releases and, of course, the software. There are many versions for different computer platforms although none for the Mac. However, there is a decoding program for the Mac called unrar.
ftp://ftp.elf.stuba.sk/pub/pc/pack/
is the official FTP site for WinRAR where you should find the latest version – along with lots of other files.

UUencode
http://execpc.com/~adw/uu.html
The homepages of UUencode and UUdecode containing DOS versions of the program.
http://www.infocom.net/~elogan/wuudoall.html
contains versions of UUencode and UUdecode for Windows in versions for 286, 386 and 486 computers. Includes links to a very busy FTP site and to a Web site which also contain the software.

Super WinUUE
http://www.neosoft.com/~pane/
houses 32-bit versions of UUencoder and UUdecoder for Windows 95 and NT.

Mac compressors
http://wwwhost.ots.utexas.edu/mac/pub-mac-compression.html
contains lots of compression software for the Mac including UULite, Compact Pro and Stuffit.

Stuffit Expander
http://www.aladdinsys.com/expander/index.html
The home of Stuffit and Stuffit Expander where you should always find the latest releases. It also includes versions for Windows and DOS.

Compact Pro
http://www.cyclos.com/macsoft.html
Contains Compact Pro as well as BinHex encoder and decoder software.

BinHex
http://www.natural-innovations.com/boo/binhex.html
Lots of information about BinHex including software for Mac, DOS and Windows plus other compression programs and utilities.
http://helpdesk.uvic.ca/how-to/support/mac/hqx.html
Download BinHex software plus documentation telling you how to use it.

The Cross-Platform Page
http://www.arrakis.com.au/~xplat/xplat.comp.html
A guide to compressing files on different computer platforms. Includes information about the compression systems and the actual software.

Audio compression
RealAudio
http://www.realaudio.com/
The RealAudio homepage – lots of info, news, help, files to play, links to sites and, of course, free software to download.

Shockwave
http://www.macromedia.com/
Shockwave is produced by Macromedia, one of the best-known developers of multimedia software such as Director, Freehand, Dreamweaver, SoundEdit 16 and so on. Shockwave supports both audio and animation and Macromedia has introduced enhanced versions of it such as Smart Shockwave which automates the selection, download and installation of Shockwave players; and ShockRave, a total 'entertainment service' using interactive games, cartoons and music. It's all here.

Beatnik
http:/www.headspace.com/
Headspace was founded by Thomas Dolby Robertson (Thomas Dolby, a musician of the 80s, of She Blinded Me With Science and Airhead fame) and specialises in software such as Beatnik for transmitting audio across the Internet. Beatnik plays a range of music files including .RMF, MIDI, .MOD, AIFF, Wave and .AU files. The Beatnik Editor imports these music files and converts them to RMF for efficient transmission over the Net.

ASF
http://www.microsoft.com./asf/
ASF (ActiveX Streaming Format) is an open file format for storing multimedia content. This area of the Microsoft site contains wads of information about it plus software to download.

Audioactive
http://www.audioactive.com/
A system of 'webcasting' which claims to be able to broadcast audio over the Net with the quality of live radio. It supports Audioactive and Shockwave formats. There's lots of info here plus a free player to download for both the Mac and PC and some impressive demos to listen to.

Emagic
http://www.emagic.de/english/products/mac/ZAP.html
Part of the Emagic Web site which contains details, features and screenshots for ZAP. In the demo area you'll find ZAP for the Mac and the UnZap decompressor, for the PC.

Waves
http://www.waves.com/
Info about TrackPac – how it works and how to use it.

INFO

RMF – Rich Music Format, a proprietary file format designed by Headspace for Beatnik which can deliver 16-bit audio files across the Internet. The company has produced several RMF files which can be licensed for use on your Web site.

Virus links

Dr Solomon's
http://www.drsolomon.com/
A veritable plethora of information from one of the pioneers of anti virus software. Loads of information including a 'So you think you've got a virus' section which helps you decide whether you have or not, plus software to download including FindVirus which scans your system and tells you if any viruses are present.

Symantec
http://www.symantec.com/
The company which took over Norton Utilities has a large Web site, and a large section of it is devoted to viruses. It contains lots of information and there are updates to download.

Protection is better than cure. Find out how to protect your files on the Symantec site.

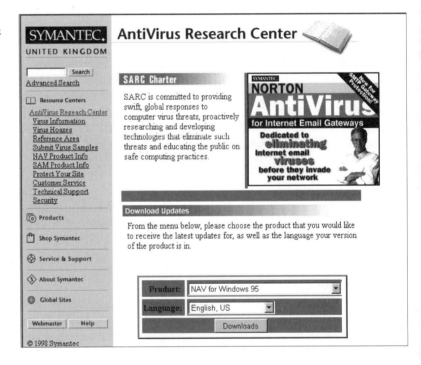

McAfee
http://www.nai.com/default_mcafee.asp
Not a lot of virus information but you can download an evaluation version of McAfee's highly-regarded Anti-Virus software.

F-Prot
http://www.DataFellows.com/f-prot.html
Data Fellows' Web site, home of the shareware F-Prot anti-virus program. Lots of info and the software, too.

Disinfectant
ftp://ftp.louisville.edu/pub/math/Larson/macstuff/
Disinfectant is the premier free anti-virus software for the Mac. It is available from sites all over the Web – a search will reveal several. The above FTP site seems to keep a fairly up-to-date version.

Anti Virus Information Page
http://www.geocities.com/SiliconValley/1710/
A collection of useful virus information including links to sites of popular anti-virus software.

Robert Chu's Anti-Virus Page
http://server.snni.com/~robertc/virus.html
Quick and dirty instructions for protecting your machine against viruses, links to virus scanners and anti-virus software companies, and utilities.

Computer Virus Myths
http://kumite.com/myths/
Not all viruses are genuine. The press and the computing community have played their part in promulgating hoax viruses and urban myths about viruses. Read all about them here.

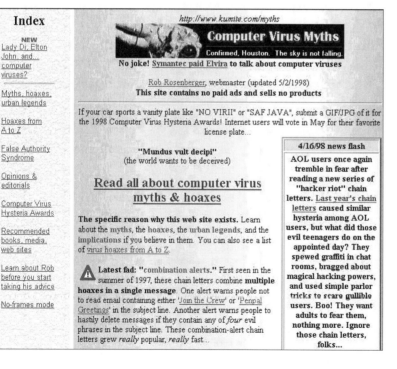

The good, the bad, the funny the sad – lots of interesting virus chit-chat on this site.

8

Troubleshooting and hints and tips

We break slightly with tradition and include the tips and troubleshooting section before the chapter which features all the links. This is to brief you on some of the problems which may occur – to be forewarned is to be forearmed and all that.

Not wired...

Before you start surfing and searching, it's worth remembering that not every organisation has a presence on the Web – at least not yet – so to contact certain organisations or to get hold of certain information you may just have to pick up the telephone...

Entering the URLs

* Most browsers do not require you to enter the http:// part of the URL and will automatically insert it after you type www.
* By convention, the vast majority of URLs are in lower-case but some sites use upper and lower-case. Some addresses will work whatever case you use but most are case-sensitive so do check this carefully if you get an error message.

The site's not there!

The URLs in this book were copied into the original text directly from a browser so it's unlikely that the address will be wrong (although in cyberspace anything can happen). So if you get an error message, check that you've entered the URL correctly.

However, it's quite possible – so much so that I guarantee it! – that some of the sites will have moved, changed location or ceased to exist altogether. You may get an error message which says:

DNS Entry not found error

This is a common error. The DNS (Domain Name Server) is a program which runs when you access the Net. It turns the alphabetic address of a site into the numerical one which computers use. If this error occurs it means that the browser could not contact your DNS or that the DNS was not aware of the site. The most common cause of this is a spelling mistake in the URL so double check that this is absolutely correct.

File not found

Many Web sites with downloadable software don't hold the software on their own server. Instead, they use a hyperlink to get the file directly from a host site. It saves space on their own server and the Webmaster at the host site can update the file without the reference sites having to upload a new file or change the hyperlink. You can usually tell where the file is by looking at the URL at the bottom of the browser page when resting the cursor on the filename.

However, sometimes trying to access a file will throw up an error telling you that the URL could not be found on the server as in Figure 8.1. Actually, this can happen sometimes even if the file is on the same server.

Figure 8.1 You will see this message if the URL cannot be found.

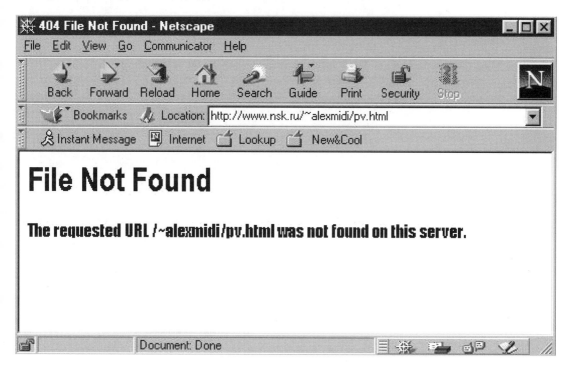

This often occurs because the Webmaster in charge of the page has changed the filename, perhaps to a later version. Let's say the original link was:

```
http://www.website.com/software/widget1.zip
```

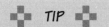 **TIP**

If you can't access a file which was available once upon a time, search the Web for other occurrences of it. It would be rare if it was only available at one site and it may well be on another server.

and the Webmaster removes that file and updates it to widget2.zip. Then the above error message will appear.

But all may not be lost. Delete the last part of the address – widget1.zip – and see if you can access the 'software' part of the address. If you can you will probably see all the files available for download and you may wee see a widget2.zip.

Occasionally, however, the file may have been removed completely or you will not be allowed to access the 'software' part of the site. But in many cases you will and in any event, you tried.

Slow downloads

No matter how fast your modem, you will inevitably hit a site which is downloading data at a few K per second. Here are a few options to try to speed up the transfer.

* Sometimes, simply clicking on the Reload button in the browser will cure the problem.
* Sometimes closing the browser and opening it again will work.
* The slowness may be due to heavy traffic – lots of people trying to access the site at the same time – and this is probably the most common cause of slow downloads. Educational sites are particularly prone to this. Check the local time where the site is situated and try again at off-peak hours. Most users seem to log on during the afternoon and early evening. Alternatively, see if you can find the file you're looking for elsewhere on the Net.
* The problem could be caused by a slow connection route. Switch to another site – try one in your home country – then try the first one again. If you had a slow route the first time, the second route may be quicker.
* Occasionally you may connect via a bad telephone line. If there's noise on the line this will slow down the transfer. You'll probably know if you have a problem with this or not – pick up the phone and listen and if you hear any crackles, it's noisy. The best solution is to get it fixed (see Chapter 6) but sometimes if you log on again you will connect via a quieter line.
* Downloads from FTP sites are often quicker than those from a Web site. Try accessing an FTP site with your browser but using dedicated FTP software may be quicker.

News and info

* Many companies post press releases on their site at the same time as they send them out to magazines. As it can take a mag several

weeks to get this into print – and even a weekly mag can take a week or longer – you can stay more up-to-date than your friends – and companies, shops and so on – who are not on-line!

* Join newsgroups and mailing lists as many are frequented by people who develop the software or who work in the companies you're interested in and you'll often pick up advanced bits of information here.
* Several music companies with Web sites now have mailing lists which automatically update you with information and new developments.
* Use software which tells you when Web sites have changed (see Chapter 4) to keep up-to-date with sites of special interest to you.

Don't use the Net!

* Check the cover CDs of computer magazines before spending time downloading Internet software. Many magazines put the latest versions of Web software, utilities and applications on their CD. It's often easier and cheaper to get software from a CD than to pay the telephone bill incurred downloading a large file. However, you may also want to check the download Web site to make sure the CD has the latest version.
* Several music magazines also have cover CDs which include music software as well as audio demos and samples.

Call costs

* Beware of telecomm companies bearing gifts. Some companies, such as BT, advertise a low-cost rate for local calls. At mid-1998 for example, at weekends a local call is 1p per minute. However, what they don't tell you is that this is subject to a minimum connection charge of 5p so if you log on and off in a minute to collect your email, you'll still be charged 5p. Many telecomm companies have a similar minimum connection charge so each time you log on, make the most of the time by staying on-line until you've used your initial connection charge's worth. Plan what you want to do before logging on.
* Currently, weekend call rate are significantly cheaper than calls at other times so do most of your surfing at the weekends. Next, use evenings.
* If you have more than one telecomm company in your area, it's well worth checking their prices as they can vary considerably. However, none of them will help you through the small print

which shows where they are *more* expensive than their competitors.
*   Cable lines currently seem to be cheap.

Web site addresses

With the information presented in the earlier parts of this book, particularly in Chapter 4 on searching the Web, you should be able to find most items you set out to look for. Some sites, however, can still take a little while to track down and many seem to avoid the spider bots like politicians avoid the truth. That's why you can often discover new and interesting sites by surfing and following links from other related sites whose designers have surfed there before you.

This is fun to do when you have a spare few hours but in an attempt to save you from Clicker's Finger, in this chapter you'll find almost 600 URLs pointing to a wide range of Web sites covering a spectrum of musical interests.

It's by no means an exhaustive list – there never could be one as the ever-changing Web is impossible to map – but it's a representative sample of what is out there and it is intended to save you much surfing time.

Among these sites there are likely to be many of which you were previously unaware offering information, new ideas, and software which you may not have known existed. One of the joys of surfing is the discovery of such sites and by including them here I hope they will be enjoyed by a greater audience.

To make it easier to find specific information, the addresses have been divided into the following topics:

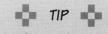

TIP

When you find an interesting site, do bookmark it otherwise you may well lose the address. I have the T-shirt. Create a number of different Bookmark folders, too, such as hardware, software, virtual synths or whatever topics you're interested in to make the sites easier to find. In fact, I have two T-shirts...

Artists	Shareware, Freeware and small developers
Composition	Record companies
Copyright and legal information	Music magazines
Music hardware manufacturers	Music and music book publishers
Musical Instruments	Music retailers and distributors
Museums	Industry and Trade Organisations
Soundcards, digital audio cards, MIDI interfaces/boxes	User groups and support sites
	Newsgroups and Mailing lists
Signal processors, mixers, amps, external audio gear	Music information
Speakers	Music and MIDI
Duplication	Recording and digital audio
Computing	Band and musician stuff
Music software developers	Computer and electronic music
	Links

The categories, of necessity, are a little loose. Many sites could easily be in more than one topic so if you don't find what you're looking for in one, try another. The index should be quite useful, too.

Artists

21st Century Design
http://www.21stcentury.co.uk/
A site run by musician and composer Clifford White who specialises in music for relaxation and inspiration – New Age-ish – but it also contains albums by other musicians.

Included are descriptions of the albums and Wave file extracts from them to download.

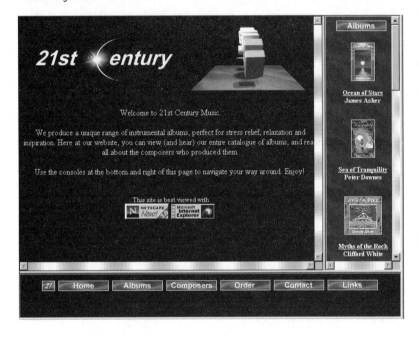

Ash Ra Tempel
http://www.ashra.com/
The official homepage containing a biography of Manuel Göttsching, discography, info on the studio, interviews and offers.

J.S. Bach
http://www.jsbach.org/
A discussion of his life, a listing of his complete works, recommended (and not-recommended!) recordings, a list of up-coming events plus links to Bach sites and Bach information around the world. You can also join a Bach discussion list.

Ian Boddy
http://www.demon.co.uk/SomethingElse/
Ian Boddy has been at the forefront of the UK independent electronic music scene since 1983 when he performed at the first ever UK

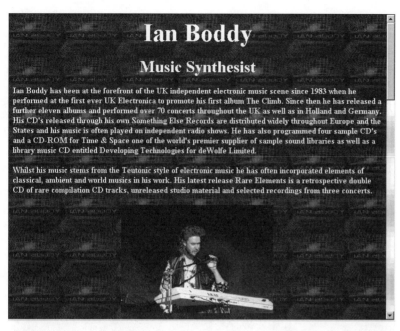

Ian Boddy

Music Synthesist

Ian Boddy has been at the forefront of the UK independent electronic music scene since 1983 when he performed at the first ever UK Electronica to promote his first album The Climb. Since then he has released a further eleven albums and performed over 70 concerts throughout the UK as well as in Holland and Germany. His CD's released through his own Something Else Records are distributed widely throughout Europe and the States and his music is often played on independent radio shows. He has also programmed four sample CD's and a CD-ROM for Time & Space one of the world's premier supplier of sample sound libraries as well as a library music CD entitled Developing Technologies for deWolfe Limited.

Whilst his music stems from the Teutonic style of electronic music he has often incorporated elements of classical, ambient and world musics in his work. His latest release Rare Elements is a retrospective double CD of rare compilation CD tracks, unreleased studio material and selected recordings from three concerts.

The site contains details of Ian's albums along with extracts in Wave and AIFF formats. There is also details of concerts, and various other projects such as the Sample CDs he has created. Also includes lots of links.

Electronica to promote his first album, The Climb. Since then he has released a further eleven albums and performed over 70 concerts throughout the UK as well as in Holland and Germany. His CDs released through his own Something Else Records are distributed widely throughout Europe and the States and his music is often played on independent radio shows.

Wendy Carlos
http://www.wendycarlos.com/

Welcome to the Official Wendy Carlos Online Information Source!

Wendy Carlos is one of the most important composers living today. While primarily connected to the field of electronic music, her compositions transcend the genre. It is certain that her music will be remembered as major milestones of 20th century music.

- Recent News -- (the most recent releases, concerts, etc.)
- Biography -- (a trim biographical sketch, with links)
- Discography -- (what's currently available & why; releases to come)
- Solar Eclipse -- (some of the finest eclipse images anywhere)
- Photo Archive -- (the studio, historical, personal, & Wendy)
- Wendy's Artwork -- (drawings, graphics, computer images)
- Resources -- (files to download: articles, music, MIDI)
- Metapage -- (a page about this page, including What's New)
- Write Wendy -- (includes Wendy's Open Letter -- replies to yours)

A Living Page

The official Wendy Carlos homepage contains news, a biography (but nothing about Walter...), discography, a photo archive, collections of Wendy's sketches, and you can write to her. There are also music resources and files to download.

Suzanne Ciani
http://www.sevwave.com/ciani/
The official homepage containing a brief biography, concert details, and you can order CDs, books and a T-shirt.

Emerson, Lake & Palmer
http://www.dynrec.com/elp/

The official Web site and a good 'un, too, with lots of info about the band and individual members – discography, biogs, tour dates, behind the scenes, sound samples, photos, stuff to buy... Cool graphics, too.

ELP Digest
http://bliss.berkeley.edu/elp/
Another set of pages for ELP fans with links to sites of the individual members and links to lots of other ELP-related sites across the world.

Enigma
http://www.five.no/enigma/
Pages about Enigma and the man behind it, Michael Cretu. Also information about Sandra, the German singer and voice behind Enigma with a link to her Web page. News, lyrics, articles, interviews, reviews...

Brian Eno
http://www.hyperreal.org/music/artists/brian_eno/
It's unthinkable that one of the seminal influences in modern music could not have a Web site and there are, in fact, several. This is probably the most complete and contains a wealth of info for Eno fans – news, interviews, lyrics and the Enocyclopaedia! There's also an intriguing piece on why Eno does not want to hear from you via email – and, no, his email address is not posted here.

Enya
http://sunsite.auc.dk/enya/

The unofficial Enya pages – a nice headline but there are more ads on the page than info. When I checked it, the layout was confused and the ads totally spoiled the site. However, if you can get past them, there is a lot here for Enya fans so don't let the layout put you off.

Robert Fripp
http://www.elephant-talk.com/

Robert Fripp and King Crimson – psychedelia from the 70s. This is a digest-format newsletter distributed by email which is occasionally, so it says, contributed to by the man himself.

There's lots of info here including the usual discography (and very well done it is, too), photos, reviews, tour dates et al.

Future Sound Of London
http://raft.vmg.co.uk/fsol/

Yes, an official FSOL home site for all you wannabes to check out. Suitably street-wise, suitably up front, suitably hip, suitably hop with movies and graphics and lots of fancy stuff. And a bit of info. There are several other FSOL sites and references on the Web which you'll discover with a search, too.

Philip Glass
http://www.uni-paderborn.de/~pg/glass.html
http://www.lsi.upc.es/~jpetit/pg/glass.html

A German and a Spanish site respectively for Philip Glass. Both seem identical and they're both in English. There is a multitude of info here including info, discography, biography, articles, photos, links, and details about his music including screen shots of some of his scores. It also has a jokes section which includes this one attributed to Emo Philips: 'A friend of mine gave me a Philip Glass record. I listened to it for five hours before I realised it had a scratch on. it'. In all, an excellent site well worth a visit.

Jan Hammer

http://www.hut.fi/~tahola/jhammer/

Best known for the Miami Vice theme (which he's probably heartily tired of playing by now), Jan Hammer is a very accomplished musician with many more strings to his bow and this site tells you a little more about him.

Jean Michel Jarre

http://www.jarre.com/

The official homepage with lots of info, sounds, remixes – yes – news and so on. Other JMJ sites to check include:

http://www.free-spirit.demon.co.uk/urlguide/

http://www.library.tudelft.nl/~blouw/

http://www.xs4all.nl/~roko/jean.html

http://www.bekkoame.or.jp/~ummo/jarre.html

http://www.studiomagazine.demon.nl/oxygene4all/

Jean Michel Jarre's home page – info, sounds, remixes, and news

Karl Jenkins/Adiemus

http://www.noahgrey.com/adiemus/

Unofficial site devoted to Karl Jenkins and the Adiemus albums including Songs of Sanctuary. Lots of information, music extracts and links to other Adiemus-related sites.

Kraftwerk

http://www.kraftwerk.com/

The official site. Plain. Matter-of-fact. As befits the group which invented robotic music! But do also check out the other Kraftwerk sites:

http://www.webring.org/cgi-bin/webring?ring=kraftwerk&list
http://www.geocities.com/SunsetStrip/8880/
http://home.t-online.de/home/Zaepke/kraftwer.htm
http://www.xs4all.nl/~bwe/index2.htm

Kraftwerk 's plain site

Paul Nagle

http://www.softroom.demon.co.uk/

Paul Nagle is an musician in the electronic music vein. The site is extensive and contains lots of information, samples from Paul's albums plus lots of patches for instruments such as the Waldorf Microwave and Pulse, Korg Prophecy, Roland VS-880 and Emu Vintage Keys. The site also includes a host of links covering electronic music, musicians, MIDI data, software, synths, shops, magazines, and Net-related stuff.

Neuronium

http://www.neuronium.com/

This is the virtual domain of Neuronium. The psychotronic music by Michel Huygen. A little alternative but Neuronium fans will appreciate it. Also check out:

http://www.earthportals.com/Portal_Market/huygen.html
http://www.amazings.com/galleries/gallery0001.html
http://www.geocities.com/Area51/Zone/4737/shiva.html

Mike Oldfield
http://www.pcug.co.uk/~darkstar/

The homepages of Dark Star which is the official Mike Oldfield fan zine. Includes news, views, a discography and biography, goodies to buy and, of course, lots of opportunities to subscribe to the magazine. It also features an enormous collection of links to other Mike Oldfield pages.

The Orb
http://www.theorb.com/net_index.html

A site design a wee bit too cute for its own good – or at least for current comms technology. Put the cursor on one of the worlds surrounding the central globe and the server fetches and displays a description of the area that world takes you to. But that's The Orb for you.

Images, discography, sounds, texture. There's info for Orb fans and software to download including Orb fonts and screensavers.

Redshift and Mark Shreeve
http://www.users.dircon.co.uk/~redshift/

Redshift is Mark Shreeve's 'electronic music' band and the site provides news, information and demos of the band. Their music uses a lot of analogue electronic instruments and encompasses a range of styles – ambient, chill out, New Age... There's also a Mark Shreeve page at:
http://sonicimages.com/markshreeve/

Klaus Schulze
http://www.klaus-schulze.com/

The official site of this Tangerine Dream man is set out like other sites such as the Ash Ra Tempel site, for example. The colours are different but it's no surprise to learn that the sites were developed by the same person.

Morton Subotnick
http://newalbion.com/artists/subotnickm/
One of the US's premier composers of electronic music and an innovator in works involving instruments and other media, including interactive computer music systems. Most of his music calls for a computer part. His oeuvre utilises many of the important technological breakthroughs in the history of the genre. Yes, a wee bit academic but worth a visit.

Synergy and Larry Fast
http://www.eclipse.net/~synergy/
One of the pioneers of popular electronic music in the mid-70s and 80s, Larry Fast released several albums under the Synergy name around that time. This site contains the usual discography and biography, plus news and other Synergy info.

Tangerine Dream
http://www.netstore.de/tadream/
The official site. Lots and lots of info about the original electronic music band. Pages include a discography, biography, interviews, pictures, movie clips, lyrics (for some pieces which had them) and 101 FAQs.

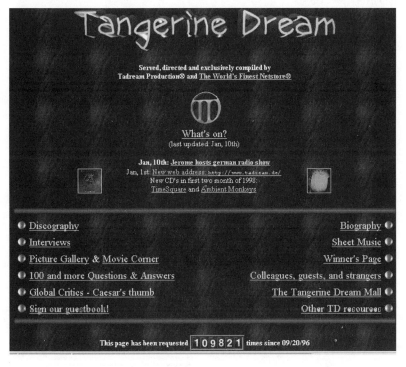

Includes a What's On guide, a merchandising section, and a rather interesting page of critical comments which TD fans will find very amusing. The site also has lots of links to other TD sites.

Tomita
http://weber.ucg.ie/tomita/welcome.html
An unofficial site but holding a wealth of information about Tomita, his music and the technology, images and links.

Vangelis

http://www.vangelisworld.com/

The official homepages, under construction as we go to press, but watch this space... However, fully working at the time was the unofficial homepage:

http://bornova.ege.edu.tr/~lyurga/vangelis/main.html

which includes pictures, interviews and a discography. Fans should also check out:

http://wwwperso.hol.fr/~antas/vwr.htm

http://www.engelen.demon.nl/

http://www.il.fontys.nl/~lodewks/elsewher.htm

http://www.cs.uit.no/Music/ViewGrp?grp_id=94

http://bau2.uibk.ac.at/perki/Vangelis.html

Yanni

http://www.teleport.com/~celinec/yanni.shtml

Unofficial pages but with lots of info about this pianist/composer – photos, news, the fans...

Yello

http://www.yello.ch/

Best viewed with a Java-enabled browser, this site is official and suitably techy and accessing the main pages reorganises your browser, removing the toolbar and making it nigh on impossible to move back through other pages... Hmm!!!

Yellow Magic Orchestra

http://www.tezcat.com/~klee/ymo.html

Yellow Magic Orchestra's site has lots of areas and lots of info including sound bytes to download and listen to.

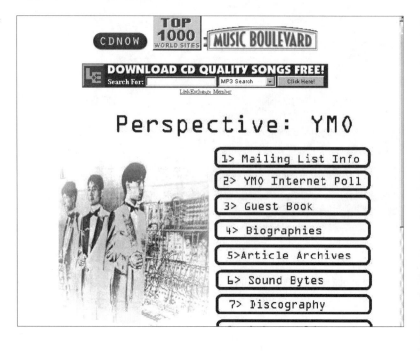

Links and associated information

BBC Soundscapes
http://www.zoo.co.uk/~nw/soundscapes/
The Web page of BBC Derby's weekly cult contemporary electronic music show. Soundscapes, presented and produced by Ashley Franklin, is a weekly aural voyage through musical landscapes on the mainstream cutting edge, encompassing Electronica, Ambient, New Age, Experimental, Classic Rock, Contemporary Classical, Fusion and Film Music. The programme for those who feel disenfranchised by Radio 1, and disillusioned by Virgin Radio. It broadcasts to central England on Sundays from 3:00pm to 6:00pm every week.

The British Music Page
http://easyweb.easynet.co.uk/~snc/british.htm
Dedicated to 20th centruy British classical music. There's a magazine, concert details, information about composers and you can listen to the Sound Clip of the Month.

KLEM Electronic Music Megalinks
http://www.sem.hhs.nl/void/klem/
A mammoth collection of links to electronic music artists official and unofficial Web sites. Organised alphabetically, the list includes hundreds of artists and sites. It lists electronic music magazines and organisations, radio stations, record labels, mail order outlets and music stores. A must to bookmark.

The on-line directory of electronic music
http://members.tripod.com/~emusic/index.html
Another large list of links to electronic music artists' Web sites, official and unofficial.

MEMO
http://www.atiainc.com/memo.htm
The Midwest Electronic Music Organisation Incorporated, or MEMO, evolved from a growing trend catering to the needs of a vast audience, exploring progressive, instrumental, and electronic music. MEMO held its first meeting in February, 1997, setting guidelines, developing strategies, and creating more accessibility for recording artists and labels to exchange information regarding the establishment of future goals. 'The association's philosophy deals primarily with this segment of the market.'

Music Internet
Ultimate Band List
On AOL. A search engine to track down the sites of your favourite bands. It contains tens of thousands of bands. If your favourite isn't here it must be obscure!

Composition

Composition is one of the least-discussed areas of musicianship. Trawl the Web, however, and you will find many references to it, articles to read and composition software to play with. The sites here come mainly from an academic background but any composer ought to find them worth visiting. Also check in the Software and Shareware sections for details of software which can be used for composing.

C-Thru's Home Page
http://www.c-thru-music.co.uk/
This is interesting. 'The site is primarily for musicians, composers, arrangers, music students (at whatever level) and music teachers – in fact anyone who is currently learning or who is considering learning music. C-Thru Music was set up to aid musicians with the understanding and creation of music through use of the Melodic Table. These pages have been created so you can discover the 'Melodic Table' for yourself. You will be able to start using the ideas straight away.' A little alternative but there's lots of info as you might expect and demos to download.

The C-Thru site is primarily for musicians, composers, arrangers, music students (at whatever level) and music teachers.

Communal Groove Machine
http://ctdnet.acns.nwu.edu/cmbecker/techno/techno.html
Try this for size. The Communal Groove Machine (CGM) is Canton Becker's algorithmic techno music composing agent that generates songs by interacting with people in CTDMOO, where it lives... The site includes samples of the songs it 'spat out' and you can Telnet into the Groove machine and do your own thing.

Check out the Electronic
Arts Research site for an
alternative slant on
composition.

Electronic Arts Research
http://autoinfo.smartlink.net/ray/

Much of the site revolves around GSMP (Genetic Spectrum Modelling
Program, a Fractal Melody Generator. To quote: 'GSMP is a program that
can act as a source of melodic material. It primarily concentrates on structure by forcing the melodies to have a specific target spectrum. GSMP
does not work on sound, the spectral signatures are those of the note list.
This program allows the user to specify some aspects of the 'target' spectrum while controlling others.' The site includes sample MIDI files and
Wave files and you can download the software and try it for yourself.

EMF
http://www.emf.org/

Not the European Monetary Fund but the Electronic Music Foundation.
Rather academic. The founder speaks for us all when he says: 'We're in the
process of major change in the world as the electronic technologies developed throughout the century become mature and increasingly intertwined
and meshed with every aspect of our daily lives. New tools and concepts
are leading to new approaches to art and universal possibilities for human
creativity. Yet the fundamental work of pioneering artists is often difficult
to find. Our mission is to provide public access to the materials and information that are essential to understanding the history and current development of music and related art forms in our technological age.'

Fractal Music Project
http://www-ks.rus.uni-stuttgart.de/people/schulz/fmusic/
'Fractal music is a result of a recursive process where an algorithm is applied multiple times to process its previous output. In a wider perspective, all musical forms, both in micro and macro level can be modelled with this process. Fractals provide extremely interesting musical results and the field is becoming one of the most exciting fields of new music research. Fractal music enthusiasts are encouraged to publish their works here. Links to physics, mathematics, algorithms and artificial intelligence, and further ideas concerning these pages are also welcomed.' A one stop source for everything connected with fractal music including articles, demo files and software.

Music Composition Resource
http://www.und.nodak.edu/dept/mcr/
Lists sources essential for today's composers, including books, articles, Internet sites, sound recordings and FAQs for beginning composers.

Music Composition Resource includes a list of interesting music composition FAQs which discusses motivation, getting through dry spells and creative principles.

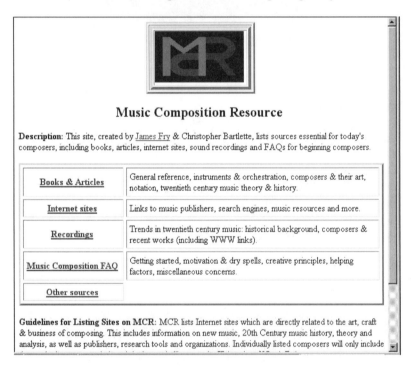

MusiNum
See entry in Shareware, page 167.

Oblique Strategies
http://www.msn.fullfeed.com/~gtaylor/ObliqueStrategies/
A collection of 'strategies' devised by Brian Eno to assist with the compositional process. The original strategies were on a set of cards which you would draw at random and act upon the suggestion but now they are available in electronic format.

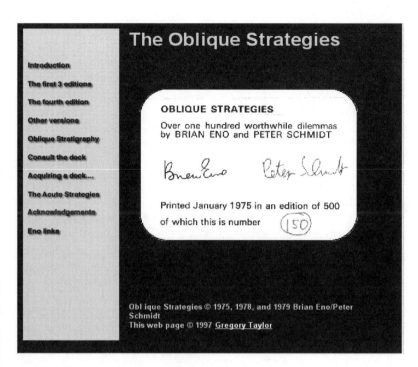

Oblique Strategies – a must to visit for anyone involved in composition and who has occasionally searched for the muse in vain.

RTPS Systems
See entry in Software, page 156.

Tonality Systems
See entry in Software, page 160.

Xen Web Site Meta-Index
http://www.tiac.net/users/xen/
A set of links to pages concerned with microtonality. They include: Interval, the Journal of Music Research and Development, 'a quarterly publication growing out of the flowering of creative activity in the micro-tonal field'; 'Pitch for the International Microtonalist is a complete set of reference materials designed to facilitate independent development in microtonal music'; 'Xenharmonikôn, an Informal Journal of Experimental Music, devoted to all aspects of microtonal and xenharmonic music.'

There's also Scala, a software tool for experimentation with musical tunings such as just intonation scales, equal and historical temperaments, microtonal and macrotonal scales, and non-Western scales. There's lots of info about the program and you can download it and make microtunes yourself!

Copyright and legal information

The Band Register
http://www.bandreg.com/legal/legalcontents.html
See entry in Music Information, page 224.

Copyright and Rights: A Hitch-Hiker's Guide from the Open University
http://ibis.life.nottingham.ac.uk/guidelines/ch7/CHAP7-Title.html
Contains the text – modified and updated – of a paper given at the multi-media courseware developer's conference at the University of Nottingham in September 1992.

Copyright law in Cyprus
http://www.cyprus.com.cy/copyrt.html
Read before you start that overseas bar gig!

The Copyright Website
http://www.benedict.com/
'This site endeavours to provide real world, practical and relevant copyright information of interest to infonauts, netsurfers, webspinners, content providers, musicians, appropriationists, activists, infringers, outlaws, and law abiding citizens. Launched on May Day '95, this site seeks to encourage discourse and invite solutions to the myriad of copyright tangles that currently permeate the Web. The Copyright Website strives to lubricate the machinations of information delivery. As spice is to Dune, information is to the Web – the spice must flow.'

Information about fundamental copyright principles, problems of sampling samples, ten famous copyright myths, famous copyright infringements (with audio examples!), issues involving copyright on the Net, Copyright law and music licensing for distribution on the Web including a synopsis of 'The Art of Music Licensing' plus links to other copyright-related sites. Bookmark.

ERA – Educational Recording Agency
http://www.era.org.uk/
If you're in education and record TV or radio programs, this site may be helpful. Section 35(1) of the 1988 Copyright, Design and Patents Act which came into force on 1 August 1989, gave educational establishments the right to record off-air for educational purposes any radio and televi-

sion broadcasts and cable programmes without infringing copyright. However, Section 35(2) of this Act states that this right does not apply if a certified licensing scheme is in place. The Secretary of State has to be satisfied with the terms and conditions of any proposed licensing scheme before it can be certified.

Free Music Philosophy
http://www.ram.org/ramblings/philosophy/fmp.html
The site describes itself as '...an anarchistic grass-roots, but high-tech system of spreading music: the idea that creating, copying, and distributing music must be as unrestricted as breathing air, plucking a blade of grass, or basking in the rays of the sun. The idea is similar to the notion of Free Software and like with freeware, the word 'free' refers to freedom, not price. Specifically, Free Music means that any individual has the freedom of copying, distributing, and modifying music for personal, non-commercial purposes. Free Music does not mean that musicians cannot charge for records, tapes, CDs, or DATs.'

Freibank
http://www.freibank.com/
Originally set up to administer the copyrights of German avant-garde artists Einstürzende Neubauten as effectively as possible, Freibank later began to offer its swift and efficient copyright collection and administration services to friends like Nick Cave, The Young Gods, Diamanda Galas and Foetus amongst others. It handles copyright matters for a catalogue of some 5,000 works with a broad variety of musical styles, however, with an emphasis on 'alternative' bands and the more progressive forms of contemporary dance music like drum 'n' bass, techno, house, hip-hop and other. The site includes information on European copyright control.

Kalvos & Damian's New Music Bazaar
http://www.goddard.edu/wgdr/kalvos/mres12.html
Wads and wads of links to legal and copyright material on the Web for composers including links about intellectual rights, the Universal Copyright Convention, a Fair Use essay, free Copyright forms, and the Berne Convention.

Library of Congress Copyright Office
gopher://marvel.loc.gov:70/11/copyright
American, but it contains a wealth of on-line copyright documentation relating to music.

MCPS – Mechanical-Copyright Protection Society
See entry in Organisations, page 206.

MIDI Loops
http://www.midiloops.com/copyrite.htm
A site licensing MIDI files for use on the Net. It includes a lot of informa-

midi-LOOPS – info on licensing and copyright for MIDI files

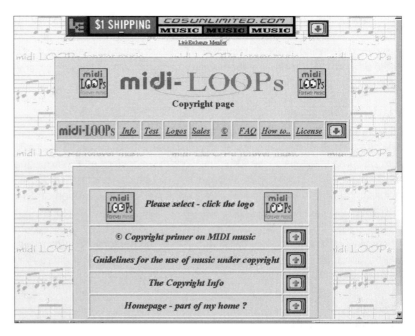

tion about copyright – a copyright primer on MIDI music, guidelines for the use of MIDI music under copyright, how to get permission to use files, MIDI files and shareware and so on.

MPA (Music Publishers Association) of America
http://www.mpa.org/crc.html
Copyright Resource Centre. Wads of copyright information.

Music in the Public Domain
http://ne1.bright.net/pdinfo/pdm2/
A site designed to help you work out what is and what isn't public domain. US-based but a lot of good and useful information here.

PRS – Copyright information
http://www.prs.co.uk/4_0.html
An excellent guide to copyright in the UK on the PRS web site. Topics include The Rights Of A Copyright Owner, How PRS Fits Into The Copyright System, Infringement Of Copyright, Moral Rights, No Formal Registration Required To Protect Copyright, and Further Information and Useful Contacts. See also entry in Organisations, page 208.

Songwriter and Music Copyright resources
http://www.copyright.net/resource.htm
It has an American slant but it contains many pointers to sources of UK information on copyright. Topics include Copyright Resources, Performance Rights Organisations, Mechanical Rights Organisations, International Organisations, Publishers, Songwriter Resources, Other Music Organisations, General Music Resources, On-line Resources, Books, Trades, Magazines and Publications.

Music hardware manufacturers

Musical instruments

Akai
http://www.akai.com/

Akai is best-known as the developer of 'the' sampler and although this is still one of its core products it has branched out to produce a wide range of high quality digital equipment such as digital recorders, post-production equipment, sound modules and support software. The site contains news, detailed info on all the company's range, reviews, FAQs, manuals to download, software to update equipment and samples to download. There's also a forum for discussion between users.

Big Briar
http://www.bigbriar.com/

'Theremins and innovative electronic musical instruments designed by Bob Moog.' Now there's a name to conjure with. The site contains product information, news, a newsletter, a section reserved for comments by the good Doctor and a Q&A session.

Product information, news, a newsletter, a section reserved for comments by the good Doctor and a Q&A session.

Buchla
http://www.buchla.com/

One time developer of analogue and custom synthesisers and modules, the company now describes itself as 'designers of unusual electro-acoustic instrumentation for electronic music'. Currently, it's two main pieces of equipment are the Thunder and Lightning MIDI controllers.

Clavia

http://www.clavia.se/

Swedish company Clavia became famous over the past few years for its innovative range of Nord synthesisers. The site includes details of these plus the DDrum along with sounds for it for PC and Mac (using Virtual PC). You can also download the Nord Modular Editor software.

Doepfer

http://www.doepfer.de/

German company and manufacturer of a range of analogue synth modules. If you hanker after the days of wall-covering synths and spaghetti patchchord cables then this is for you. Lists new products, overseas dealers and prices.

Emu Systems

http://www.emu.com/

Emu is probably best-know as a manufacturer of synthesisers, samplers and sound modules but it is also involved with the SoundFonts technology used in the Creative Labs sound cards and has produced several sets of sampled sounds.

This excellent site contains a plethora of information about the company, a complete list of product details, a support section, a set of downloadable factory presets, and links.

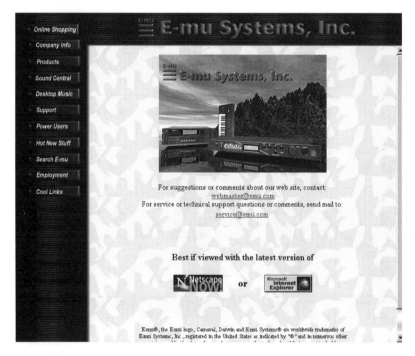

Ensoniq

http://www.ensoniq.com/

Another musical instrument manufacturer which also produces effects, multimedia soundcards, digital systems and semiconductors. The site is attractive and extensive and contains detailed information on Ensoniq products including the instruments and soundcards, technical support, press releases, and company information. There is a download section containing the latest drivers, MIDI and audio demo files and utilities.

Fatar
http://www.musicindustries.com/fatar_.htm
Manufacturer of MIDI master keyboards and pedal boards. The site contains info about the products plus pricing in US dollars – it's always interesting to compare the 'proper' price with that which customers in the UK get charged.

Your chance to compare prices in sterling with US dollar prices!

Generalmusic
http://www.Generalmusic.com/
The company previously known as GEM, coming a little later than most into the hi tech keyboard market but with an interesting and impressive range of products. There's lots of information on the site, details of new releases, updated operating systems to download, free music files, and a list of distributors worldwide.

Hinton Instruments
http://www.hinton.demon.co.uk/
A rather hideous backdrop to an otherwise interesting site of a company which specialises in MIDI solutions such as MIDI interfaces, MIDI automation, MIDI routers and customised equipment. There are interesting music software downloads and links to other sites.

Kawai
http://www.kawai.co.jp/english/index.html
http://www.kawaius.com/
The first link is to the Japanese HQ which currently only has the home page in English. The second is the US Web site which is all in English. Well, American. It lists the company's pianos, digital keyboards, home keyboards and synths, and there are sound demos, patch libraries and operating system updates to download plus links to sites containing patches, librarians and other info of interest to Kawai instrument owners.

Korg
http://www.korg.com/

Korg Online, the site of one of the world's leading musical instrument manufacturers.

Product info on keyboards, synths, sound modules, digital pianos, tuners, effects processors and digital recording systems –plus details of related third-party products.

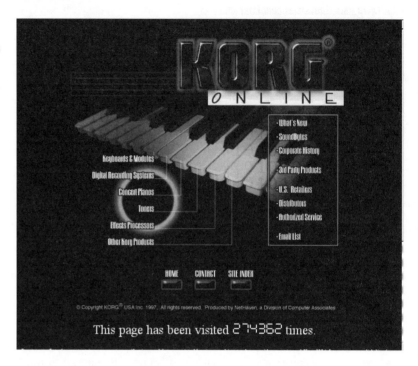

Kurzweil
http://www.youngchang.com/kurzweil/

Original developer of the top-end Kurzweil workstations, the company has since been acquired by Young Chang. The site includes information about the range, and you can access an FTP site to download files for Kurzweil instruments. There is also links to other Kurzweil-related sites.

Moog Music
http://www.moogmusic.com/

Robert Moog (rhymes with 'vogue') was one of the original synthesiser developers and although he left the company, Moog Music continues to produce new Moog synths to delight the modern synthesist. These include the Minimoog and mouth-watering, rack-filling modular synths. The site includes information on current product (although not all have photos) and there's an archive of older, classic instruments. There's a news section, a tech support area including FAQs, patch sheets and an on-line store.

Novation
http://www.nova-uk.com/

The company made a name for itself with the BassStation bass module and has branched out into drum and synth modules. The site includes product details, dealers, a long list of help information and there are patches to download for a range of instruments.

Oberheim
http://www.gibson.com/products/oberheim/
Classic synth manufacturer Oberheim is still manufacturing classic synths such as the Matrix 1000 and OB-Mx plus the OB-3 drawbar expander, a keyboard, FX units and MIDI processors. The site contains info on all Oberheim products plus downloadable manuals.

Panasonic
http://www.panasonic.co.uk/
Manufacturer of a range of musical equipment from consumer electronics such as hi fis, TVs and video recorders to notebook computers and the Technics range of keyboards. The site is extremely lacklustre and the information is presented very matter-of-factly. Includes lots of links to other Panasonic and Matsushita sites. See also the Technics entry, page 123.

Peavey Electronics
http://www.peavey.com/
Highly regarded US company developing musical instruments ranging from guitars and amps to drums and keyboards. The site contains information about the products, user ads, and job opportunities. You can subscribe, free, to the Key Issues on-line magazine and the company produces a quarterly magazine called Monitor which is also available on-line. You can download instrument presets and Wave files.

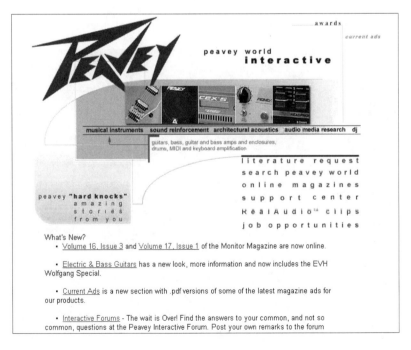

You must read the Hard Knocks section which tells of users' experiences of subjecting Peavey gear to falls, floods, hot water, car wrecks and more but which still continue to work. Heck, they must be using our roadies!

PPG
http://www.nashville.net/~antarct/ppg.htm
Synthesiser manufacturer whose range includes modular analogue synthesisers, keyboards, sequencers and drum machines. There are details of a PPG editor programmed in Logic's Environment – very neat – and a page of MIDI info. Lots of stuff for the hi tech retro artist to wallow in.

Quasimidi
http://www.quasimidi.com/
German manufacturer of hi tech synths such as the Sirius, Raven and Polymorph. Lots of info, news, nice piccies and links to interesting sites.

Roland
http://www.roland.co.uk/home2.htm
http://www.rolandgroove.com/
http://www.rolandcorp.com/
http://www.rolandus.com/
One of the major musical instrument manufacturers, Roland also has a heavy interest in software. The site includes info about instruments, news and road shows, and you can download software, applications, samples and so on. You can also access the Groovezone – you'll need Shockwave (see Chapter 7) – and groove along to, er, phab and phunky sounds.

The Roland Corp site has a much more corporate look and feel as you might expect but it's packed with info about Roland, BOSS and DTM products, plus details about GM and GS and there are patches, drivers and sample files for both PC and Mac to download.

The US site is a bit more relaxed and contains an equal amount of product info and downloads. The company has removed the on-line price list so you can't compare US with UK prices – darn shame! – but you can

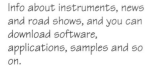
Info about instruments, news and road shows, and you can download software, applications, samples and so on.

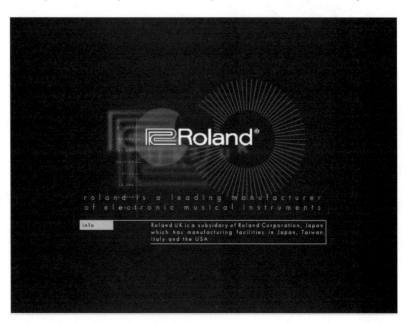

get them via a FaxBack service. It also includes links to user groups. Also check out Edirol, a member of the Roland group:
http://www.edirol.com/

Technics
http://www.technics.co.uk/
A site devoted to the Technics range of pianos, organs and keyboards. See also the Panasonic entry.

Lots of product information, dealer lists, some software downloads and details of the Technics Music Academy where you can go to learn to play.

Waldorf
http://www.waldorf-gmbh.de/index.html
The site contains details of products such as the Wave, (arguably described as the biggest synth ever built!), the MicroWave and MicroWave XT and II, Pulse and the 4-Pole filter module. The company has also developed the D-Pole plug-in for Cubase VST and there are demos for downloading. There's a news section, you can download manuals and there are a few links, too. Distribution is through TSi and you can check out that site at:
http://www.tsi-gmbh.de/

Wernick
http://homepages.webleicester.co.uk/wernick/
Manufacturer of MIDI percussion instruments such as the XyloSynth, the NotePad (electronic drum pad) and the KikNotePad (an electronic kick drum). Details, news, reviews and prices.

Yamaha
http://www.yamaha.com/
http://www.yamaha.co.jp/english/index.html
http://www.yamaha.co.uk/
Yamaha is best known as a manufacturer of musical instruments hence its

Yamaha's UK-based European homepage includes an XG area; Synth Zone with lots of information, FAQs and downloads for popular Yamaha synths; a section on home keyboards; a pro audio section (a mirror of the Japanese site); and a virtual shop where you can buy some goodies.

inclusion in this section. However, the company is also involved with many software developments and often releases support software for its products. The first URL is the American site, the second is the Japanese site (where you can often find items which don't make it to the UK) from where you can access the XG area which contains lots of information and files to download.

Museums

For want of a more suitable category, these sites find themselves here.

EMIS
http://dspace.dial.pipex.com/emis/museum/museum.htm
The EMIS Synthesiser Museum is a real collection of instruments, based in Bristol. This link contains details of the instruments – around 400 – with information about each one. See also entry in Retailers.

Synth & MIDI Museum
http://www.synthony.com/museum.html
A database of the larger, older electronic synths and MIDI equipment. This is a fascinating site, a mine of almost-forgotten information. There are hundreds of old instruments here, specs carefully detailed and many with a photograph. An essential site to visit for anyone interested in synthesisers. Bookmark it now.

Soundcards, digital audio cards, MIDI interfaces/boxes

AdB
http://www.adbdigital.com/
Manufacturer of professional 24-bit digital audio products, specifically the Multi!Wave (yes, that's how they spell it!) Pro 24 sound card for the PC.

Alesis
http://www.alesis.com/
Alesis is probably most famous for the ADAT digital audio recorder whose interface at least has become a de facto standard for connecting pieces of digital equipment. The company also produces synthesisers, the Nano range of synth modules, amps and speakers, signal processors and mixers.

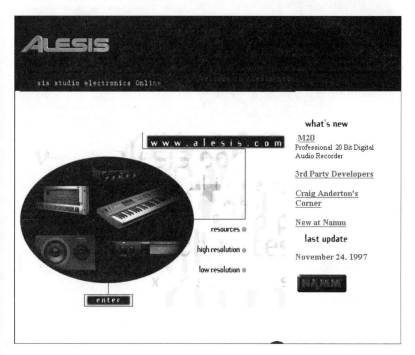

There's lots of info here about Alesis products and the company, and lots of files to download.

Altech Systems
http://www.altechsystems.com/
MIDI interfaces for PC notebooks and Apple Mac computers plus sound-cards for PC notebooks and MIDI/SMPTE cards for desktops.

Aardvark
http://www.aardvark-pro.com/
Manufacturer of hard disk multi-track cards for the PC including the Aark 20/20 and the Aark TDIF, an eight-channel digital interface. The site includes product details, driver downloads and details of the company's worldwide distributors.

CreamWare
http://www.creamware.com/
One of Germany's leading manufacturers of digital audio hardware and software. The company's best-known product is the tripleDAT card and direct-to-disk recording software for the PC. The site includes product information, tech specs, news, on-line workshops, and job opportunities.

Creative Labs
http://www.creaf.com/home.html
The site of the company which virtually invented the PC sound card (regardless of the fact that the early ones were powered by a Yamaha chip).

The site contains lots of info about the cards, new drivers, info, competitions, SoundFonts to download and lots of other goodies. The company also produces speakers, graphic and video products, and a range of accessories. A bookmark must for anyone with a Creative card.

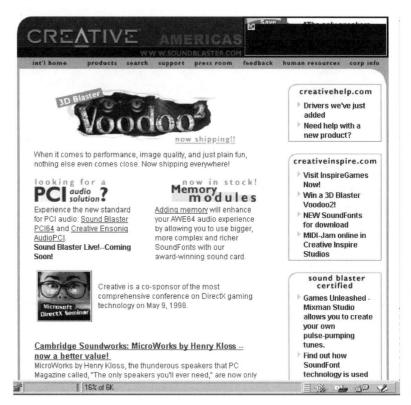

DAL – Digital Audio Labs
http://www.digitalaudio.com/
Best known for its CardD Plus, a high quality digital audio card for the PC, DAL also has a range of other digital audio cards including the V8, a high-quality hardware system designed to integrate all the digital bits in your studio. The site includes lots of information about the products, company info, the latest software and drivers, FAQs and on-line tech support.

Digidesign
http://www.digidesign.com/index1.html
Developer of the ubiquitous Pro Tools direct-to-disk recording system,

Digidesign began by specialising in high quality digital audio hardware and software for the Apple Mac and has now taken the PC under its wing. The site contains a wealth of information about Digidesign products and includes details of how you can get a free copy of Pro Tools v3.4 for the PowerMac. Worth logging on, eh?

Digigram
http://www.digigram.com/
Developer of professional digital audio sound cards such as the PCX and the LCM ranges. The site includes news, product information, a technology information section, and a download area with updated drivers, sample files and utilities.

EES – Technik fur Musik
http://www.ees-musik.de/
A German company although with an English option on the Web site specialising in MIDI interfaces, MIDI switchers and MIDI controllers. The site contains information about the products and the latest drivers to download.

Event Electronics
http://www.event1.com/
A company set on producing affordable digital audio equipment and known for the Gina, Darla and Layla sound cards by Echo, some of which had a protracted delivery.

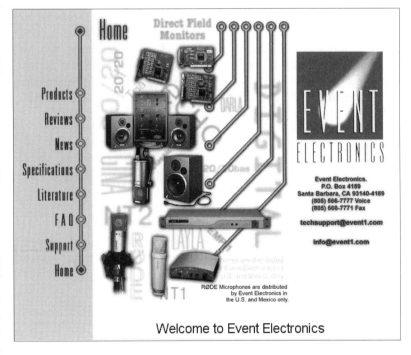

Welcome to Event Electronics

There's lots of product information on the site plus software updates to download. There's also Echo Reporter which analyses your PC system for its suitability for digital recording with the Darla/Gina cards, although the report will be of interest to PC users using any sound card.

Fender
http://www.fender.com/
Site of the most famous guitars of all.

Frontier Design Group
http://www.frontierdesign.com/
Developer of computer-based high quality digital audio converters such as Zulu, Tango and the WaveCenter card. There's lots of product information on the site, FAQs and a tech support area.

Gadget Labs
http://www.gadgetlabs.com/
PC digital audio card, multi-track recording software, analogue audio processing software and Wave file compression software are all on the Gadget Labs site. Product info and demos to download.

Guillemot
http://www.guillemot.com/uk/index.html
Guillemot is a French company best known for its range of MAXi soundcards for the PC although it also produces speakers, Mics, DVD systems, 3D accelerators and scanners. The site is in English and contains a wealth of information about the products, the latest drivers to download, Soundbanks and demo files. You can access technical support and there are a few links to other sites of interest to MAXi users.

Kenton Electronics
http://www.kenton.co.uk/
Kenton made its name as developer of MIDI-to-CV interfaces and has since expanded into MIDI boxes and performing MIDI retrofits on analogue equipment. It's a bright site where you can browse product information, read reviews, check prices, and download manuals and a catalogue.

Lyrrus
http://www.lyrrus.com/
Developer of G-Vox – the link between your guitar and computer.

Mediatrix
http://www.mediatrix.com/
Developer of soundcards and daughterboards. The site includes product information, news, reviews, press releases, technical information, drivers and so on.

Mark of the Unicorn
See entry in Software, page 151.

MidiMan
http://www.midiman.net/
Manufacturer of MIDI interfaces for Mac and PC, digital and audio patch-

bays, digital-to-analogue converters, synchronisers, line mixers and MIDI accessories. Lots of product information, a big list of FAQs to browse, press releases, and drivers and utilities to download.

Orchid
http://www.orchid.com/
Developer of 3D accellerators, mainly for the games market, but has also dabbled in soundcards including the NuSound 3D. Product and company information and driver updates.

Philip Rees
http://www.philrees.co.uk/
UK manufacturer of a wide range of MIDI boxes – MIDI-to-CV converters, MIDI Thru boxes, MIDI switchers, MIDI selector boxes, MIDI merge units and line drivers (to transmit MIDI data over long distances). The site has a wealth of information about the products plus technical articles by Philip Rees himself including how to wire a DIN plug for MIDI and details about MIDI Thru boxes and MIDI mergers. There's also a news page and lots of info to download in Acrobat format.

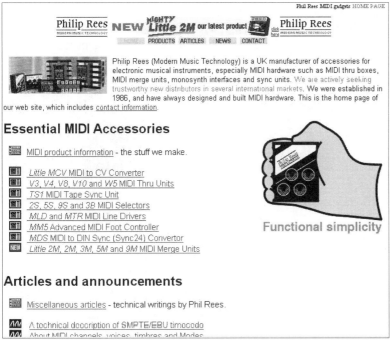

There's a wealth of information about every conceivable kind of MIDI box on the Philip Rees Web site.

Soundscape
http://www.soundscape-digital.com/
Soundscape is a pro-quality direct-to-disk recording system for the PC and a British development to boot. The site includes product information, news, reviews, technical support and links to companies which are developing supporting software for the system.

SADiE – Studio Audio & Video
http://www.sadie.com/

A UK company and developer of the SADiE and Octavia digital audio workstations, the Portia JPEG card system which can integrate with them and the SASCiA real-time networking system for transferring audio between the workstations. The site contains product information, news, FAQs and software updates. You can subscribe to a user forum and there are links to other sites of interest.

Symbolic Sound
http://www.symbolicsound.com/

Symbolic Sound designs, manufactures, and markets hardware and software for computer-based digital audio. This includes the Kyma sound design workstation, a visual sound design language with associated Capybara multi-DSP hardware accelerator. Kyma is being used for sound design for music, film, advertising, television, virtual environments, speech and hearing research, computer games, and other virtual environments. The site has info on the products as well as company background and a newsletter on the activities of Kyma users.

Turtle Beach
http://www.tbeach.com/

A division of Voyetra Technologies and manufacturer of digital audio cards such as the Montego, Pinnacle, Malibu and MultiSound cards for the PC.

Technical support, files and drivers to download, news and a Fun Stuff area which contains hints, tips and competitions.

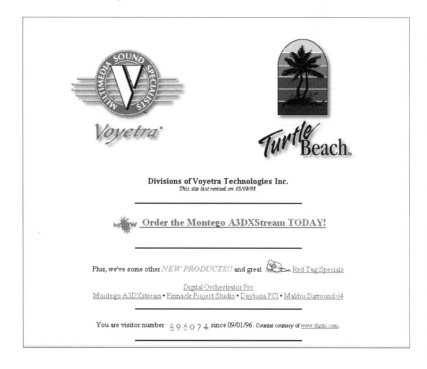

Signal processors, mixers, amps, external audio gear

AKG
http://www.akg-acoustics.com/
Manufacturer of Mics, headphones, sound processing equipment and mixers. The site carries lots of information about the ranges, news, distributors and links to other companies.

Amek
http://www.amek.com/
Mixer manufacturer. The site includes product details, news, tech support and details of automation software.

AMS Neve
http://www.ams-neve.com/
Best known for its legendary mixing consoles, AMS Neve produces mixers for all kinds of applications. The site includes information on the products, news, contacts, job opportunities and the quarterly Talk Back magazine.

Aphex
http://www.aphex.com/
Perhaps best known for its Aural Exciter, Aphex has a range of effects, amps and signal processors. Details, along with prices, are here. The company has also branched out into software with a couple of digital audio plug-ins for Pro Tools TDM.

There are demos to download along with Acrobat info on other products.

APT – Audio Processing Technology
http://www.aptx.com/
Developer of the apt-X 4:1 digital audio compression system used by many manufacturers in professional audio applications.

ART – Applied Research and Technology
http://www.artroch.com/
Manufacturer of programmable guitar amplifiers, signal processors, compressors, EQ and foot controllers. You'll find product details here, new products, FAQs, and a listing of artists who use the gear.

Ashly
http://www.ashly.com/
Power amplifiers, signal processors and mixers. Info, specs, photos, company history.

Audio Toys
http://www.audiotoys.com/
Manufacturer of mixer and signal processors. The Web site, sometimes slow, contains info on the products, contacts and tech support.

Behringer
http://www.behringer.de/
German manufacturer of signal processors, mixers, microphones and amplifiers.

The Behringer site includes lots of info about the products, news information, manuals, job opportunities, and software updates for products along with dire warnings not to open up your equipment.

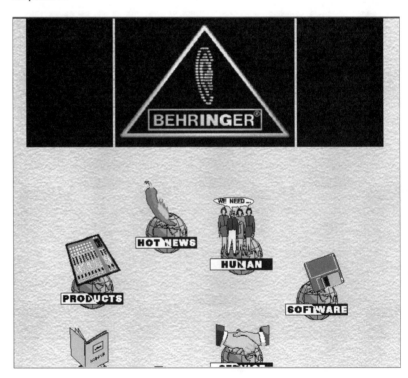

BSS Audio

http://www.bssaudio.co.uk/

Manufacturer of a range of signal processors including dynamics processors, equalisers, frequency dividing systems and active signal distribution systems. The site contains a lot of product and technical information, online manuals, and support details.

Canford

http://www.canford.co.uk/

Manufacturer and distributor of pro audio equipment including DAT cassettes, mixers, headphones, transformers, microphones, minidiscs and so on. Product information on site and catalogue available to pro audio users.

Carlsbro

http://www.carlsbro.co.uk/

One of the most famous names in amplification. The site was under construction as of writing.

Cedar Audio

http://dialspace.dial.pipex.com/town/estate/vg65/

Manufacturer of audio restoration systems. Lots of info about a range of products including Cedar for Windows, tech specs, news and info on audio restoration.

JL Cooper Electronics

http://www.jlcooper.com/

Developer of professional audio products including control, automation, interfacing and synchronisation products.

About JLCooper Electronics

For over a decade JLCooper Electronics has been a pioneer in the development of professional products. Our solid reputation for design innovation is a testimony to the quality, reliability and performance of every product we make. JLCooper's rapid double-digit growth can be attributed to our remarkable versatility.

JLCooper Electronics has grown to a modern 20,000 sq. ft. facility, encompassing all aspects of design and manufacturing. We offer a complete line of mixing console automation systems, synchronizers, MIDI and computer peripherals for the professional audio, video and multimedia markets. Our products are sold through dealers and distributors worldwide.

Lots of information on the site including service and technical info.

Dbx
http://www.dbxpro.com/

Best known for its dbx noise reduction systems, the company also produces associated equipment such as compression/limiters, EQ and preamplifiers. The site contains some techy and semi-techy information and offers a choice of using frames or not.

Denon
http://www.denon.com/

Denon is probably best-known for its speakers and in-car hi fi systems but it also produces a range of CD and DVD players and pro audio products. The site has details of all these, news items, links, FAQs and dealer lists. The Denon Active Media department is involved with CD replication and offers a range of MPEG services.

DigiTech
http://www.digitech.com/

Lots of information on the company's products divided into guitar, studio and harmony sections. There's also an upgrade information section, on-line documents and new products info.

The DigiTech site contains sections on guitar, studio and harmony effects.

DNA
http://www.dna.nl/

Developer of pro audio equipment such as the Dymand compressor, the Dictator stereo peak program limiter, and the Symon distribution amplifier. The site includes product descriptions, technical specifications and downloadable manuals.

DOD
http://www.dod.com/
DOD manufacturers a wide range of FX, amplification and sound reinforcement equipment. It's all here.

Dolby Laboratories
http://www.dolby.com/
The company which virtually invented noise reduction has a large site containing wads of information. Areas include: New Information, Press Releases, Dolby News, Statistics, Cassettes, Technical Information, Movies and Cinema, Home Theatre, Multimedia, Cinema Products, Professional Products, Literature. Dolby Digital, DVD, Company Information, People, Career Opportunities, and Trademark Information. What more could you want? Ah, no free samples, though.

Drawmer
http://www.proaudio.co.uk/drawmer.htm
Noise gates, compressors, amplifiers, tube pre-amps and TDM plug-ins are all here along with reviews, news, details of old products and access to technical support.

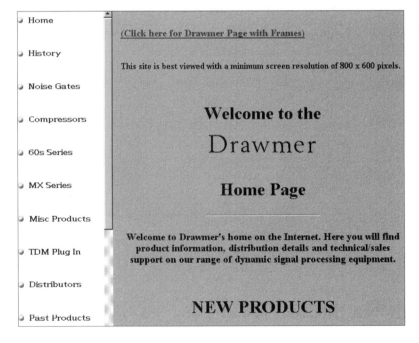

Product info, reviews, news and tech support at the Drawmer site.

Euphonix
http://www.euphonix.com/
Euphonix manufacturers digitally-controlled mixing consoles for the pro audio industry based on the CS3000. The site contains a multitude of data including 45 web pages of information about the system plus lots of downloadable brochures and manuals. It also has a news & events area, a

support area, sections for music, post production, broadcast and live use, and there's an area dedicated to Euphonix users.

Eventide
http://www.eventide.com/

Eventide says it is a manufacturer and purveyor of neat science toys. Musically, it is best-known for its harmoniser effects processors and you'll find details about them on this site along with technical specs. There is also some edit software to download.

Filmtech
http://www.filmtech.co.uk/

Manufacturer of the LSP4 Location Mixer and the Universal Microphone Power Unit.

Focusrite
http://www.focusrite.com/

Founded by legendary designer Robert Neve (of Neve mixing console fame), Focusrite is a manufacturer of high quality audio products such as amplifiers, pre-amplifiers, compressor/limiters and equalisers.

Fostex
http://www.fostex.com/

Manufacturer of hard disk recording systems, DATs, mixers and multi-trackers. The site has lots of detailed product information, there's a FAQ on recording techniques and links to a wide range of music-related sites.

Lots of information about recording on the Fostex site.

Joe Meek
http://www.joemeek.co.uk

Under construction as of writing but the site will include information on Joe Meek products, sounds to download and info about stars using the products.

Lexicon
http://www.lexicon.com/

Manufacturer of digital effects processors, amplifiers and outboard guitar electronics. Product info and support info plus links to other industry sites.

Digital effects info and links to other industry sites at Lexicon.

Mackie Designs
http://www.mackie.com/

A name well-known in the UK as a manufacturer of quality, affordable mixers. The site includes product information, a list of dealers: there's a technical support area, news, reviews, and an area with information about famous Mackie users.

NuReality
http://www.nureality.com/

Manufacturer of boxes designed to improve the 3D spatial awareness of audio systems from in-car audio to PC sound. A graphic site with lots of info about the products and the technology they use.

QSC Audio
http://www.qscaudio.com/

Developer of the PowerLite power amplifiers series and the RAVE system which routes audio via a fast Ethernet system. A busy and colourful site with lots of info, photos and downloadable Adobe Acrobat files.

Rolls/RFX/Bellari
http://www.rolls.com/
An audio electronics manufacturer specialising in signal processors, amplifiers, mixers, signal sources and interface accessories. The Web site contains information about the products produced by the divisions – Rolls, RFX and Bellari – news and reviews.

Sennheiser
http://www.sennheiser.com/
Manufacturers of microphones and headphones using the latest technology.

Soundcraft
http://www.soundcraft.com/
Manufacturer of professional audio mixing consoles for live, recording, post production, broadcast and disco applications. On most pages, information about consoles is colour-coded by application.

Soundtracs
http://www.soundtracs.co.uk/
Manufacturer of digital audio mixing consoles. The site contains details of the current range of products and a list of worldwide distributors.

Request a brochure on the latest products, check out the specs, how much they cost, and discover which famous people use them. Annoying windowed site but graphic and informative.

Spirit By Soundcraft
http://www.spirit-by-soundcraft.co.uk/
Designer of the world's coolest mixers and speakers. It says here.

Speck
http://www.speck.com/
Manufacturers of high quality audio mixers, equalisers and other audio products. Product and company information.

Studiomaster
http://www.studiomaster.com/
Best known for its mixers, Studiomaster also produces a range of professional audio equipment including amplifiers, Mics, speakers and accessories. They're all here along with news, tech specs and links.

TC Electronic
http://www.tcelectronic.com
Developer of high-end signal processors for the studio, PA and broadcast industries. The site contains product info, software updates, distributor lists, manuals to download, news, press releases and employment opportunities.

Teac/Tascam
http://www.teac.com/
Possibly best-known, in earlier days, for its multi-track reel-to-reel recorders, the company produces a range of data storage products, consumer audio equipment, mixers, DATs, and so on. The site contains information on them all plus FAQs, a tech support area and a list of repair centres.

Product info, FAQs and tech support at Tascam.

Speakers

Bose
http://www.bose.com/
Probably best known as a speaker manufacturer, Bose has invested in a range of sound technologies and the company's site is crammed with product info, sound reproduction information, car audio systems, details of new developments, technical info and corporate information.

Bose is more than just a speaker manufacturer.

EAW – Eastern Acoustic Works
http://www.eaw.com/
Manufacturer of a wide range of professional loudspeaker systems. All the info you could need is here along with a host of other information such as tour info, installations, product development, features about EAW, links and so on.

Epos
http://www.musichallaudio.com/epos/
Speaker manufacturer. The site includes info on products both old and new.

Tannoy
http://www.tannoy.com/
One of the best-known names in speakers. The site has product information, and a section on design philosophy.

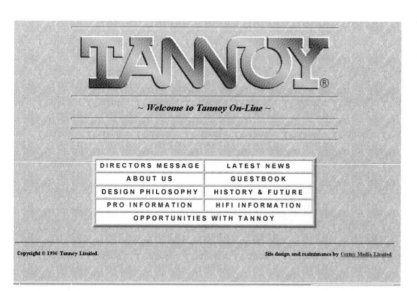

You can read about the company's design philosophy on the Tannoy site.

Duplication

COPS
http://www.cops/co/uk/cops/
COPS offers CD replication, cassette duplication, vinyl pressing (still?), artwork and printing. The company offers an all-in-one service at affordable prices.

Ablex
http://www.ablex.co.uk/
A duplication company set up by Decca in 1969 and still going strong. Handles CDs, cassettes, CD ROM, Minidisc, floppy disk formats. Includes a host of specifications and information sheets for CD and cassette inserts to download.

Computing

As you might expect, many computer manufacturers have a Web site but these are slightly outside the scope of this book. However, here are a couple of computer-related sites worth pointing your browser to.

Apple
http://www.apple.com/
A site which must be bookmarked by every Mac user. News, info, updates, software downloads...

EveryMac
http://www.everymac.com/
Lists every Mac made, including clones, by manufacturer and processor. Well worth stopping by if you're in the market for a new Mac or want to mug up on a second-hand bargain.

A must for Apple
aficionados.

Includes a glossary and lots of links to Mac manufacturers and to other sites of interest covering Mac news, OS info, resources, magazines and technical information.

Tom's Hardware Guide
http://sysdoc.pair.com/hdd.html
You want to know about computers? Stop by Tom's.

Lots of information in an easily-accessible format. Covers hard disks, motherboards, video, RAM, CPU and so on.

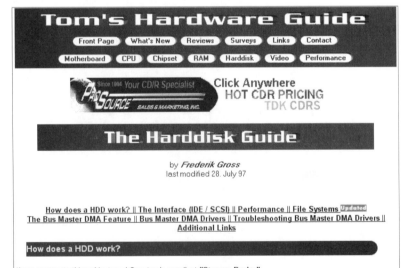

Music software developers

Sometimes the line between 'commercial' software developer and share-ware software developer blurs but we've had a brave attempt at drawing it. In particular, most of the entries here are sites of larger companies.

If you don't see what you want here, check the Shareware section. Also, bear in mind the fact that many companies develop both hardware and software so check there, too.

Adamation
http://www.adamation.com/
Developer of digital media applications for BeOS (an alternative Mac oper-ating system) including ImageElements, AudioElements, and StudioBuilder. AudioElements is an object-oriented application that allows the creation, editing and compilation of audio effects. Lots of info. If you're not familiar with BeOS, check it out.

AnTares
http://www.antares-systems.com/
Digital signal processing software for pro audio use. A bland Web site but informative, nevertheless. Auto-Tune does automatic and graphical into-nation correction for voices and solo instruments. Infinity is a well-known sample looping program for the Mac. The Multiband Dynamics Tool is a 5-band dynamics controller and the JVP Voice Processor is a de-esser, compressor, 3 band EQ and Delay FX processor for vocals. The site includes details of the software, demos to download, access to tech sup-port, news and links to a few other sites.

Apogee Electronics
http://www.apogeedigital.com/
Apogee is an American developer of digital audio software and hardware. The site includes product info, product manuals to download, lots of hints and tips and software updates. It also includes links, news and a number of support documents.

Arboretum Systems
http://www.arboretum.com/
Developer of digital audio software for the Mac and PC. The company's most famous product is Hyperprism which lets you change a wide range of effects in real-time by moving the mouse around the famous blue screen. Brian Eno describes it as: 'a wonderful invention'. You can access and download all Arboretum manuals here, check out new products, download demos and subscribe to the Arboretum Newsgroup and Mailing list. There are some interesting links here and you may even find some free plug-ins to download.

Audioworks
http://www.audioworks.com/
Developer of Sound2MIDI, PC software which converts audio data into MIDI data. Lots of info about the software, reviews and links.

Beatboy
http://www.beatboy.com/
Drum pattern programmers made up of drummers in New York and Pennsylvania. Product info and demos to download.

Bias
http://www.bias-inc.com/
Developer primarily of Mac-based digital audio software including Peak and plug-ins such as SFX Machine. The site contains lots of information about the products, news, updates, demos to download, and job opportunities.

CALMUS
http://rvik.ismennt.is/~kjol/
CALMUS (calculated music) is a computer program designed for music composition. It is specially constructed for 20th century music and deals with musical problems that occur in this music, providing specially designed tools and options to handle them. The compositional process in CALMUS is both sequential and parallel. The program sequentially calculates values of musical objects in a composition, while at the same time constructing melodies for each object. Among concepts used in the program are musical objects, polyphony, harmony, melody, MIDI and graphical representation. A bit techy, a bit academic but there is lots of info here, samples to download and a demo if you want to learn more.

CALMUS (calculated music) is a computer program designed for music composition.

CALMUS

Calculated Music (1988-1998)

CALMUS is a computer program for musical composition. A demo version is available for <u>download</u> . For registered version of CALMUS press <u>here</u> for further information.

- <u>Introduction</u>
- <u>Hierarchy of CALMUS</u>
- <u>Compositions from CALMUS</u>
- <u>WHY CALMUS ?</u>
- <u>CALMUS Library</u> NEW (ftp://ftp.ismennt.is/pub/Macintosh/Tonlist/calmus/)

Cakewalk

http://www.cakewalk.com/

Developer of the eponymous Cakewalk range of sequencers for the PC which is claimed to be the best-selling sequencer software in the US.

There's lots of information about the products, press releases, product reviews, demos to download, tech support patches and updates, StudioWare panels, CAL (Cakewalk Application Language) files and instrument definitions. A must for anyone with a Cakewalk sequencer.

Clixsounds

http://www.clixsounds.com/

Developer of the shareware program, Agent Audio, which has been released in a professional version. Among other facilities, it allows you to replace a program's sounds with your own. The company specialises in sounds and sample CDs for the Apple Mac and there are sounds for sale and demos to download plus lots of news and info.

Clockwork

http://ourworld.compuserve.com/homepages/clockworkmusic/

A small company involved in the design, creation and direct marketing of music and studio related software. Products include a tutor for CAL (**see** Cakewalk).

Coda

http://www.codamusic.com/

Developer of a range of music software programs including the ubiquitous Finale, a pro-end notation and printing package used by many profession-al music typesetters. The site includes details of current and new products, there's a tech support and a FAQ area and demos to download. There's also a list of related sites which support Finale including a forum and mailing list.

Crystal River Engineering
http://www.cre.com/
Developer of AudioReality 3D processing technology used in high-end systems such as VR rides, simulators and so on but also available as the Proton plug-in for Digidesign's Pro Tools. The site contains some info about the process and has a link to its parent company, Aureal.

Csound
http://www.leeds.ac.uk/music/Man/c_front.html
The Leeds Csound site from the Department of Music at Leeds University with information for users of Barry Vercoe's Csound programme from the Music and Cognition Group of the MIT Media Lab. Csound is a rather techy but incredibly powerful music programming language based, as its name suggests, on the C programming language. If you're into it, this is the site for you. If you're not but you're of a programming bent, check it out.

Cycling '74
http://www.cycling74.com/
A site for the distribution and support of software by David Zicarelli. He was largely responsible for developing Max (which originated at IRCAM) into a commercial product for the Mac and he's still involved in its development. He has also released MSP, a set of extensions to Max 3.5 that let you do real-time synthesis and signal processing with a PowerPC Mac. It consists of over 60 objects that synthesise, process, analyse, delay, and generally mess around with audio signals in real-time. You'll also find M at the site. This is one of the original algorithmic composition programs, first published by Intelligent Music in 1987. Lots to read about and demos to download.

D-Lusion
http://www.d-lusion.com/
A German company, currently composed entirely of students, responsible for a range of cutting-edge products such as the RD 30 Bass Line, the X-Tracker tracker, and Creator, a four-track MOD editor. Info and files to download. Pay it a visit.

DUY
http://www.duy.es/
Developer of digital audio plug-ins for the Mac. Lots of info, feature lists and demos.

Emagic

http://www.emagic.de/

http://www.emagicusa.com/

The first URL is to the original German site but it offers you an English version. The second is to the US site which is currently a front end whose hyperlinks take you to the German site. Emagic is the developer of the Logic and Logic Audio sequencers for the Mac and PC and formerly of Notator for the Atari ST.

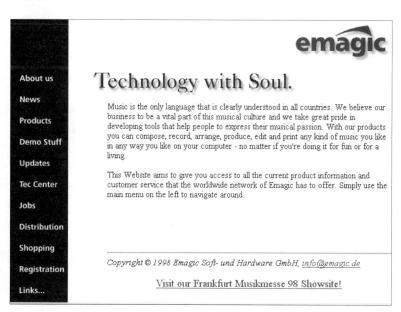

The site lists the products by platform and includes a news area. You can download demos of many programs and you'll find software updates here, too. The Tec Centre includes Q&As, tips & tricks, and some files Logic users may find useful. There's also an interesting collection of links.

Emu Systems, inc

http://www.emu.com/

See entry in Music hardware manufacturers, page 118.

Evolution Electronics

http://www.evolution-uk.com/

Developer and distributor of the Sound Studio Gold sequencer with direct-to-disk recording facilities, various other software programs and MIDI keyboards. There's lots of information on the site about the products including loads of demos, patches and help files.

Gallery Software

http://www.demon.co.uk/gallery/

Gallery is a Digidesign Software Partner and develops a range of software, some hardware utilities and accessories for Digidesign products. The site contains lots of information about them, software updates and demo versions and you can download the on-line version of the Gallery catalogue.

Giebler
http://www.giebler.com/
Manufacturer and distributor of disk management and sequencer conversion software for musical keyboards and sequencers. The sequencer conversion packages can convert Standard MIDI Files into files which load directly into many keyboards and sequencers. Supported products include those from Alesis, Ensoniq, Korg, Kawai, Roland and Yamaha. The company also offers a disk recovery service for a range of keyboards.

Heavenly Music
http://www.ortiz.demon.co.uk/
Programmers of high quality MIDI files and developer of a multitude of MIDI building block files and AWE SoundFonts.

Download the catalogue, download demos and find out more about the musical husband and wife team.

Last update 9th May 1998

Why is she smiling?

She's heard our files - of course!

Heavenly Music Productions is a premiere MIDI/Music and Sound company serving working musicians, arrangers and producers world-wide. Founded in 1992, Heavenly has been at the forefront in their field with over 40 products and services. All music at this site has been produced using one or more of the products in our catalogue. Enjoy your visit and remember - if it ain't heavenly ... no comment. Click HERE to enter up to thirty pages of MIDI / AUDIO and music related information.

What's New ???

HiSoft
http://194.159.249.123/
http://www.hisoft.co.uk
Developer of low-cost sampling systems for the Atari and Amiga, HiSoft continues to market products which include CD ROM packages, video, sampling and a miscellaneous collection of utilities.

Howling Dog
http://www.howlingdog.com/
Developer of Power Chords, a guitar-oriented sequencer but also of interest to users who like working with chords rather than the note-based system of most sequencers. There's lots of info and specs, demos to download plus MOD files and links.

Innovative Quality Software
http://www.iqsoft.com/
Developer of SAW (Software Audio Workshop), multi-track direct-to-disk recording software for the PC which currently comes in three versions. The company also has a range of plug-ins for SAW and third-party developers have produced some, too.

The site contains company info, product support details; you can get updates here and download demos. There are dozens of links to SAW users' sites, links to Newsgroups and related manufacturers, recording, broadcast and theatre sites.

IRCAM
http://www.ircam.fr/index-e.html
http://www-old.ircam.fr/index-e.html
IRCAM (Institut de Recherche et Coordination Acoustique/Musique), the famous French music academy. The site, available in French and English, gives details of its activities and supports a range of music software for computer-assisted composition and sound creation including Opcode's Max. There are worthy papers to read and software to download although the main programs require you to be a member of the Forum. Not the easiest site to navigate your way around but well worth stopping by to see what the academics are doing. Try this site for easier access to the FTP archives:
http://www-old.ircam.fr/index-e.html

Justonic Tuning
http://www.justonic.com/
To quote: 'Some synthesisers on the market today allow you to create an harmonic scale. For example, you can retune your synth to a C harmonic scale. You can then play a beautiful C chord or C melody. However, when you move to a D, E or other chord, you are hopelessly out of tune. Likewise, you can tune guitar strings to pure harmonics, but when you do

this the the two E-strings are out of tune, and as you play up the neck, the frets are not in tune with the harmonics. You're stuck.

The Solution: Justonic Tuning's revolutionary new software – Justonic Pitch Palette. To play pure harmony, all notes must be flexible, and they must be precisely retuned, on the fly, in real-time as you play. The Justonic software makes tuning adjustments to the pitch tables of your microtunable synthesiser. It accomplishes the task in under 3 milliseconds. This allows pianos and guitars with a MIDI interface to play and modulate in just, or any other intonation, in real time.' So now you know. Fascinating, and a site you must visit at least once. Downloadable files, too.

Justonic Pitch Palette – revolutionary new software to keep everything in tune – perfectly.

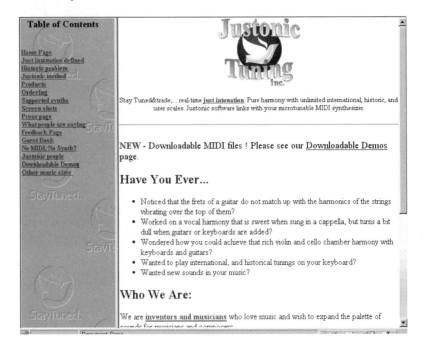

Karnataka
http://www.audioarchitect.com/
Developer of Audio Architect, the software-based modular synthesiser. The Web site contains information about the program, quotes from reviews and users, details of features due in the next version, a set of tutorials, samples produced by the program and you can download an evaluation version. There are also links to other music sites.

Kid Nepro
http://www.kidnepro.com/
'The Patch King' Developer of a vast range of sounds for a vast range of instruments. View the catalogue, order on-line, get great deals...

Lyrrus
See entry in Music hardware manufacturers, page 128.

ManyMIDI
http://www.manymidi.com/
Produces a large range of synthesiser sound libraries. Read the catalogue, order on-line.

Mark of the Unicorn
http://www.motu.com/
Best know for its Performer sequencer software which was one of the first high-end MIDI sequencers for the Mac.

Digital Performer integrates 24-bit digital audio and the company now produces a range of MIDI and audio interfaces as well as other music software for the Mac and the PC.

MediaTech Innovations
http://www.midibrainz.com/
Developer of the Drumz Wizard and the Muzical Wizard, PC programs which assist with the composition of drum tracks and patterns. Lots of info, FAQs, MIDI files to try and demos to download.

Mixman
http://www.mixman.com/
The Mixman Studio is a sort of DIY song construction kit using sample loops. Lots of info, additional CDs to buy, tips, tricks, and links.

Musicator
http://www.musicator.com/
Developer of the Musicator sequencer for Windows. The site includes lots of information about the program and how it works, new features in the latest version plus a demo to download along with a range of utilities.

Musitek
http://musitek.com/
Developer of MIDIScan, software for the PC which scans printed music and converts it into MIDI data. Information, tech support, upgrades and a demo to download.

Native Instruments
http://www.native-instruments.com/
Developer of Generator, a real-time synthesiser for the PC (a Mac version is planned as of writing). It uses a highly graphic front end to let you create synthesised sounds on your computer which can be played in real-time. Lots of info and a demo version to download. Could this be the future of synthesis?

Newtronic
http://www.newtronic.com/
Supplier and developer of high-end tools for MIDI programmers particularly in the field of Dance and electronic music. The company produces MIDI files and sample CDs, and retails a range of MIDI programming books, software and synth sounds which you can order from the on-line shop.

Newtronic's site includes an on-line shop for dance music aficionados

Ntonyx
http://www.ru.com/ntonyx/
Here's something of a rarity – a Russian music site promoting Russian-developed music software. In particular, Style Enhancer which puts expression into MIDI files and Pattern Variator which creates sequences from patterns and lets you manipulate them in real-time. Fascinating stuff. There's a lot of info about the products and how they work, news, reviews and, of course, demos and MIDI files which show what the programs can do. Fascinating. A site you must visit.

Opcode
http://www.opcode.com/
Developer of Vision and Studio Vision sequencers and integrated digital recording software as well as OMS, Galaxy, notation software, digital audio plug-ins and, of late, MIDI interfaces. The company started develop-

ment on the Mac but has been porting its products to the PC. The site includes lots of product info, news and events as well as product updates and the most recent version of OMS to download.

PACE
http://www.paceap.com/
The company responsible for most of the hard disk install copy-protection systems used by music software developers. It is capable of a great many more features than most developers use. Interlok is the latest system. Read about it all here. Some of the installs can do dire things to your system if it detects uncomplimentary software on it. See also Syndey Urshan Music.

Padworld
http://www.padworld.demon.co.uk/
The Web site of musician, author, writer and bon viveur, Peter Buick. An eclectic collection of the weird and wonderful – software, book promotions, the KIP University for the remote and distance learning of music and multimedia, songs, the Kurzweil owners group, a Spice Girls game... 'Seven goldfish can't be wrong,' it says. No they can't – check it out!

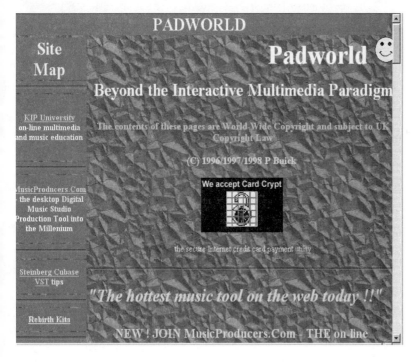

Padworld – a veritable Aladdin's cave for the curious muso. Don't miss it!

Passport Designs
http://206.15.71.82/
http://www.passportdesigns.com/
As of writing, the first URL worked while the second reported that the site was unavailable. Passport is best known as developer of Master Tracks (later Master Tracks Pro), one of the earliest MIDI sequencers for

the Mac and PC. Development was somewhat stilted and the program features were rapidly overtaken by other developers but the program has still continued to develop. The Web site is a slightly confusing collection of what appear to be links to a couple of 'home' pages. However, you can soon click your way around to find lots of info about the program, and a large number of downloads from MIDI files, many by Passport users, to software demos. There are also on-line music lessons. An eclectic site but worth a visit.

Personal Composer
http://www.pcomposer.com/
Personal Composer for Windows from the eponymous company. Read about the product, download a demo.

PG Music
http://www.pgmusic.com/
A busy site from the developer of Band-In-A-Box accompaniment software. News, updates, demos by the score, information, technical support, a wish list, reviews, press releases and links. Phew!

Lots and lots of info from the developer of Band-In-A-Box accompaniment software

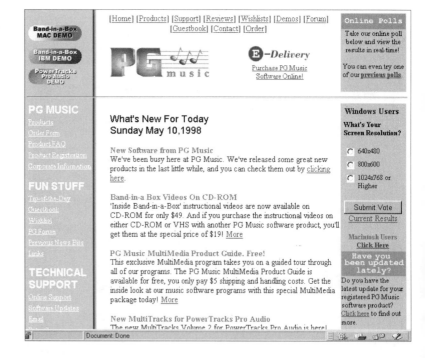

Power Technology
http://www.dspfx.com/
Developer of DSP/FX digital audio DirectX plug-ins for the PC. The original plug-ins used a hardware card but now a set is available which uses the native power of the PC. The site contains lots of information about the effects, magazine reviews, user comments, press releases and you can download a demo.

Propellerhead
http://www.propellerheads.se/
Developer of Steinbeg's ReBirth RB-338, an emulation of Roland Bass and Drum machines. There's tons of support on this site for RB users, including songs, drum loops and software kits to let you customise ReBirth. You'll also find news of new products and press releases. Phunky.

Pro-Rec
http://members.aol.com/prorec/
Producer of synth sounds, sample CDs and MIDI files. The site includes product info and special offers.

Prosoniq
http://www.prosoniq.com/
Developer of Sonic Worx software – audio tools for the Apple Mac – and digital audio plug-ins for Cubase VST.

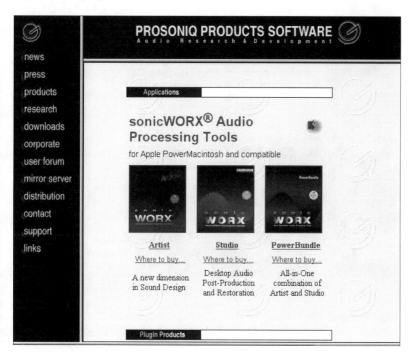

Lots of product information, news and press releases. There are updates and demos to download and you can join a Prosoniq mailing list.

RealNetworks
http://www.real.com/
Developer of RealAudio, RealVideo and RealFlash which deliver streamed data from the Web to your computer in real-time. Lots of info about the technology, samples to try and free plug-ins download. Check out the UK site, too at:
http://www.real.co.uk/

RTPS Systems
http://www.rtps.com/
UK developer of The Mirrormaker, a fascinating program which mirrors MIDI files by flipping the notes around a central pivot point, making high notes low and vice versa. It's capable of producing some very musical result. Available for both Mac and PC and sample MIDI files are available so you can hear what it does to the music.

Seer Systems
http://www.seersystems.com/
Developer of a real-time software synthesiser for the PC called Reality. The clever thing is, the latency is so low you can play it in real-time from a MIDI keyboard.

The site has lots and lots of information about the product, reviews, FAQs, a users' forum, patches for users to download and audio demos. Is this the future of music synthesis, we ask again?

SEK'D
http://www.sekd.com/
German developer of the Samplitude range of multi-track direct-to-disk recording software plus a range of digital audio cards for the PC. The site is packed full of info about the products and new releases and there are files, demos and updated drivers to download.

Sion
http://www.infoserve.net/quickscore/
Developer of QuickScore Elite and Copyist for Windows. Rather spartan pages but there are demos and files to download, reviews and lots of links.

Softlab
http://www.softlab-nsk.com/
Specialists in multimedia and computer graphics. Includes DDClip, a non-linear, non-destructive real-time audio and video multi-track editor. Demos to download.

Software Technology
See entry in Music retailers and distributors, page 202.

Sonic Foundry
http://www.sfoundry.com/
Canadian developer of Sound Forge wave edit software for the PC, CD Architect audio CD burner, digital audio plug-ins and utilities. A bright site (in a dark sort of way) with news, product info, tech support, updates and demos to download.

Soundscape
See entry in Music hardware manufacturers, page 129.

Soundtrek
http://www.soundtrek.com/
Developer of The Jammer and The Jammer Pro, music composition software which composes music in a wide range of styles. The site contains information, demos and MIDI files to download and lots of information about the software.

SSEYO
http://www.sseyo.com/
UK developer of Koan, a generative music composition program which has been used by Brian Eno to compose an album – on floppy disk. There are several versions of the Koan program which enable the user simply to listen to compositions or to generate their own using the minimum amount of musical knowledge and these are available for download free of charge or for a nominal sum. The site is packed with examples of Koan music with links to sites which use it. You can put Koan music on your Web site, too. There is news and reviews, links to users' sites, MIDI files, press releases, a Koanmail newsletter... The site's a must to visit for any computer musician.

Steinberg
http://www.steinberg.de/
http://www.steinberg-us.com/
http://www.us.steinberg.net/
http://dialspace.dial.pipex.com/town/road/gbp97/
The German home site and some other ones, too. Check out them all. Lots of info on the latest products, demos, software updates, drivers, free plug-ins, dealer lists and info on compatible ancillary equipment such as CD-R drives. In particular, the last URL is the Steinberg UK site, semi-offi-

cial and put up by Arbiter, the UK distributor. Information here varies but it often has hints and tips, soundcard information (what works with VST) and updates. There's a wealth of info in these sites which are essential bookmarks for anyone who uses Steinberg software.

Essential bookmarks for anyone who uses Steinberg software.

Swiftkick Productions
http://www.swiftkick.com/
Developer of the Environment Toolkit, a book and disk offering a complete set of tools for customising Logic's Environment to your MIDI studio. The book takes up where the tutorial included on the Logic CD leaves off. There are detailed descriptions of the advanced features of the Environment, numerous construction tips and an extensive collection of easy-to-import Environments that can stand-alone or be integrated into your own constructions. There's also the ET4, a quarterly electronic journal of Environment news. Each issue contains new tools, plug-ins and control panels plus articles on the Environment and news on recent changes & updates. A must to visit for any Logic user.

Synchro Arts
http://www.SynchroArts.co.uk/
A Digidesign Development Partner which specialises in Pro Tools plug-ins. Lots of info, users' comments and downloadable demos.

Synoptic
http://www.synoptic.net/
A company specialising in computer-based digital audio software. It's range includes Virtual Waves, a program for sound synthesis, processing

and analysis allowing you to create virtual sound generating machines by connecting the program's various modules together. Virtual Waves Light is the OEM version of Virtual Waves, available for bundling with soundcards. Voice FX is a program for voice processing which includes 40 effects like Reverberation, Echoes, Alien Voices, Robot Voices, Resonant Filters, Flanger, Underwater, and many others. Easy Synth is a virtual real-time analogue synthesiser with an interface which looks like a modular synth front panel with lots of knobs and buttons. It emulates an analogue machine with 4 oscillators, 4 multimode resonant filters, 8 LFOs, and 8 ADSR envelopes. Includes downloads and demos. Definitely a site to visit if you're into synthesis.

Syntrillium
http://www.syntrillium.com/
Developer of the shareware program Cool Edit and the up-market multi-track software, Cool Edit Pro. Lots of info, a technical FAQ section, news, and program demos, updates, manuals and utilities to download.

TC Works
http://www.tcworks.de/
Developer of digital audio plug-ins based on TC Electronic (see entry on page 139) hardware designs. They include TC Native Reverb, Native EQ and Native Essentials. Info, news and demo downloads here.

Techno Toys
http://www.technotoys.com/
Software for electronic music. The range includes Seq-303, an analogue sequencer emulator for Windows 95 and NT. Midi Thruway is a comprehensive MIDI merge/thru/filtering/channelisation utility which lets you control several sound cards or synths from any combination of controllers and applications. Download the programs, get other freebies and check out the sounds and MIDI files. The site also has a large list of links.

Terzoid
http://www.terzoid.com/
The company's main product is NoiZe for Windows, a Universal MIDI Patch Editor/Librarian. There is also WaveShop, a DirectX plug-in for Cakewalk 6.x and other DirectX compatible programs that does Compression, Limiting, Noise Gating, and Gain Levelling. There's a Sys Ex page which explains some of the mysteries of System Exclusive messages – check this out if you do nothing else – and you can download software demos, too.

Time+Space
See entry in Music retailers and distributors, page 203.

Titan Designs
http://ourworld.compuserve.com/homepages/titanweb/
A company which made its name through the Atari and which still sup-

ports the platform (along with the Falcon) and which also has a range of hardware and software accessories. Includes information and software demos to download.

Tonality Systems
http://www.xs4all.nl/~psto/
Developer of Symbolic Composer, a LISP-like composition program much favoured by academics and a few cognoscenti.

Lots of information on the software, technical information, audio samples, news and a demo to download. Very interesting.

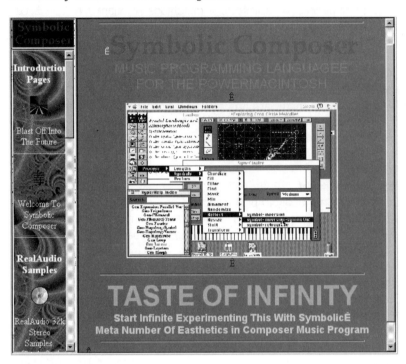

Syndey Urshan Music
http://www.urshan.com/
http://www.urshan.com/cgi-bin/sum/sum.cgi
The man and the company determined to free users from the vagaries, uncertainties and downright unreliability of hard disk installs and dongle-based copy protection. The company's main product is the Terminator which allegedly lets you backup a disk and restore it in order to preserve your hard disk installs. There's lots of info about the program and a con-fusing array of options to choose from should you wish to order – which you can do on-line. There's a freeware version to try (use wisely and very carefully), press releases, reviews, and an interesting page of 'scare' sto-ries put about by companies to dissuade users from using Terminator. If you hate hard disk installs and copy-protection systems, this is a must to visit. See also PACE, page 153.

Voicecrystal
http://www.voicecrystal.com/
The music products division of Eye & I Productions. Developer of sounds

and voices for many synthesisers on floppy disk, CD and RAM cards. Also supplies sample CDs and music software which you can order on-line. There are a lot of products here with lots of info and sound clips to download. You can join the mailing list and check out the latest news.

Voyetra
http://www.tbeach.com/vywelcome.htm
A sub-page within the Turtle Beach Web site although Voyetra is the parent company. It specialises in software and this area includes info on the vast range of music software in its catalogue.

Waves
http://www.waves.com/
Originating from Israel but with an office in the USA, Waves specialises in the production of digital audio software and plug-ins for most of the major digital audio software programs on both Mac and PC. The extensive site includes a list of products and the platforms they support, details of new products, demos to download and there are generally several free software updates for existing users. You can join the Waves mailing list, there are hints and tips on using the software, a FAQ section and lots of links to other interesting sites.

Wildcat Canyon Software
http://www.wildcat.com/
Developer of software which includes Autoscore which lets you record MIDI music by singing or playing an acoustic instrument, and the Internet Music Kit which helps you add music to your Web site. There are free downloads on the site and a tech support areas in case they give you problems.

Yamaha
http://www.yamaha.co.jp/english/xg/
Yamaha site devoted to XG instruments. Lots of product info, MIDI files and plug-ins to download. See entry on page 123.

Shareware, freeware and small developers

You don't have to be one of the big software developers to create useful and interesting music software and an increasing number of smaller companies and even one-man companies are doing just that and releasing their wares as shareware. Some even give them away for free!

This section is an attempt to highlight the sites and products produced by smaller companies although the difference between 'small' and 'major' is growing increasingly meaningless, particularly in the commercial world of the Net.

So, apologies if some companies, particularly those not dealing regularly with the UK market, find themselves in this section when they may actually be the world's third-largest music software developer. Let us know and we'll correct it in the next issue.

Some of the developers don't have a company name so in some cases the entry is by listed by the name of the software rather than the developer.

One of the fascinating aspects of surfing the Web is that you never know what you might discover next. There are many small sites containing exciting information and fascinating software. In this list you may find the software you knew was available but not where from – but you may also discover lots of software and information which are among the Web's best-kept secrets. Tell your friends...

ArborRhythms
http://www.teleport.com/~mantra/
Home of the ArborRhythms Music Processor, an algorithmic composition program for Windows 95. It can generate music using mathematical and linguistic formulas (there are over 60 functions), play/edit wave files (6-track potential with DirectX), generate wave files using mathematical formulas, and process input from a MIDI keyboard in real time.

Arnold's Web Page
http://www.planete.net/~amasson/
Arnold who? He's actually Arnaud Masson and he writes shareware and freeware for PCs and Macs. He's probably most famous for Arnold's MIDI Player, a shareware application that plays any MIDI or Karaoke file on the Mac through the internal speaker via QuickTime or through an external MIDI device. There is also a Windows version. And there's MIDIPlugin, a freeware plug-in for Netscape and Explorer that allows you to play MIDI songs inside HTML pages.

Awave
See FMJ, page 163.

David Brown's Plug-ins
http://www.dbrown.force9.co.uk/
The philanthropic David Brown has developed some plug-ins for Cubase VST which he is giving away free of charge, gratis and for nothing on his Web site. There are also some shareware plug-ins here, an FAQ and some links.

Buena
http://www.buena.com/
Dedicated to the production of inexpensive video and audio software. Products include Stomp Box Delay and Stomp Box Tremolo, and the site has a couple of freebies, too.

Classical MIDI Archives
http://www.prs.net/midi.html#index
The premier site for classical MIDI files. Arranged alphabetically by composer and there's a search engine, too.

CNet Shareware.Com
http://www.shareware.com
An excellent source of shareware for all computer platforms including the ST and the Amiga. The emphaisis is definitiely on the PC as is to be expected but the Mac is well represented, too. Not music-specific.

Shareware for all computer platforms including the ST and the Amiga

Cosmiksquirrel
http://www.geocities.com/SiliconValley/Bay/2891/
What a name, eh? This is actually a useful site listing a range of software including soft synths (virtual synths and samplers), MIDI editors, sounds and patches, and there are links to sites containing music and theory information.

DiAS
See Gistix

Erehwon
http://macware.erehwon.org/
A wadge of freeware and shareware for the Mac and Newton. They are divided into categories and they include Sound, Multimedia and Audio & MIDI. Lots to look at, lots to download.

FMJ Software
http://hem.passagen.se/fmj/fmjsoft.html
Famous for Awave for the PC, a very well respected audio and wavetable instrument file format converter, editor and player. Get it here.

Gistix
http://www.gistix.com/dias
Mainly a developer of high quality mapping products and bespoke software but also of DiAS (Digital Analogue Sequencer) which emulates the function of an analogue sequencer in software – with several extras. It has two 32-channel modules with note parameters such as MIDI channel, voice, pitch, octave, duration, gate, velocity, pan and glide. You can play the modules in parallel or in series, adjust all the controls in real-time, store settings in presets and save the output as a MIDI file. Just the thing for electro and retro musicians. Lots of info and the program to download, too.

GetRight and Headlight Software
http://www.headlightsw.com/
HeadLight Software and GetRight.Com provide download utilities and services to allow users to easily download files and recover (resume downloading) if errors occur. Software for Windows 95/NT and a Java version for the Mac and other platforms.

Hermann Seib's MIDI Page
http://netbase.t0.or.at/~seib/midi.htm
MIDI software developed by Austrian, Hermann Sieb. The range includes WBMan, a preset editor/librarian for the Waveblaster daughterboard. GMKbd is a General MIDI-compatible keyboard simulator for Windows which can be used as a stand-alone program or, with appropriate MIDI drivers, it can be used to send MIDI messages to other applications, such as sequencers. There's also the useful MultiMID which lets you run more than one MIDI program in Windows at the same time.

Illogik
http://www.illogik.org.uk/
A site created by a band of enthusiasts devoted to the creation of tracker music. Lots of files to download and several trackers, too, in case you don't already have one.

KAE Labs
http://kaelabs.com/
Developer of a shareware program called VocalWriter for the PowerMac which sings your lyrics in English. Fascinating stuff. Download a fully-working version and see if you can put the Spice Girls out of business.

Kelly Industries
http://www.wstuff.com/KellyIndustries/
Digital audio plug-ins – the PanHandler32, Ambience Extractor32, Dither32, BigTime32, and Stereo To Mono Plug-ins for SAW32. Information, some free stuff, demos to download and you can order on-line.

KeyKit
http://www.nosuch.com/keykit/
One of the Web's best-kept secrets, KeyKit (formerly known as Keynote), is a programming language and graphical user interface for MIDI, useful for both algorithmic and real-time musical experimentation. It was originally written for the PC but a Mac version is also available – and it's free to download. See also Tim Thompson. Also, check out a site containing compositions produced with the help of KeyKit:
http://www.unangst.com/music_du.htm

LiSa
http://www.xs4all.nl/~steim/lisa.html
This is one of those programs and 'companies' which are difficult to categorise. It looks like a one-man show but the software is available through distributors. Check it out yourself. LiSa (Live Sampling) is a real-time audio manipulation environment that runs on a PowerMac. It uses the 16-bit AD/DA converters and the computing power of the PPC processor to turn the Mac into a versatile audio sampler able to generate up to 64 voices on a fast PPC604e machine. Complete program control is possible via MIDI, allowing the user to work with this system in a performance environment.

Eric Lyon's WWW Presence
http://ringo.sfc.keio.ac.jp/~eric/
A site about Eric Lyon – of course – his compositions and software including BashFest, a virtual drum machine front end to the popular synthesis language CMIX. Some other interesting programmer/techy stuff here, too. Also check out a site which uses BashFest:
http://ringo.sfc.keio.ac.jp/dotcom/dotcom2.html

Nexor
http://www.nexor.com/public/mac/archive/welcome.html
A catalogue of Mac software divided into nine sections – Development, Games, Graphics, Hypercard, Misc, PowerMac, Sound, System Extensions, and Utils.

Macintosh MIDI User's Internet Guide
http://www.aitech.ac.jp/~ckelly/mmuig.html
A collection of information and links for the Mac-based musician. A What's New section lists updates and new products and there's lots of useful Getting Started info. Pay it a visit.

Maxim
http://www.abel.co.uk/~maxim/
Digital audio freeware. An interesting collection of programs and utilities including one which enables a PC to write and format Akai S-series sampler floppy disks. There is also a list of Cubase VST plug-ins, all free to download.

MIDI Editor

http://perso.magic.fr/llebot/

'MIDI Editor is the most powerful MIDI manager ever made! A revolution in the world of MIDI (System Exclusive) communication! Designed to work with any MIDI device: just enter the parameters of your device, plug in the MIDI cables, and there you go... You can even design your own editor windows! Two help files are available (English and French version). Numerous presets are furnished for Alesis, Casio, Emu, Kawai, Korg, Roland, Sequential, Yamaha...' Lots of info and a demo to download.

MIDI Editor – Lots of info and a demo to download.

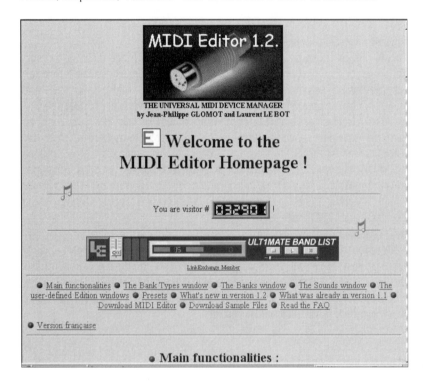

MIDI Farm

See entry in Music information, page 218.

MIDI Karaoke

http://www.teleport.com/~labrat/karplayers.shtml

Don't let the name put you off! Yes, the site does list programs which play karaoke files but there are also some MIDI file players. Programs for Windows, DOS, Mac and Amiga.

MIDI-Ox

http://ourworld.compuserve.com/homepages/JamieOConnell/midiox.html

MIDI-OX – 'the greatest all-purpose MIDI utility'. It's a Windows 95/NT 32-bit program, both a diagnostic tool and System Exclusive librarian. It can perform filtering and mapping of MIDI data streams. It displays incoming MIDI streams, and passes the data to a MIDI output driver or the MIDI Mapper. You can generate MIDI data using the computer keyboard or the built-in control panel. You can even record and log MIDI data and then convert it to a Standard MIDI File for playback by a sequencer. It's freeware.

MIDI Music Web Site
http://www.quicknet.se/ftp/dialup/q-112005/
A large site with a massive collection of information, links, software, MIDI files, and samples. The programs are for the Mac, Atari and the PC and there's a list of music links divided in various categories.

A massive collection of information, links, software, MIDI files, and samples

Mod4Win
http://www.mod4win.com/
The guys who write trackers always seem to be good at graphics, too. This site, visually impressive, is host to the Mod4Win tracker. You can join the mailing list and browse through lots of other files, MODs and links.

Music of Cyberspace
http://elbs.uel.ac.uk/walthius/
This Web site features the original MIDI sequences of multimedia composer Michael D. Walthius, a tribute to the efficiency of the Cakewalk software which he uses. Lots of files to download in XG and GM format and a FAQ.

MusiNum
http://www.forwiss.uni-erlangen.de/~kinderma/musinum/musinum.html
'MusiNum is a free sonification program which turns numbers into gener-ative fractal music. Everybody can create unique royalty free music for his

homepage within few minutes. Interesting for mathematicians and other people who like to play. Fractal concepts, self-similarity and a new kind of symmetry are audible now!' That just about says it all. Lots of info, the ability to compose on-line and links to fractal music and music composition software sites.

Polyphony
http://www.flash.net/~mikegar/polyphony/
'Polyphony is the only Emu Proteus configuration editor and librarian designed for Microsoft Windows. It is designed to be useful to anyone using the Proteus for MIDI sequencing work. If you dislike the tiny LCD on the front or your Proteus, download the demo and see the difference!' Essentially a commercial product but a demo is available.

Quadratic
http://www.quadratic.com/
Develops shareware for Macintosh and Power Macintosh systems. There is shareware and freeware here, utilities rather than music applications but the world is hardly overrun by Mac shareware developers so the site is worth listing.

Thomas Rehaag
http://www.netcologne.de/~nc-rehaagth/tr.htm
Developer of VST plug-ins including AUM which gives you the sound of a low pass filter with resonance as it was used in classic analogue synthesisers. It does about the same as Steinberg's Trancemitter but it needs about a third of its processor power. There's also PSI (Phase Shift Iterator) which is a phaser/flanger plug-in which needs minimal processor power. Demos to download.

Redshift
http://users.iafrica.com/r/re/redshift/
'Featuring the biggest collection of editors and patches on the planet.' If you want an editor for your synths or some patches to load into it, try here first. There is software for Mac, PC, Atari, Amiga and Unix, and a whole load of links too.

Roni Music
http://home1.swipnet.se/~w-11396/
Roni's main program is Sweet Sixteen which first saw light of day on the Atari and which is very reminiscent of C-Lab's (now Emagic) Notator. Hmm. It was originally a commercial program but Roni made it shareware and it has since been ported to the PC. Other Roni products include the Musician's CD Player, Sweet MIDI Arpeggiator, Sweet MIDI Harmoniser and Sweet Little Piano.

Setsu Home Page

http://www.tcp-ip.or.jp/~setsu/

Japanese programmer who has developed several music programs for the Mac. These include several librarians and some MIDI utilities.

Shareware Music Machine

http://www.hitsquad.com/smm/

'Welcome to the World's Biggest Music Software Site!' it says. There are areas for all platforms – Mac, Windows 3.1, Windows 95/NT, DOS, Atari, OS/2 and Linux. What! No Amiga or Archimedes? Oh well. There are lists to help you find what you want. One to bookmark.

For wads of shareware bookmark this site!

Simtel.Net

http://www.simtel.net/simtel.net/

A large collection of shareware, freeware and public domain software for the Mac, Windows 3.1 and Windows 95. There's also a list of alternate servers in several countries.

Software Forge

http://subnet.virtual-pc.com/ma407651/Forge//CuteFX/

A UK-based shareware organisation specialising in music-related and Internet software. CuteFX is a digital effects unit program that requires no special hardware and runs with a standard PC and soundcard. It provides effects familiar to musicians from hardware 'effects boxes', such as distortion, phaser and delay. Other utilities include CuteLoops, the simple/live MIDI loop sequencer; CuteBreaks, the drum-loop (breakbeat) creator; SysEx Solution, the system exclusive data storage, librarian; and a program editor for the Korg M1.

SoundApp
http://www-cs-students.stanford.edu/~franke/SoundApp/
SoundApp is one of the better-know pieces of Mac shareware. It can play or convert files dropped onto it into a variety of formats. It supports Play Lists which are lists of sound files that can be saved for later use. Files in a Play List can be played or converted as a group or individually. It supports a randomised shuffle playback mode and repeated playback of Play Lists. Useful if you need to convert files. Free to download.

St. Clair Software
http://www.stclairsw.com/
Developer of Mac shareware. Not specifically music related but good utilities.

SuperCollider
http://www.audiosynth.com/
SuperCollider is an environment for real time audio synthesis which runs on a Power Macintosh with no additional hardware. It features a built in programming language with a mini GUI builder for creating a patch control panel, a graphical interface for creating wave tables and breakpoint envelopes, MIDI control, and a large library of signal processing and synthesis functions a few of which are found nowhere else. Lots of info and a demo to download.

Synth Edit Page
http://www.cybertheque.fr/galerie/GGregson/
The home page of Gary Gregson, programmer of XGEdit for Mac and PC, the essential utility for anyone with a Yamaha XG sound module. There is also edit software here for the Yamaha AN1x and Roland GS instruments. There is a ton of info, too, for XG users and lots of links to XG stuff.

Tim Thompson
http://www.nosuch.com/tjt.html
The KeyKit developer's site with more software to download as well as compositions. There's a list of programming languages which are used for music and some interesting links. See also KeyKit.

Tontata
http://ux01.so-net.or.jp/~mmaeda/indexe.html
Mr Tontata is the Japanese developer of MIDIGraphy, one of the very few shareware MIDI sequencers for the Mac. Mr Tontata has produced other programs, too, which are also here.

Uncertain Music Corps
http://www.umcorps.demon.co.uk/
'It don't mean a thing if it ain't got that doubt.' A site dedicated to bringing you ever-changing, generative music using the Koan authoring system

(see SSEYO entry in Software). Lots of fascinating downloads, especially for users with an AWE card – some pieces include vocal SoundFonts – eerie.

Vellocet
http://www.cs.uwa.edu.au/~skot/vellocet/
If you want to know what Vellocett is/means you'll have to read Clockwork Orange or log onto the web site. The developers are in a band called Vellocet and have created free plug-ins for Cubase VST for both Mac and PC. Info on the plug-ins, info on the boys, gig dates, background info, and, of course, the downloads.

Jim Walker's Software Source
http://members.aol.com/jwwalker/
Nothing in the way of music but some utilities for the Mac which many people swear by including Dialog View and Manual Maker. Check it out.

Walnut Creek CD ROM
http://www.cdrom.com/pub/demos/music/
The URL to a long list of music software in a range of categories.

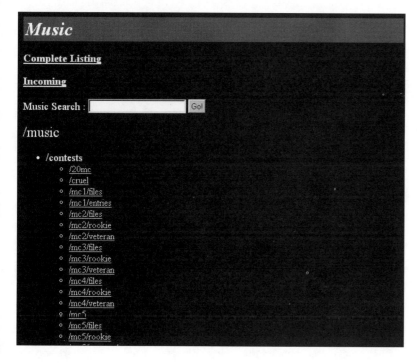

Walnut Creek – One to explore.

Yav.com
http://www.yav.com/
The home pages of Christopher Yavelow, author of the mammoth Music & Sound Bible for the Mac and developer of several interesting composition programs including Push Button Bach and Cyber Mozart. There is

also a host of links to music, Apple and multimedia-based sites. An interesting visit for anyone into computer-assisted composition – and you can download the software.

XGEdit
See Synth Edit Page, page 170.

Zerius
http://zerius.com/
Developer of several music programs including the Zerius Software Vocoder and the Zerius Synth. Virtually no info about the company but lots about the products Seems a bit techy and the preferred code seems to be Java – who needs Windows anyway!? – although some are available as C code. You'll also find MOD players here and lots of files to play.

Record companies

A&M Records
http://www.amrecords.com/
A plethora of info including links to all current A&M artist sites, news, tours and A&M merchandise. There's lots of information here including how to submit a demo, how to get a job at A&M, and other stuff like tracking down old records.

AD Music Ltd
http://tile.net/admusic/
AD Music Limited was established in 1995 to market electronic music in the UK and world-wide. It inherits the existing catalogue previously marketed by the AD Music & FX Music private labels run by David Wright and Robert Fox, since 1989. The musical territory in which AD Music Ltd operates is described by the company as "electronic, experimental and esoteric", which perhaps also indicates just how difficult it is to pigeonhole.

Much of, although not all, the AD catalogue follows in the tradition of European Electronic Music, a style typified by such exponents as Tangerine Dream or Vangelis. However, it is also the company's intention to present music which crosses over into other musical territories such as ambient and dance. Examples of these are the Code Indigo, Jan Hanford and Witchcraft albums.

Arista Records
http://www.aristarec.com/
Offers hi and low bandwidth access. It's very graphics-oriented and the pages can take a while to load. Contents include info on artists, a weekly word section where you can listen to news items via RealAudio and there are lots of audio and video clips. There's also a chat area where you can, er, chat to other on-line visitors.

Atlantic Records – there's a chat room and a toy box page where you can play on-line pinball. If you must. You can also join mailing lists and artist newsgroups.

Atlantic Records
http://www.atlantic-records.com/
A very graphic site with areas on artists, news, events and tours.

Blue Note Records
http://www.bluenote.com/
It's cool, it's hot, and it's everything in-between. It's jazz. Info, artists, a catalogue, shopping, new releases, an FAQ page, the history of the company – it's all here.

Loads of info and RealAudio extracts from dozens of artists.

Capitol
http://www.hollywoodandvine.com/
Information about current releases, tours, a chance to win some goodies, listen to album extracts and you can join the monthly newsletter. There's also information about Capitol Studios if you want to know what gear the big boys play with in a major recording studio.

Dawn Awakening
http://www.words.demon.co.uk/dawn/index.htm
One of the UK's leading independent New Age music publishers with a large catalogue of CD and cassette recordings of music for relaxation, therapy, easy listening and quiet contemplation. Browse the catalogue and order on-line.

Chill out, calm down and relax while browsing through Dawn Awakening's on-line catalogue of CDs and cassettes.

Dawn Awakening Music
Music for Relaxation, Therapy, Easy Listening & Quiet Contemplation

....Welcome to the Dawn Awakening On-line Music Catalogue....

At Dawn Awakening we pride ourselves on having a range of original and unique recordings of relaxing instrumental music that is second to none. We are the second-largest publisher of this type of music in the UK. We choose our recordings with great care and our catalogue includes many top-selling titles.

The Catalogue - See what makes our titles so popular!

Top 30 - Check out this month's Top 30 titles!

New Releases - See our latest releases!

Order - Get a free CD or cassette!
Order details are here. You can order by email, fax, phone or post. Cassettes are £6.95 each and CDs are £11.95. However, order four of either type and get another of the same type absolutely free!

Music Categories
To help in your choice of music, we have devised four categories, although many titles fall into two or more:-

A Massage & Healing Arts

Decca
http://www.decca-nashville.com/
Straight to the point with Decca. Click on the Win Free Stuff! Link on the home page and then browse the site! It's for country fans with lots of info, news and sound bites to delight in.

Deutsche Grammophon
http://www.dgclassics.com/
One of the best-known classical music record labels. Check out new releases, tour dates and take a peek behind the scenes in the new DG studio.

Domo
http://www.domo.com/

A sort of major alternative label covering music styles which you could categorise as New Age, World Music and Rock/Alternative. Publishers of Kitaro and Horny Toad. Check the site for info on Domo artists, tours, biographies, discographies, new releases and so on.

Elektra
http://www.elektra.com/

A new design makes it easy to find individual artists, search music topics (alternative, ambient, dance, country and so on), browse the archives, check tour dates and see what's for sale in the store. You can also download loads of audio and video clips.

Island Records
http://www.island.co.uk/

Read the catalogue, check the noticeboard, enter the chat room or the staff room, see what's new, check out tour dates, read about the history of Island Records and listen to RealAudio extracts.

Island Records sexy home page

M&M Records
http://www2.gol.com/users/davidr/index.html

News, top stories, new releases, discography, future releases, featured artists, and a history of M&M – including where the name came from – are all here.

MCA – Universal Music
http://www.mcamei.com/
http://www.universalmusic.co.uk/

The UK site uses Shockwave and features artists, club information, tour dates, new releases and interviews. Nashville cats check out:

http://www.mca-nashville.com/

Motown
http://www.motown.com/
Information about Motown, music, featured artists, and games and trivia, too!

Motown's home page.

Naxos
http://www.hnh.com/
Naxos is famous for its budget-priced CDs and also for being one of the most fertile of the Cycladic islands in the Aegean. If you want to go on holiday go to:

http://www.vacation.net.gr/p/naxos.html

otherwise the above URL will take you to an info-packed site with sections on classical music, composers, critical reviews, how to build a classical CD collection, an introduction to Chinese music (a very popular site with the Chinese), new releases, future releases, and the Naxos catalogue. There are also lots of RealAudio music clips to listen to.

Parlophone
http://www.parlophone.co.uk/
Contains details of new releases and tours, and it has a Fanzine area with info on favourite artists.

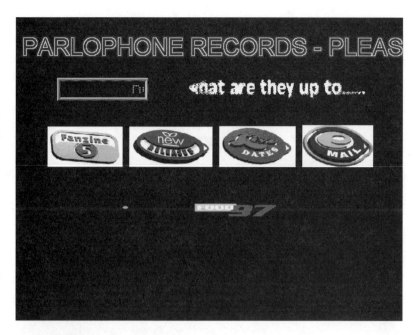

Find out where your favourite
Parlophone artists are
touring on the Web site.

Philips Classics
http://www.philclas.polygram.nl/
A list of artists and composers including Philip Glass. Lots of information
and recording details here.

Polygram
http://www.polygram.com/
http://www.polygram.com/polygram/Music.html
You can search this site by artist, label, country, film & video title or by
company.

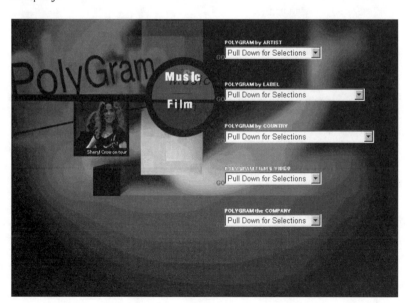

Includes financial results and
links to the music and the
video side of the company.
There are also details of new
releases, tours, the
catalogue, divisions of the
music by genre, and
competitions – but for US
contestants only.

RCA Victor
http://www.rcavictor.com/
The dog and the gramophone company.

Areas for jazz, Broadway, film music and Celtic music. Info on albums and artists and music and video clips, too.

Sony

http://www.music.sony.com/Music/index1.html
A large site with lots and lots of information – artists, tours, new releases, back catalogue info, news, live Web broadcasts, multimedia material, interviews and music clips.

It's a big site, it's Sony's site

You can also check out Sony's European presence at:

http://www.musiceurope.com/

This even has free downloads where you can get Mac and PC screensavers of your favourite Sony artists. There are also trimmed-down versions of files to give a flavour of the combined music, video, lyrics, and interactive excitement of the CD Extra medium.

Sun Records
http://www.sunrecco.com/
This is where rock and roll began – the home of Elvis (Presley, not Costello), Jerry Lee Lewis, Johnny Cash, B.B. King, Roy Orbison and many other rockers from the Golden Age. The site has a history of Sun's development and info on its major artists.

Virgin
http://www.vmg.co.uk/
You can have a stab at the URL of many sites but would you seriously have tried 'vmg'? 'www.virgin.co.uk' will take you to the Virgin corporate site. Use the first URL to go right to the music stuff. Also check out

http://www.virginrecords.com/

The site includes a page of Virgin people who may be able to help with technical queries, student union services and it tells you who to send your demo tapes to. There are sections on artists, one for trance, dance, ambient rock and funked up techno dub and one for the Spice Girls. We show the front page here for any readers under 7.

... and then there were four.

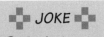
Walt Disney Records
http://www.disney.com/
http://www.disney.com/DisneyRecords/index.html

Trust Walt Disney to have an interesting and visually attractive site. Safe surfing here, folks! The second link is the Record link with simply wads and wads of info, pictures, new releases, audio and video downloads. A super site for Disney fans and kids of all ages.

Warner Bros
http://www.wbr.com/

This is a bi-i-i-i-i-g site. Check out Warner's currently heavily-promoted feature artists, look up any of the company's artists, new releases, look for job opportunities and read the Newswire to see what's new at Warner's. There is an artists' message board, tour dates and info, a FAQ, and you can subscribe to the Warner's mailing list. The site also contains audio and video clips and if you want to know what Dub really is, go to:

http://www.ear1.com/cgi-bin/WebObjects/WMAmbientDanceGenre

Artists, new releases, job opportunities, message board, tour dates – this site has the lot.

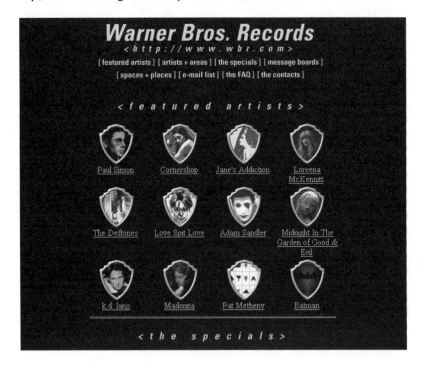

Links

Bigmouth
http://www.bigmouth.co.uk/
For UK contacts, check this one out. It includes links to over 700 UK artists plus a list of UK record labels.

Dirty Linen – Record Company Addresses
http://www.futuris.net/linen/special/label.html
See entry in Magazines, page 185.

Entertainment Extra – Record Label Links
http://www.ddc.com/extra/labels.htm
Links to over 100 record label sites here.

HandiLinks to Music Labels
http://ahandyguide.com/cat1/m/m354.htm
Links to over 500 record labels spanning the world and covering every possible type of music from Contemporary Middle Eastern Progressive Folk (http://xdot25.com/) to music by artists who live real Christian lives (http://www.pamplinmusic.com/).

Jump City – Record Labels and Recording Studios
http://users.aol.com/Jumpcity/record.html
Not a massive list of record companies but lots of interesting links to other music sites at:

http://users.aol.com/Jumpcity/more.html

Try browsing around here on a wet afternoon.

LAMA – Lowland's Alternative Music Archives
http://www.masadsign.nl/llama/llama.html
Lots of info on bands, artists, lyrics, radio and audio including links to around 500 record labels.

Music Guild Directory
http://www.musicguild.org/directory/record.htm
Another list of links, many with a few sentences about the companies.

R&R
http://www.rronline.com/reclabel.htm
A list of sites created by the R&R on-line newspaper. See the entry in Magazines.

A Rancid Amoeba – Record labels on the Web
http://www.arancidamoeba.com/labels.html
Don't let the name put you off – but don't eat while you surf! Make this your first stop if you're looking for a record label. It contains over 2900 links!

Sonic State – UK Record Label Directory
http://www.sonicstate.com/directories/recordcos/ukrecordindex.html
Not links but names, addresses and contact details for UK record labels. Besides addresses and phone numbers, you'll also find details of current staff, and either details of their musical preferences or a listing of the bands they've signed/look after. Now you can send your tapes to the person whose musical taste is in the same area as yours.

Not links but names, addresses and contact details for UK record labels.

Tiller Video Productions – Record Labels on the Web
http://www.tillervideo.com/html/labels.htm
Over 700 links.

The Ultimate Band List – Record labels
http://www.ubl.com/label/
Hundreds, maybe a thousand record labels here, arranged alphabetically.

Music magazines

Most companies now, it seems, have a 'Web presence' and what more natural step could there be for a publisher printing magazines than to put them on the Web, too. Of course, with the Web you don't even need a paper magazine. You can create, edit and publish far faster and reach a potentially larger market, too, for virtually nil cost.

So the sites here are a mix of on-line magazines and paper magazines with an on-line presence.

AMP – Alternate Music Press
http://www.tiac.net/users/elements/amp/
AMP describes itself as the on-line multimedia magazine of new music. It's a big site with lots of information. There's news pages and features on a varied range of subjects. There's a review section divided into five categories – Acoustic, Celtic & Folk; New Age & World Music; Ambient & Electronic Music; Jazz & Blues; and Classical and New Music. Send your CD to the Editor if you'd like it reviewed. There are links to the home pages of well over 100 musicians, bands, record companies and associated sites. And there are links to well over 100 sites containing MIDI files and software. Worth reading.

The on-line multimedia magazine for new music.

Billboard
http://www.billboard.com/
Billboard magazine, on-line. News, views, reviews and previews as well as the usual chart info. Dragging itself into the technological age, a relatively new feature is a look at how hi tech is affecting the music industry.

British Music Page
http://easyweb.easynet.co.uk/~snc/british.htm
Devoted, in the main, to 20th century British classical music. The page features an on-line magazine containing a host of articles and features, a

recommended listening list, details of composers, concert information, lots of links to other music pages and a sound clip of the month. Low on graphical excitement but feature-packed and an excellent source of information, not readily available elsewhere.

CCM
http://www.ccmcom.com/
CCM? American lifestyle/music magazine. Will it catch on in the UK? Read it and see.

Computer Buyer
http://www.comp-buyer.co.uk/
The UK mag which lab tests equipment and gives you best buy info in no uncertain terms.

Computer Music
See Future Publishing.

Computer Music Journal
http://mitpress.mit.edu/e-journals/Computer-Music-Journal/
The Computer Music Journal is a quarterly Journal that covers a wide range of topics relating to digital audio signal processing and electro-acoustic music. It is published, as hard copy, by MIT Press and is now in its 21st year. The topics addressed include software and hardware for digital audio signal processing; electro-acoustic, electronic, and computer music; software for music notation, printing, and archival systems; music

The on-line area includes sounds, code, references and documents. It can be a wee bit techy but if you're interested in computers and music you must pay it a visit.

Computer Music Journal
Published by MIT Press
Douglas Keislar, Editor
Curtis Roads, Stephen Travis Pope, and Anne Deane, Associate Editors
P. O. Box 14043, Santa Barbara, California, 93107 USA
cmj@create.ucsb.edu — http://mitpress.mit.edu/Computer-Music-Journal

Computer Music Journal WWW/FTP Archives

Serving the Electroacoustic Music and Digital Audio Community for 21 Years

Overview

The files in the directory named /pub/Computer-Music-Journal on the server mitpress.mit.edu at MIT can be accessed via the World-Wide Web, Internet ftp file transfer, or the gopher protocol; they are available to anyone provided that the copyright notices included in them are maintained.

The paragraphs below describe the contents of the *Computer Music Journal* archives and provide WWW hypertext pointers for viewing the various documents stored there. For ftp access to the archive files, select FTP-access. The WWW home page (that you're looking at) is URL http://mitpress.mit.edu/Computer-Music-Journal/.

- Contents: Tables of Contents and Abstracts of *Computer Music Journal*

representation languages and music cognition; new physical performance interfaces; sound localisation and 3-D sound spatialisation; sound in computer user interfaces and virtual realities; aesthetics of contemporary music, and other areas.

Dirty Linen
http://www.futuris.net/linen/
The on-line version of an American magazine sold through distributors rather than newsagents. Lots of features on various artists, a gig guide, news and reviews. The site also has two particularly useful lists, one of record company addresses with links to sites if available:

http://www.futuris.net/linen/special/label.html

and one of concert listings by artist:

http://www.futuris.net/linen/special/by-artist.html

Dotmusic
http://www.dotmusic.com/
The fastest charts, the hottest talent and the latest industry news. That's what Dotmusic is about. It includes links to Music Week, Record Mirror, Music Business International, Gavin (the United States' definitive music industry magazine, it says here), plus links to Miro and Promo newsletters.

The fastest charts from Dotmusic on-line.

Electronic Musician
http://www.emusician.com/
The on-line home of Electronic Musician magazine. 'EM is the premier resource for musicians interested in personal music production. emusi-

cian.com allows net musicians to interact with our editors and get valuable tips, news and commentary that you will not find in our print magazine. You also get direct access to our music industry and article databases where you can download past features and reviews for free!' Sounds like a bargain.

The premier on-line magazine for electronic musicians

Future Music
See Future Publishing, next.

Future Publishing
http://www.futurenet.com/
Future is probably the UK's major publisher of music-related magazines as well as a host of computing and other miscellaneous titles and many of them are on-line. The above URL will take you to the list. This one:

http://www.futurenet.com/musiciansnet/

will take you to Musicians Net which hosts the music mags including The Mix, Future Music, Hip Hop Connection, Guitarist, Guitar Techniques, Total Guitar, Bassist and Rhythm. You may also see vestiges of the now-defunct, The Band.

The areas contain reviews, features, competitions and techniques although not from the current issues, plus links to software and books and lots of other music sites. There's a hi tech forum and you can post classified ads here. In all, the areas contain a wealth of useful information. A must to bookmark.

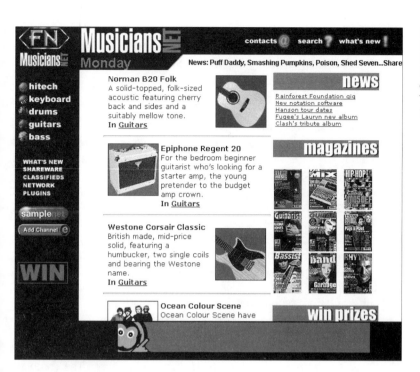

Musicians Net which hosts Future's music mags including The Mix, Future Music, Hip Hop Connection, Guitarist, Guitar Techniques, Total Guitar, Bassist and Rhythm – a must

GiG produced by The Band Register
See entry in Bands and musician stuff in Music Information, page 224.

Keyboard Player
http://www.keyboardplayer.com/
The longest-running keyboard magazine in the UK. The site contains sample reviews including a full listing of every item reviewed in the magazine, plus readers' problems from The Clinic.

Making Music
http://www.cerbernet.co.uk/makingmusic/
The on-line version of the free magazine which is given away in your local music shop – if you're up early enough to get a copy. But you can always subscribe. The site has a few articles to tempt you but it's real raison d'être is to get you to subscribe.

Mix
http://www.mixonline.com/index.html
The American magazine (not to be confused with Future's The Mix) for commercial and project studio recording, concert sound, and audio for film and video. It contains news, features, opinions, tests, links and more.

The Mix
See Future Publishing, page 186.

Music & Computers
http://www.music-and-computers.com/
The American magazine. Lots of info and extracts from various issues and a whole load of links.

Musicworks
http://www.musicworks-mag.com/
'Musicworks is about the excitement of creative engagement in sound exploration. We offer an inclusive context in which ideas can be discussed and understanding can be nurtured, helping to bridge the gap that has developed during this century between listeners and the sounds and ideas that interest contemporary musicians. At one time we had a theme for each issue such as Animals and Music (MW20), Women Voicing (MW31), Cross-Cultural Exchange (MW47), or Radiophonics (MW53). In the past few years we have continued to explore similar thematic areas, but the themes have become sequential, continuing from issue to issue.' Sounds like the blurb was written by a spin doctor but do give the site the benefit of your visit before removing it from your bookmark list.

New Age Voice
http://www.newagevoice.com/
The New Age Music Industry's Official Trade Magazine. 'The complete source for radio airplay and retail sales for the New Age music Industry. NAV is the only monthly trade magazine promoting New Age, Ambient/Space, Electronic, Acoustic Instrumental, Celtic, Native American,

The New Age Voice site includes the Top 50 plays and has links to a host of other music and industry-related sites.

Neo-Classical and related styles to the industry. Hundreds of musicians, record labels, retail stores, radio stations, promoters, marketers and industry executives depend on NAV's timely and useful information.'

POPi Music Magazine
http://www.popi.com/

Music Journalism with Digital Penetration, it says. It features album reviews, interviews with musicians and other 'music-related pablum to numb your mind'. Includes 'the most irritating sound of the week' and 'Riff of the Day' spots.

ProRec
http://www.webculture.net/prorec/prorec.nsf

An on-line zine of professional and home recording resources on the Net.

Pro Sound News
http://www.prostudio.com/psne/

All the latest news for the Pro Sound industry with sections on hardware, software, mastering, broadcasting, recording and so on.

R&R Online
http://www.rronline.com/

Radio & Records – the Industry's Newspaper. A mammoth collection of information, facts and figures and useful links to a wide range of sources including record labels and industry sites. The Industry Site topics include Broadcast-related sites; Industry, Government and Educational

A mammoth collection of information, facts and figures and useful links to a wide range of sources.

Organisations; Program Suppliers; Voice Talent; Archives, Directories & Reference; Hardware/Software Technology Suppliers; Music Industry sites; Research & Programming Consultants; Promotions, Sales & Marketing; Legal & Finance; Show Prep; Air Personalities; Internet Broadcasters; and Broadcasting Companies. Phew!

Rock Online
http://www.rockonline.com/

A combination of features, artist and label info, club dates, college radio and chat rooms. Lots of Indie content and references.

SOS
http://www.sospubs.co.uk/html/home.htm

Sound On Sound is one of the longest-established hi tech music magazines in the UK. The Web site lists the contents of all the issues but there are no full reviews. There is a selection of readers' letters – Crosstalk – readers' ads, a hi tech music glossary plus news items and you can order a wealth of goodies from the SOS secure server.

Magazine contents, letters, ads – and goodies to buy from the on-line shop.

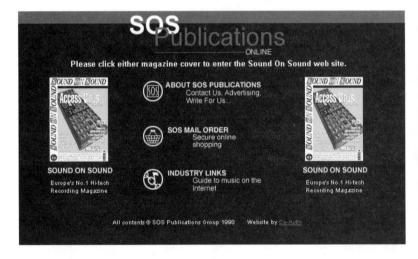

Studio Sound
http://www.prostudio.com/studiosound/

Features from current and past issues of Studio Sound are available to read and download. A wealth of information for studio-based sound generation and production.

Ziff Davis
http://www.zdnet.co.uk/mags/

Publisher of several UK mags (or UK versions of the company's US mags) we'll let Ziff Davis speak for itself:

'PC Magazine. Every month we bring you the most extensive and indepth product reviews and analysis in the UK – just take a look at what's in this month's issue. Take advantage of our special ZDNet UK subscription offer and get 12 copies for...' Okay, guys that's enough of the plug.

'PC Direct. PC Direct is the ultimate direct buyers resource – here's a look at what's in the magazine this month. For just £19.97 you'll get a year's issues plus a free CD ROM thanks to the special ZDNet UK subscription offer...' Okay, we get the picture.

'PCGW. Join the Gaming revolution. If you like the look of this month's PC Gaming World, why not take up our special ZDNet UK subscription offer and get 12 games-packed CDs plus this great magazine...' Okay, okay, we heard.

'Education Direct. Education Direct is the ultimate resource for schools and colleges looking to keep up with the computing revolution. Delve into the latest issue for the best hardware and software reviews, buying advice and tips on making the most of the Internet. Available twice a year with news-stand editions of PC Direct, Education Direct is also available to suitably qualified readers who contact the editor at: fcorless@zd.com. Don't forget to check out the education channel for weekly news, reviews and the hottest educational links.'

'IT Week. For senior IT professionals at large sites, IT Week will be the first place for hard news; technical and informed product coverage with the best UK and world analysis; targeted reporting of strategic and management issues; plus structured, focused coverage of IT across the enterprise.'

The site contains a mine of information and downloads – you may never actually need to buy a mag in spite of all the hard sell... In all, an excellent site, well worth visiting regularly. Also check out the site in the US where the company publishes even more magazines:

http://www3.zdnet.com/findit/mags.html

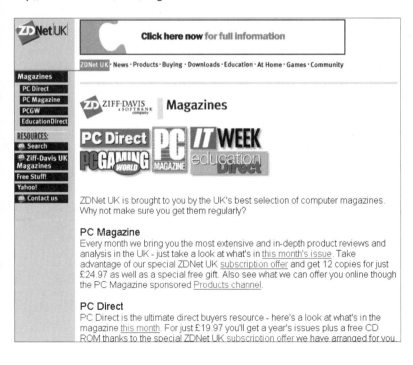

A mine of information for computer freaks – but watch for those subscription hyperlinks!

Magazine links

Alternative Music Magazines
http://www.prospernet.com/newsmagazines/music/alternative.html
A nice list or around 40 magazines including a brief description of the magazines' contents.

UK Music Magazines
http://www.ukdirectory.co.uk/ent/mag.htm
A directory of UK-based mags covering a wide range of interests from BritPop to Welsh music.

Music magazines
http://www.palatka.net/music/mmag.html
Lots and lots of links to lots and lots of music mags.

Music Magazines On-line
http://www.bib.lu.se/elbibl/projekt5/homepage.html
A detailed list of on-line magazines divided into the following categories: traditional rock and pop, alternative, metal, punk/skate, country, folk rock, jazz, soul/blues, hip hop, and techno/dance. It also has lists of other of sites which have lists of music mags...

A categorised list of on-line music magazines.

MUSIC MAGAZINES ONLINE

Here you can find the most interesting music magazines of popular music on the web, listed by genre. All of the magazines included in this list are in English except a few in Swedish. Of course there are music magazines in other languages on the web, but not on these pages. All the magazines you find here are possible to read immediately in fulltext free of charge. This collection is not a complete list of all the music magazines online.(Alphabetic order)

These are the genres

- **trad. pop/rock** Here you find mainstream rock and pop.
- **alternative** Includes indie, industrial, gothic, lo-fi and grunge.
- **metal** Unfortunately no magazines here yet.
- **punk/skate** Here you can find some noisy pop and hardcore as well.
- **country** Almost only contemporary country.
- **folk rock** Here you can find world music, roots and some traditional folk music too.

- **jazz** From traditional jazz to acid jazz.
- **soul/blues**
- **hip hop** Here you can find some trip-hop and jungle as well.
- **techno/dance** This genre includes ambient, trance, rave and trip-hop.
- **mixed contents** Here you can find magazines including more than one genre or magazines covering very limited genres.

Similar collections Here you can find other sites that lists music magazines.

Musicsearch Magazine Listings
http://www.musicsearch.com/NewsRoom/Magazines.html
From the Musicsearch Web sites, a lorra lorra mags are listed alphabetically, a few with a one-line description of their content and subject matter.

UK Piano Page
http://www.airtime.co.uk/forte/mag.htm
This URL takes you to a list of UK-based on-line music magazines covering everything from classic to underground dance music.

Music and music book publishers

Many record companies also publish music – they make more out of it, that way – so check the Record Company sites, too.

A-R Editions
http://www.areditions.com/
Mainly publishers of modern editions of early music but it also has an academic hi tech side called the Computer Music and Digital Audio Series which includes various tomes about the use of computers in composition and music production. These aren't generally available in the UK and the site is well worth a visit to see what you can get over there but not over here.

The Alfred Charles Co.
http://www.alfred-charles-co.com/
MIDI recordings of original music by contemporary composers including floppy disk albums of some of the world's foremost authors of classical, popular and children's music. Includes composer pages and files to listen to and you can submit original MIDI music to the company for publication.

Arsis Press
http://www.instantweb.com/~arsis/
Specialist publisher of Concert and Sacred Music by Women Composers. Arsis means 'upbeat' in Latin and is the preparatory movement of a conductor's baton. Not a lot of people know that. Who aren't orchestral musicians. Or conductors. Or who haven't done Latin.

Belmont
http://www.schoenberg.org/
Belmont publisher Arnold Schoenberg's music. Wonder if they play it on the house speaker system as background music.

Boosey & Hawkes
http://www.boosey.com/
Boosey & Hawkes is an international music publisher as well as a manufacturer of acoustic instruments. There's lots of info on this up-market site but as of writing the publishing side was under construction.

Captain Fiddle Music
http://www.tiac.net/users/cfiddle/
How can you resist having a look around a site with a name like that! If you're a fiddler, stop here.

Carl Fischer
http://www.carlfischer.com/
The site lists new publications, retail stores and includes information for anyone wanting to submit a manuscript.

Creative Music
http://www.creativemusic.com/

Fun stuff, on-line shopping, even files to download.

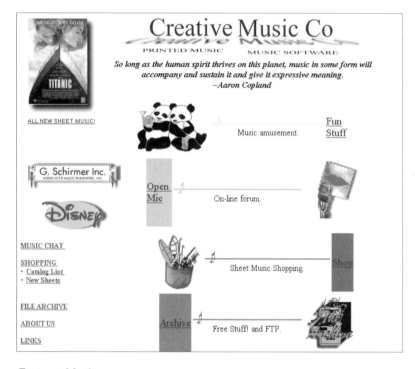

Fentone Music
http://www.fentone.com/
Fentone Music is a publisher of classical, educational and recreational music for players of all ages and of all instruments. Browse the catalogue, look at new publications, order from the on-line store.

Hal Leonard
http://www.halleonard.com/hal/index.icl
Large and well-known publisher of popular books, sheet music, software and videos. Search the site by title, artist or category.

Music Sales
http://www.musicsales.co.uk/
One of the world's leading publishers of a vast range of music including many popular titles for guitar, piano, keyboard and organ. The on-line Internet Music Shop lets you select titles to add to your shopping basket. See also Sheet Music Direct in Retailers, page 202.

Oxford University Press
http://www1.oup.co.uk/
One of the largest and most respected music publishers in the world, OUP has an impressive catalogue of over 4,000 titles covering the education, scholarly, and performance fields.

PC Publishing
http://www.pc-pubs.demon.co.uk/
UK publisher specialising in affordable hi tech music books – and publisher of this book, too! The company has a growing range of books, something to interest all hi tech musicians, covering MIDI, digital audio, multimedia, sequencing, sound engineering, electronic projects and more. Bookmark and browse regularly (you knew I'd say that, didn't you!).

The UK's premier publisher of affordable hi tech music books

G. Schirmer
http://www.schirmer.com/
A large site with details about the composers the company publishes, catalogue listings, premiers and so on. Includes a very large list of links to a wide range of music sites. Part of the Music Sales group.

Schott Music
http://www.schott-music.com/
A long-established publisher, mainly of modern classical pieces. The site includes composer pages, a concert diary, news and sound clips.

Digital music publishing and on-line sheet music at Sunhawk's site.

SEARCH REGISTER ORDER DOWNLOAD

welcome to *sunhawk*.com

The Future of Music Publishing is Here.®

Sunhawk Corporation is a digital music publisher and on-line sheet music store. From the comfort of your PC, you can use our **Solero™** technology to hear the music as well as make engraving-quality print-outs of anything you purchase. But you can listen to a sample — for free! — even when you're just browsing through our <u>catalog</u>.

Free Song of the Week

Catalog

SOLERO™
Software

Search

May 1998
1. Download the Viewer
2. Browse our catalog
3. Make a purchase
4. Tips for first-time visitors

Check out our star-studded <u>Warner Bros.</u> collection, which ranges from pop standards by <u>Sondheim</u> and <u>Gershwin</u> to the latest hits by

Sunhawk
http://www.sunhawk.com/
Is this the future of music publishing? 'Sunhawk Corporation is a digital music publisher and on-line sheet music store. From the comfort of your PC, you can use our Solero technology to hear the music as well as make engraving-quality print-outs of anything you purchase. But you can listen to a sample – for free! – even when you're just browsing through our catalogue.' Check it out.

Universal Editions
http://www.uemusic.co.at/
Publishers of contemporary music. Lots of info to file through.

Links

AcqWeb's Directory of Music Publishers
http://www.library.vanderbilt.edu/law/acqs/pubr/music.html
A list of links plus links to other reference pages.

Washington Music Publishers and Dealers list
http://www.lib.washington.edu/libinfo/libunits/soc-hum/music/publishers.html
You'll find this hiding several levels down in the University of Washington library database.

William and Gayle Cook Music Library Indiana University School of Music
http://www.music.indiana.edu/music_resources/publ.html
Links to well over 100 music publishers plus links to other sites with lists.

Music retailers and distributors

ABG – Audio Broadcast Group
http://www.abg.com/
American distributor of pro audio products. Lots of info on the site about the products the company handles.

Arbiter
http://www.arbitergroup.com/
Specialists in computer music solutions and UK distributor for Fatar, Kawai, Passport, PG Music, Voyetra, Music-PC and Altech Systems among others. The site has extensive areas for all the company's products, news and links to other sites of interest.

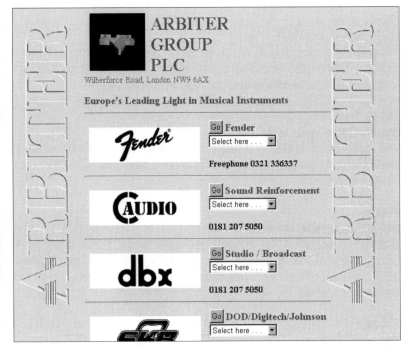

Lots of info about lots of products from lots of manufacturers

Blue Systems
http://www.bluesystems.com/
A professional audio retail, distribution, design service and manufacturing company, geared towards the needs of record and management companies, artists, education and recording studios. The site is informative and lists the equipment the company handles. There's also news and a sales and wants area.

Cameo

http://www.cameoworld.com/

USA-based distributor of multimedia and audio products – Digidesign Pro Tools plug-ins, hardware, and stand-alone audio/multimedia software. Lots of info about products from a range of companies.

CIE

http://www.cie-ltd.co.uk/

Previously known as Canadian Instruments and Electronics, CIE is a manufacturer's agent marketing a range of audio products. The Web site has news information and you can request catalogues on various products.

Cimple Solutions

http://www.cimplesolutions.demon.co.uk/

A service centre and a distributor for a range of products. Cimple Solutions is an approved Akai and Emu service centre and distributes a range of equipment such as MIDI-to-CV converters and MIDI interfaces. The site includes information about the company and a massive number of links to manufacturers and distributors.

Dawsons Music

http://www.dawsons.co.uk/

Pro audio Web site of a large UK retailer. Lots of info about software, modules, keyboards, recording equipment and so on. Shop on-line, get software updates, news and details of special offers.

Digital Media

http://www.digital-media.co.uk/

The Atari Falcon is alive and well. Digital Media distributes music hardware and software for it and for Mac and PC platforms, too. Well, you need to look ahead.

EMIS

http://dspace.dial.pipex.com/emis/

EMIS is the exclusive UK distributor of Doepfer products (see Music hardware, page 118) and, usefully, the site includes prices. There's news, details of the products including second-hand sales, and links. Check out the museum details, too – it's a real museum in Bristol.

Emusic

http://www.emusic.com/

'The Downloadable Music Site is the future of music distribution,' says Emusic. You can listen to samples of every song on every album before you buy, then buy only the songs you like. Why pay for a whole album when you only want one or two songs? The company currently uses CyberCoin for its on-line transactions.

Welcome
to Et Cetera Distribution

and welcome to our Web Site - the guide to what is currently available in the world of computer music and sound from Et Cetera Distribution.
You will find these pages packed with some of the most innovative and quality products currently on the market, from brand new releases to tried and tested favourites.
Explore our web site, and find out more.
Welcome to Et Cetera Distribution the source for PC music and sound

Home
News
Press
Products
Tech Support
Links
Downloads
Company

- Turtle Beach <u>Malibu</u> Sound Card
- <u>Cool Edit Pro</u> Now shipping.
- <u>Music Master</u> Professional, Notation and sequencing program.
- <u>Cakewalk Metro MAC Sequencing Software</u>.
- Guitar Coach, Multimedia Guitar tuition.
- Apex Sound Card now shipping.
- Cakewalk Upgraded to Version 6.01.
- Gadget Labs <u>Wave/4</u>, 4 in 4 out digital audio soundcard for PC now shipping.
- Jammer upgraded to version 3.0
- Pinnacle <u>Project Studio</u>.
- Frontier Designs <u>Wavecenter</u> 8 in 10 digital audio soundcard with SPDIF I/O, adat interface, MIDI in and 3 MIDI out.
- Maxi Sound Home Studio pro 64

Product info on a wide range of PC related kit, plus a download area, a links page and copies of press releases.

Et Cetera
http://www.etcetera.co.uk/
One of the UK's major music software distributors which specialises primarily in products for the PC. The site includes information about them and they include products by AdB, Cakewalk, Coda, Digital Audio Labs, Datasonics, Frontier Design, Gadget Labs, Jump Music, Musicworks, Personal Composer, Sion Software, Syntrillium, Turtle Beach, UbiSoft and Yamaha.

FX Rentals
http://www.fxrentals.co.uk/
Service round the clock. If you need some gear in a hurry, you know where to come. The site contains equipment lists and charges plus a large number of links.

Harman
http://www.harman.co.uk/
UK distributor of music hardware and software. Web site off-line as of writing but the international site is up and running at:

http://www.harman.com/

Very much a corporate site and alongside stock quotes it lists products and brand information.

HHB Communications
http://www.hhb.co.uk/
Leading UK supplier of its own HHB products and a wide range of pro audio gear by Sony, Panasonic and Pioneer. The site includes equipment lists, dealers and technical support.

InterStudio
http://www.interstudio.co.uk/

International valuers and dealers in broadcast, video, film, post-production and pro audio equipment. The site lists both new and used equipment by category. It includes pro audio equipment such as microphones, radio microphones, mixing consoles, processors, players, digital recorders, analogue recorders, and amplifiers. There are also guitar, Beatles memorabilia, vintage tubes and wanted sections.

Key Audio Systems
http://www.keyaudio.co.uk/keyaudio/

UK distributor for Mackie, Ensoniq, Clavia, Event Electronics, Hosa and Art. Lots of info about the companies and products, you can request product information and there are FAQs for each of the manufacturers and links to the manufacturers' sites.

Larking Audio
http://www.larking.com/

UK distributor of Soundtracs Studio Consoles and suppliers of professional recording equipment. Main dealers for a host of professional musical equipment manufacturers and also suppliers of used equipment. The site details some of the main products the company handles along with some of the used items.

Millennium Music Software
http://www.millennium-music.co.uk/

Specialist in PC-based audio visual technology which supplies all sizes of digital A/V production systems for the domestic or professional set-up from soundcards to digital editing suites.

The Millennium site includes details of much of the equipment the company handles plus details of any special offers which may be available. There's a news section, a reviews section and the odd article. You can join the company's mailing list. Remember how to spell it – two Ls and two Ns.

Music Connections
http://www.musicconnections.co.uk/
'The ultimate hi tech retailer' it says, with shops throughout the UK. Lots of information about the products, promises of the best deals, lists of second-hand equipment, monthly deals and links.

Musictrack
See Mark of the Unicorn in Software, page 151.

The Music Web
http://www.compulink.co.uk/~ijb/index.htm
UK-based Internet music store selling sounds for all major synthesisers, sample CDs and RAM cards.

Newtronic
See entry in Music software developers, page 152.

Roland
See entry in Music hardware, page 122.

SCV
http://www.scvlondon.co.uk
A busy site of one of the UK's major music software and hardware distributors containing information on the product lines, product reviews, news, support, software and links.

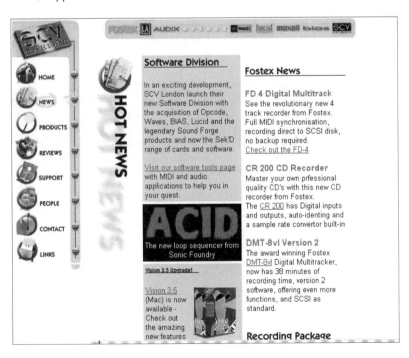

SCV is fast becoming one of the UK's major music software distributors

Sheet Music Direct
http://euro.sheetmusicdirect.com/
Part of the Music Sales group (see entry in Publishers, page 194). This site lets you browse sheet music titles, download them and print them out at home. You have to pay for them first, of course, although if you fill in a questionnaire you get a little something for nothing. The future of music publishing?

Software Technology
http://www.software-technology.com/
The company originally established in 1989 as Gajits to develop and market a range of sequencers for the Atari has now developed into a retailer and on-line supplier of computer-related products. These include support for the Atari and Amiga as well as the Mac and PC. The site lists the products available and has details on many. The company also distributes the VAZ Virtual Analogue Sequencer for the PC and you can download a working version from the site.

Soundonline
http://www.soundonline.com/
UK retailer of sample CDs, associated software and hardware such as sound cards. You can browse by category, listen to RealAudio versions of some of the samples, add selection to a shopping basket and buy on-line.

Sound Solutions
http://www.soundsol.com/
The site contains details of a large range of musical equipment – soundcards, software, sound modules, MIDI interfaces, keyboards, speakers, MIDI cables and so on.

Product reviews, price lists and you can order on-line using the company's secure server. There is also software to download and links to other sites.

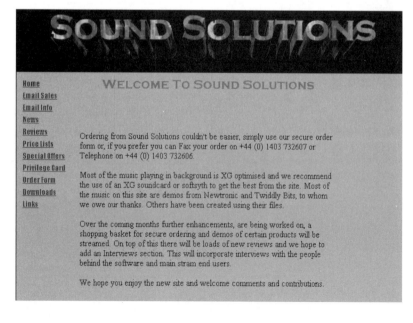

Sound Technology
http://www.soundtech.co.uk
UK distributor of pro audio hardware and software by companies such as Emagic, Samson, JL Cooper, Alesis and BBE. The site includes a product list, product information and details of events.

Stirling Audio
http://www.stirlingaudio.com/
UK distributor of mixers, monitor speakers, microphones and outboard equipment by companies such as Otari, Tascam, Panasonic, Marantz, Denon and Lexicon.

Studio Systems
http://www.studiosys.demon.co.uk/
The Web site of Studio Systems which has been working with Soundtracs consoles for over 12 years. It repairs out-of-warranty consoles and boasts that it has virtually every spare part in stock. The site also lists some 'previously enjoyed' consoles.

System Solutions
http://dialspace.dial.pipex.com/town/avenue/abr73/
Specialist in Mac, PC and Atari software with the accent on music although not exclusively.

Time+Space
http://www.timespace.com/
One of the UK's premier suppliers of sample CDs which has recently branched out into music software.

Lots and lots of info about the CDs and the software here plus samples and demos to download.

Turnkey
http://www.turnkey.uk.com/
'The UK's music technology superstore.' A large site with details of a vast range of musical hardware and software which the company handles supporting the PC, Mac and Acorn Archimedes.

Lots of descriptions of the products, there are many software demos to download, you can join the mailing list, check out the what's new pages and keep and eye open for special offers.

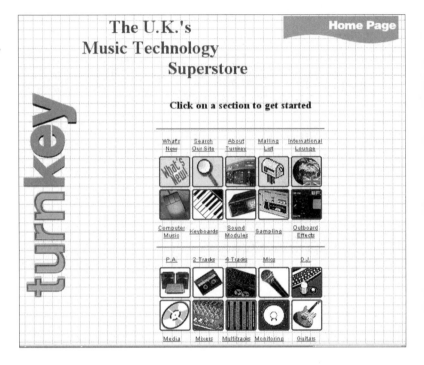

Unity Audio
http://www.unity-audio.demon.co.uk/
Pro audio software and hardware specialists. The site lists the products and there are software demos to download plus a few 'lessons' on topics such as noise reduction and audio restoration.

Washburn UK
http://www.washburn.co.uk/
Best known for its guitars, Washburn UK also distributes PRS, Crate, Ampeg, Kurzweil and Dynamix products. The site includes product information and dealer lists.

Yamaha
See entry in Music hardware, page 123.

Industry and trade organisations

ABJM – Association of British Jazz Musicians
http://dialspace.dial.pipex.com/jazz/abjm.htm
The ABJM is a non profit making organisation which represents the inter-

ABJM

What is the Association of British Jazz Musicians?

The ABJM is a non profit making organisation which represents the
interests of jazz musicians in the UK and is supported by the *Musicians'*
Union, as well as leading UK jazz personalities. It is the only lobbying
organisation for British jazz musicians. The ABJM works for the
promotion of jazz within the UK, providing regular meetings for members
to express their views, and provides a newsletter for members.

Who Can Join?

If you are a Musicians' Union member, you are eligible to join the ABJM.

How Do You Join?

For further information, contact:

Chris Hodgkins, The Association of British Jazz Musicians, c/o Jazz Services, Room 518, 5th Floor,
Africa House, 64-78 Kingsway, London WC2B 6BD tel: +44 (0) 171 405 0737/0747/0757 fax: +44 (0)
171 405 0828

Web pages designed by Steve French (stephen.french@virgin.net)

BACK TO JAZZ SERVICES HOME PAGE

Hits since 28/06/97:

`000060`

ASSOCIATION OF BRITISH JAZZ MUSICIANS

Membership info for UK
jazzers

✦ *JOKE* ✦

*Q What's the
difference between
a large pizza and a jazz
musician?*

*A A large pizza can
feed a family of
four.*

ests of jazz musicians in the UK and is supported by the Musicians' Union,
as well as leading UK jazz personalities. It is the only lobbying organisation for British jazz musicians. The ABJM works for the promotion of jazz
within the UK, providing regular meetings for members to express their
views, and provides a newsletter for members.

APRS – Association of Professional Recording Services
http://www.aprs.co.uk/
Today's APRS encompasses the full breadth of professional audio from
the traditional music studios in which it had its origins, to the new generation of project studios, to post-production and broadcast, live sound, film
soundtracks, duplication and training. The APRS is a leading force within
the British Music Industry, maintaining contact with numerous UK and
International associations, and with other bodies concerned with standards, training, technical and legal issues. It is governed by a Board of
Directors who are elected by members and normally serve for three
years. Studios can become members of the APRS which guarantees clients
a certain level of standards, quality, professionalism and service and
there's a list of associated studios on the site.

ASCAP – American Society of Composers, Authors and Publishers
http://www.ascap.com/
ASCAP has a membership of over 71,000 active composer, songwriter,
lyricist and music publisher members. It was created in 1914 to provide
the essential link between the creators of music and the users of music. It
is the only performing rights licensing organisation in the United States
whose Board of Directors is made up entirely of writers and music publishers elected by and from its membership.

BPI – British Phonographic Industry
http://www.bpi.co.uk/

The BPI is the trade association for UK record companies. If you enjoy British music, then you've come to the right place. Inside, there's all you need to know about the UK record industry, including the official UK charts and the world famous BRIT Awards. The BPI iexists to protect the interests of its members in all areas of their activity. It has over 200 members which together account for over 90% of UK record sales. Through its charity, the BRIT Trust, the BPI supports the BRIT School for Performing Arts in Croydon and other educational institutions and charities.

Broadcast Net
http://www.broadcast.net/

Lots of graphics which can make for a slow connection, although no doubt most of the members have ISDN connections anyway. It's a coalition of professional broadcast services and the site has lots of links to members and providers of associated services.

The Broadcast Industry's home page.

MCPS – Mechanical-Copyright Protection Society
http://www.mcps.co.uk/

MCPS is an organisation representing thousands of composers and publishers of music. Acting as an agent on behalf of its members, MCPS negotiates agreements with those who wish to record music, ensuring that copyright owners are rewarded for the use of their music. It collects and then distributes the 'mechanical' royalties which are generated from the recording of music onto many different formats, including CDs, cassettes, videos, audio visual, multimedia (including Web sites) and broadcast material.

If, for the time being, you are the only person making recordings, say, onto your own label, then it may not be practical to become a member since the only mechanical royalties generated would be those payable by yourself (as a record company) to yourself (as a music copyright owner). If however, your records have been recorded into broadcast material such as radio or television, you should consider becoming a member. The site also has a guide to copyright.

MMA
http://www.midi.org/
The MIDI Manufacturer's Association is the original source for information on MIDI technology, where companies work together to create the standards upon which MIDI compatibility is built. Albeit with the speed of a lame tortoise. However, as far as ratified specs go, this is the place to come.

Get the low down on the hi tech specs, download some specs and get some copyright info, too.

Musicians' Union
http://www.musiciansunion.org.uk/
If you don't know what the MU is about, this'll tell you. It includes information on local offices, press releases, FAQs, links and it has a members' area. It includes a gig list and a brief copyright section.

NMPA – National Music Publishers' Association
http://www.nmpa.org/
An American association, the NMPA has been a strong and effective cham-

pion for the protection of music copyrights in an age of rapid technological changes. NMPA was a leading voice for music publishers in connection with the enactment of the Copyright Act of 1976, and has successfully advocated amendments to that Act where necessary to protect the interests of music copyright owners.

PRS – Performing Right Society
http://www.prs.co.uk/index.html

PRS is the UK association of composers, songwriters and music publishers. It administers the 'performing right' in their music. Whenever copyright music is heard in public the people who own the copyright in the work are entitled by law to give permission and should get paid by the music user. But, the people who create and publish the music need help to give that permission (licence their music) and to collect the fees due. So they give PRS the right to do both on their behalf. See also entry in Copyright, page 116.

Re-Pro – Guild of Recording Producers, Directors and Engineers
http://www.aprs.co.uk/repro/index.html

Re-Pro is an International Association for and run by Studio and Music Producers, Sound Directors, Recording and Mixing Engineers, Programmers and Remixers. It aims to provide a forum where information can be shared by music professionals world-wide. If you are looking for a Producer, Engineer or a Remixer, look them up in the UK Members page.

Re-Pro – for the people who make the music

Re-Pro

THE GUILD OF RECORDING
PRODUCERS, DIRECTORS
AND ENGINEERS

Re-Pro is an International Association for and run
by :-

Studio and Music Producers, Sound Directors,
Recording and Mixing Engineers, Programmers

User groups and support sites

There are many official and unofficial sites on the Web which support particular instruments or music software. Here is just a handful. Check the Shareware section, too, as there are several developers producing software for specific instruments.

Alesis

MIDIWorld
http://midiworld.com/quadrasynth/
Hosted by MIDIWorld, this is an unofficial support site for the Alesis Quadrasynth range. Sounds, software, FAQs, MIDI files, mailing lists and links. Lots of material, an essential visit for all QS owners.

Apple Macintosh

I/O MUG
http://www.iomug.org/
General Mac-type group with links to Mac sites, Mac companies and software archives.

Composers' Desktop Project

CDP
http://www.bath.ac.uk/~masjpf/CDP/CDP.htm
Academic-type music composition system designed to let users make music with sounds. Academic feel to the site, too, with very few graphics. The CDP software runs on Atari, PC and the Silicon Graphics Workstation. Lots of info and details of compositions created with CDP software.

Make music with sounds with the CDP

COMPOSERS' DESKTOP PROJECT

Welcome to the CDP Home Page - 1998

~ *We help people make music with sounds* ~

How the CDP System can help *you*

With the CDP System you can:

- work towards the highest standards of innovative sound design with one of the world's most comprehensive set of sound transformation tools
- input from any type of sound source (microphone, recording - vinyl, tape, CD, DAT, synthesiser and MIDI tone generator)
- handle direct-to-disk recording and playback of soundfiles of any length (not restricted to RAM capacity)
- experiment with most types of computer synthesis of sounds (using *Csound*)
- perform editing and mixing functions
- sculpt sound with in-depth sound processing in the time (*amplitude/time*) and spectral dimensions (*amplitude/frequency*)
- explore the potential of algorithmic composition (with *Tabula Vigilans* and *Cscore*)
- constantly expand the system simply by extending the software, maintaining a fixed computer platform, such as a Pentium running Windows 95 (with a powerful upgrade path)
- create your own customised applications with the help of special CDP libraries and documentation - selected CDP source is available upon signing a non-disclosure agreement

Cubase

Club Cubase
http://www.cix.co.uk/~gal/ccd/index.html
An independent business designed to serve the large Cubase user base. Club membership is currently £18 a year which covers subscription to Basique, the club magazine, and discounts on most Steinberg products.

The site contains news, upgrade information, a price list – see how much you save buy being a member – and there's a download page and links.

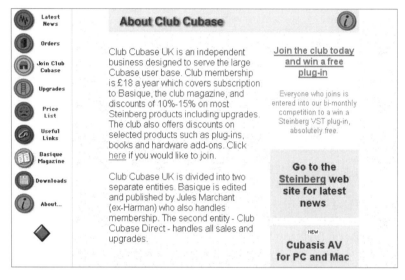

Cubase for Windows Users
http://www.instanet.com/~thedusk/
An independent support site for users of Cubase under Windows.

The site for Cubase Windows users. It offers news, upgrades, hints and tips, technical information, software to download and links.

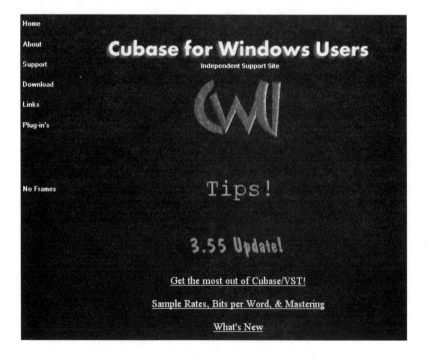

UbikMusic
http://www.ubikmusic.com/
The Web site of a music production company which has produced music and sound effects for everything from motion pictures and Top 20 records to industrials, multimedia, CD-ROM games, Web sites and presentations. It hosts a CuTips page giving out some hints and tips on using Cubase.

VST Performance Survey
http://www.padworld.demon.co.uk/vst.html
Part of Peter Buick's eclectic Padworld site (see Padworld entry in Software, page 153) which summarises the problems Cubase VST users have had with various combinations of equipment.

Digital audio workstations for the Mac

Daw Mac Homepage
http://www.bakalite.com/Pages/DAW-Mac.html
Join the mailing list browse the archives and check the FTP site. There are details of other newsgroups and mailing lists, and links. If you've got a problem, the chances are someone here has had it first.

Digidesign

Digidesign
http://www.alumni.caltech.edu/~franko/digi.html
There's lots of info, particularly about Pro Tools, tech specs, links to reviews and articles relating to Digidesign products, and you can subscribe to the Digidesign Users mailing list.

The Official Unofficial Digi Home Page. Make of that what you will!

Emu

Emulater Station 1
http://www.informatik.uni-frankfurt.de/~mickey/ES1/
A wealth of information from introductory to advanced, reviews, links, newsgroups and so on. An essential site for every Emulater owner.

Ensoniq

Ensoniq Resources on the Internet
http://www.op.net/~mikeh/ensoniq.html
That's what it says and that's what it is – a mammoth list of Web pages, commercial company sites, FTP sites and files, patches, software and mailing lists. Lovely stuff.

ESI

See Teddy's Page under Kawai (next).

Kawai

Teddy's Page
http://www.Uni-Mainz.DE/~kirss000/
Especially for the K4 and the K11, but also some info on the Emu ESI 4000.

The K5 Geek Page
http://www.neuroinformatik.ruhr-uni-bochum.de/ini/PEOPLE/heja/k5.html
The K5 was Kawai's additive synth. Cool at the time, now largely forgotten. But not on this site. Everything you wanted to know about it plus links to other related sites. Geek or gadget freak? You decide.

Koan

Moebius
http://ourworld.compuserve.com/homepages/webmoebius/moebkrnl/moebius.htm
A techy sort of site using Koan files and devoted to algorithmic music composition.

Korg

M3R LibEd Home Page
http://ciarm.ing.unibo.it/researches/m3r/
A sort of one-application site. The M3R LibEd allows you to archive programs and combinations from the Korg M3R and edit global and combination parameters. Runs under Windows 95. Lots of info, links to other M3 sites and the program is free to download.

Wavestation Trading Post
http://www.his.com/~rickg/trading.html
A place to swap your WS Performance data.

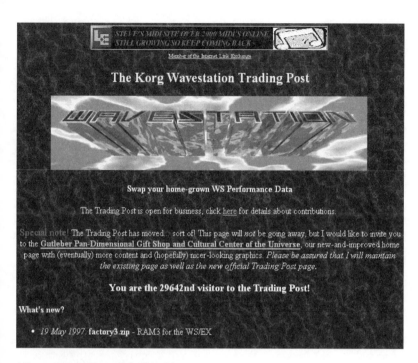

Lots and lots of material
here for Wavestation users

Wavestation Users Mailing List
http://www.magic.ca/~lost/ws.html
The Web site of and access to. Includes a FAQ and some software.

Wavestation Patch Archive
http://www.city.ac.uk/~cb170/ws_subs.html
As it says, swap your WS patches here.

MCC Wavestation FTP site
ftp://ftp.mcc.ac.uk/dir/pub/emagic/SOUNDDIVER/LIBRARIES/Korg/Wavestation/
Editors, MIDI files and more. Log on and browse.

Logic and Logic Audio

The World Wide Logic Users Group
http://www.mcc.ac.uk/~emagic/
Unofficial, but lots of info including hints and tips, a hardware guide,
tutorials, a PC soundcard survey, FAQs, a mailing list section and links.
Excellent support for the Logic user.

MAX

Opcode
http://www.opcode.com/downloads/max/
Upgrades and patches for Opcode's MAX software for the Mac. See also
Cycling '74 (page 146) and IRCAM (page 149) in Software.

Max resources
ftp://notam.uio.no/pub/mac/max/
Lots of Max programs.

Max Resource Guide
http://www.geocities.com/CapeCanaveral/Lab/7055/
A list of Max users, hardware which works with Max, a digest and more.

Berkeley Max FTP site
ftp://xcf.berkeley.edu/pub/misc/netjam/submissions/max/
Another source of archived Max programs.

Theremin

Theremin Home Page
http://www.nashville.net/~theremin/
Ah, the strains of the old wibbly wobbly Theremin rolling gently over an alien landscape. The sci fi movie score writer's favourite instrument. This page contains everything you ever wanted to know about the Theremin – what it is, who invented it – Leon Theremin, of course – where to buy one, who owns one, records they have appeared on...

All you ever wanted to know about the Theremin and the wibbly-wobbly sounds it makes

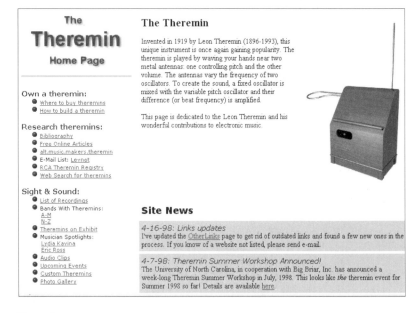

Yamaha

The Unofficial Home Page of the Yamaha MU80 Tone Generator
http://arachnid.ccs.uwo.ca/mu80/
Bit of a mouthful but that's what it is. Info, voice lists, docs in Acrobat format, links and software.

SY-List

http://www.neuroinformatik.ruhr-uni-bochum.de/ini/PEOPLE/heja/sy-list.html

There's a whole wad of data here about all thing SY-ish including info, documentation, FAQs, software, sounds and samples.

Loads here for the SY user, including links to other SY and music resources on the Web

Michael's Page

http://xgmidi.wtal.de/

If you want to know anything about XG, stop by at Michael's Page. There's a mine of information here about hardware, editors, MIDI players and utilities. There's advanced information on SysEx, effects, patches and programming. There are XG & MIDI links, an XG MIDI library and song collection, a discussion area and a composer gallery.

Synth Edit Page

See entry in Shareware, page 170.

Newsgroups and mailing lists

Many music sites have a newsgroup or mailing list which can be easily joined from the site with the minimum of hassle. The entries here give more information about newsgroups and lists and will be particularly useful to anyone looking for a particular list, who wants to join one via email or who wants to start their own.

Email Discussion Groups

http://alabanza.com/kabacoff/Inter-Links/listserv.html

Lots of info for anyone looking for a list or wanting to join one. Topics include a Directory of Scholarly E-Lists, the Liszt Directory of Email Discussion Groups (See Liszt entry below), Publicly Accessible Mailing Lists, the Tile.net List of Internet Discussion Groups (See Tile.net entry below) and you can Search the List of Lists. Lots of help files, too.

Email Discussion Groups/Lists – Resources

http://webcom.com/impulse/list.html

A one-stop information source for information about mailing lists. A mammoth site with wads and wads of info.

FindMail

http://www.findmail.com/index.html

Browse lists by category or do a search. Includes information on how to start your own list.

Findmail contains lots of info about lists

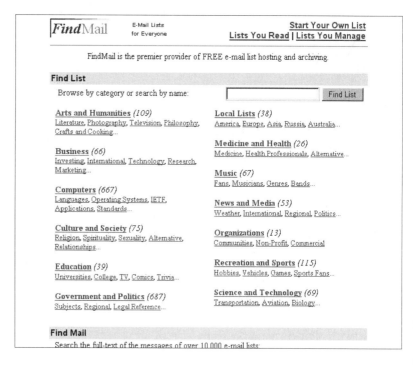

Liszt Newsgroups: uk.music

http://www.liszt.com/news/uk/music/

As it says, a list of newsgroups divided into areas which include alternative, breakbeat, folk guitar, music (general), DJing and R&B. Join a few.

List of Music Mailing Lists

http://www.shadow.net/~mwaas/lomml.html

Lists of lists and more lists of lists. The IMML (International Music Mailing

Lists) covers all 'traditional' musical genres, including classical, jazz, blues, fusion, country, bluegrass, reggae, new age and world music. Also encompasses music composition and the discussion of actual musical instruments including electronic instruments.

PMML (Popular Music Mailing Lists) covers all popular music genres – virtually any style that shows up on Billboard's Hot-100 list with any regularity, including rock, pop, alternative, progressive, metal, folk, r&b, rap, hip-hop, dance, grunge, and all similar, reasonably-popular styles.

UMML (Underground Music Mailing Lists) supports all less well-known musical genres including Acid Jazz, Ambient, BritPop, College Radio, Dark Alternative, DiY, Electro, 'Electronica', Ethereal, Funk, Gothic, Hardcore, IDM, Indie, Industrial, Jungle, New Wave, Punk, Rave, Ska, Synthpop, Techno, Trance, Trip-Hop, and related offshoots. Also contains lists for unknown artists who would normally be included within PMML. A haven for promoting unsigned, unusual and non-commercial musical styles. Bookmark it.

Majordomo
http://www.cis.ohio-state.edu/~barr/majordomo-faq.html
Majordomo is a program which automates the management of Internet mailing lists. If you're thinking of starting your own, this has all the info you need to know

Tile.net
http://tile.net/
Another excellent reference source for information about mailing lists, Usenet groups and FTP sites. You can search by name or look at the details alphabetically.

Music information

As well as the sites which fall neatly – or not so neatly – into the other categories in this chapter, there are many which contain information and support for a range of hardware, software and miscellaneous musical topics. This section loosely brings some of them together, squeezing them into a pigeon-hole with shoehorn determination.

Music and MIDI

Hardware Web
http://homepage.cistron.nl/~nctnico/
An interesting site devoted to MIDI hardware. It contains details of construction projects – MIDI interfaces for various computers, MIDI testers, MIDI switchers and mergers, and even a MIDI keyboard. There are instructions and schematic diagrams, links to other electronics sites and a music hardware FAQ.

An important site for any
musician. Go there!

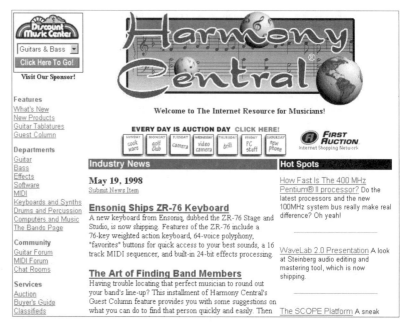

Harmony Central

http://www.harmony-central.com/

A major collection of resources for the musician. Lots of news and comment, communities, software, departments specialising in MIDI, software,
computer music and so on. An essential bookmark.

MIDI Farm

http://www.midifarm.com/

Here's another major MIDI and music site. It contains news, info on MIDI
and audio recording, press releases, a wealth of free MIDI files and music
software, an FTP site and more.

MIDI Farm – another
essential bookmark for every
computer-based musician.

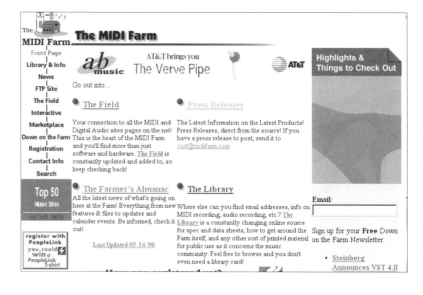

MIDI Users Group
http://www.nowopen.com/mug/

A user group on the Net with a subscription fee – how's about that! There are lists of MIDI files and wads of software much of which is shareware or freeware – but you can't download it, you have to order it! You can subscribe to a free newsletter, however, and the software lists make interesting reading (to discover stuff you can then find on the Web yourself) and there are links to other sites.

MIDIWorld
http://midiworld.com/

A humungous collection of MIDI and music-related information – MIDI basics, synthesisers, software, sounds, MIDI links, MIDI files, MIDI Lab and the marketplace. Each is a large area in itself. For example, the software section lists software by type with a few words about each program and links to relevant sites. There's PC and Mac stuff here. The MIDI Lab is for experimental MIDI music – info and downloads. Check it out.

A humungous collection of MIDI and music-related information. Bookmark it!

Mining Co MIDI Music
http://midimusic.miningco.com/index.htm

The Mining Company has lots of areas within it, each devoted to a specific interest. The MIDI music area has a vast range of features, info, hints and tips, tons of music files, details of MIDI hardware and software, newsgroups and MIDI files.

TidBITS Guide to MIDI and the Macintosh
http://www.leeds.ac.uk/music/Info/MacMIDI/Contents.html

A knowledgeable but eclectic and academic set of information about MIDI and the Mac. Well worth reading for the info, though.

Recording and digital audio

CD-ROM Digital Audio
http://www.tardis.ed.ac.uk/~psyche/cdda/
These pages have been set up primarily to provide information on the ability of various CD-ROM drives to read CD-DA discs – that's 'normal' audio CDs to the rest of us. It contains a fascinating amount of information and includes software both to do the transfer and to analyse the transfer capabilities of CD ROM drives. There's also a list of the results. Consult before buying a CD ROM if you want to lift audio from it.

Creative Musicians Coalition
http://www.aimcmc.com/
'CMC is an international organisation dedicated to the advancement of new music and the success of the independent musician. CMC represents independent artists and independent record labels world-wide. We stock their music albums and videos and make them available for purchase. Furthermore, we encourage listeners to take an active role in the music-making process by participating in an ongoing dialogue with our artists.' Get involved.

CMC – flying the flag for independent artists.

Digital Domain
http://www.digido.com/
A site primarily designed to help audio engineers and musicians make better Compact Discs and CD ROMs. It contains a lot of information about

CD and CD ROM Mastering. Well worth reading if you're burning your own or even if you intend to get a mastering house to do it for you.

Digital Sound Page
http://www.xs4all.nl/~rexbo/main.htm
Geared towards making music with a PC. The site includes getting started articles, information on PC hardware and software, samplers, news items and links.

Fraunhofer IIS
http://153.96.172.2/amm/
MPEG Layer 3? MPEG-2 ACC? The Fraunhofer research reveals all. Lots of info and software to download.

Michael Bramon's Plug-in tracker
http://www.mindspring.com/~michael.bramon/plugies.html
Here's a neat idea. With the exponential rise in the number of digital audio plug-ins, it's very difficult to keep track of them all. Well, for most people, maybe, but not for Michael Bramon who has set out to do just that. He lists every professional plug-in for most of the popular Mac-based digital audio workstations. They are divided by type – VST, TDM. Premiere-compatible, AudioSuite, Native (PPC/Stand-Alone), Logic and MAS (Digital Performer). There's also some choice comments about various digital audio-related topics and, of course, plug-in demos to download.

Mac plug-ins listed by the diligent Michael Bramon.

Pro Audio.net
http://www.soundwave.com/
Join Pro Audio.net and get news, info, discussion groups and more.

Sonicstate
http://www.sonicstate.com/
'The music and pro audio theme park'! Lots of info here, news, views, events, links to synth sites, Mac and PC software to download, Mic database, Tweak of the Week, UK and US studio listings, chat and more. Bookmark and browse.

Band and musician stuff

AMG – All Music Guide
http://205.186.189.2/amg/music_root.html
A rip-snorting database of all recorded music, it claims! Search by album, artist or song name. It also has sub-categories such as Key Artists, Key Albums, Music Styles, a Music Glossary, and Music Maps which trace the development of music Rock and Roll and Blues Rock.

CAVMS
http://www.cavms.demon.co.uk/
Cardiff And Vale Music Services which supplies music tuition to schools. Takes the torture out of teaching.

Grendel's Lyric Archive
http://www.seas.upenn.edu/~avernon/lyrics.html
Looking for the lyrics to a song? There's lots of them here, neatly arranged by artist.

Lyrics to order from
Grendel's Lyric Archive.

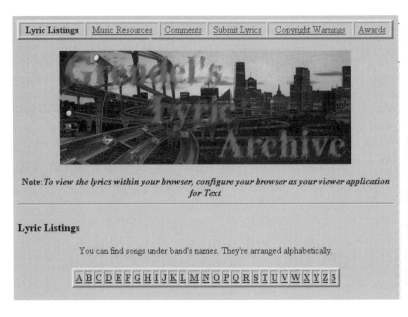

LAMA – Lowland's Alternative Music Archives
See LAMA entry on page 181.

BURBS – British Unsigned Rock Band Site
http://users.powernet.co.uk/cool/burbs.html
Yes, it really is a site where unsigned British bands can promote their music. Each band has an area on the site containing text, pictures and sound samples of their music. There's also a Noticeboard where you can post notes to the Rock Community.

Hyperreal
http://www.hyperreal.org/
Choose alternative. 'Our mission is to give a home to alternative culture, music and expression.'

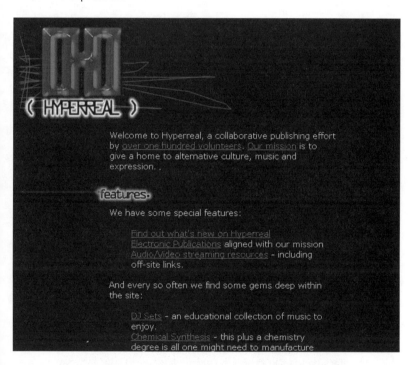

The site includes features, music resources, some software, and there's a section on raves and the drug culture.

Musart
http://musart.co.uk/
Or to give it its full title – the Musart South London & Canterbury Music Web Server. It's a collection of links to music sites and to pages produced by the Canterbury Scene Musicians. Rather garish dayglo colours but lots of info and worth exploring – or even joining if you're in the right area.

Musicians Network
http://www.musiciansnetwork.org.uk/
Beneath the wild, garish Web exterior beats a slightly confused layout containing lots of things of interest to the musician. To quote: 'The com-

bined effect of our overall activities can be summarised as follows: We introduce new music to the listening public, we introduce new music to the recording industry, we provide aspiring bands and individual musicians with the contacts and creative outlets necessary to develop their skills and determine their direction in a fast moving and rapidly changing industry.'

Mutual Music
http://www.mutual-music.com/
A free interactive music industry resource directory with supportive services, promoting contact and co-operation in all aspects of making and distributing music. We could all do with a little extra help. Drop by.

Mutual Music – when you need a little extra help.

National Band Register
http://www.bandreg.com/
This site offers bands the facility to search the world's largest database of band names and band information. Find out if your band name is in use, and if not, register it to help prevent from other bands using it. And what's more, it's free! The site also contains pages of legal advice for bands and information about CDs by the best unsigned bands. The site's magazine, GiG, features music industry news and reviews of unsigned bands' demos, and lots of other goodies.

Partners In Rhyme
http://www.partnersinrhyme.com/
Now isn't that a good name for a company which provides sounds and music for films, TV and multimedia. The site contains lots of info, lots of files and utilities for Mac and PC, a book list and more.

The Rhythm Section
http://www.demon.co.uk/andys/music.html
A guide to the London music scene including bands, listings, agencies, record companies, mail order CDs and music links. It includes the Musicians' Notice Board where you can post messages requesting musicians, announce your gigs and so on.

Route66
http://www.compulink.co.uk/~route66/
A wealth of info for the musician – news and gossip, gigs, bands, composers, producers, magazines, record labels, publishers and loads of links. This is where you get your CiX (see Chapter 5).

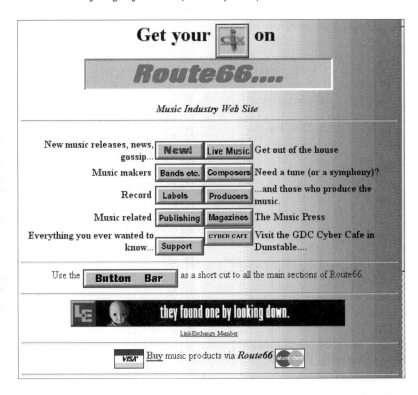

Lots of information for the musician on the journey which takes you down Route 66.

Semantic Rhyming Dictionary
http://www.link.cs.cmu.edu/dougb/rhyme-doc.html
Writing a lyric that must be satiric but nothing outlandish that no one would standish? Then you sure come to the right place.

SheepNet
http://irix.bris.ac.uk/~dm5751/sheepnet/home.html
For those interested in Indie Music – and sheep. Possibly a rare combination of interests. It was originally going to be a page all about sheep and the funny things that you can get up to with them. However, as SheepNet grew, the author started running out of things to say about sheep and so

instead turned to Indie music. Is he trying to tell us something? The site is now primarily a link to many different Indie related sites.

Studiobase
http://www.demon.co.uk/studiobase/
'The only web site dedicated to the UK professional recording industry.' Lists of recording studios, recording engineers and mixers, hire companies, studio design and construction, record companies, mastering, manufacturers, distributors, software, management and rehearsal facilities. Worth a bookmark, don't you think?

Studiobase – dedicated to the UK professional recording industry..

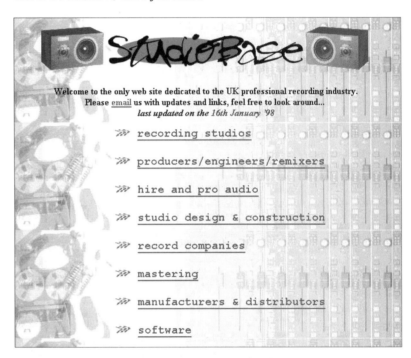

Swarming Midget Band Name Archive
http://www.geocities.com/SunsetStrip/7011/geetar.html
This site lists hundreds of names which could be used for a band and which have, some at least, been constructed by the site author. Some, obviously on an off-day but some, well, hmm, worth looking at...

Computer and electronic music

Computer Music Consulting
http://www.computer-music.com/
A company which has produced music and sound effects for many games. There's lots of info here about making music with computers including several articles to help you get started.

Emusic-L Page
http://sunsite.unc.edu/mcmahon/emusic-l/index.html
EMUSIC-L and SYNTH-L are Internet electronic mailing lists coming from
the American University in Washington, DC. They are a synergistic pair of
discussion groups: EMUSIC-L discusses more esoteric aspects of electronic
music – performance, music theory, composition, and synthesis, while
SYNTH-L discusses the technical details of composing, recording and performing electronic music – hardware, software, recording technique, and
the like. There is some small overlap between the two lists, and many of
the same people may be found on both.

International Computer Music Association
http://music.dartmouth.edu/~icma/
Bringing art and science together. Academic but a little learning never did
anyone any harm. Members' home pages and lots of links including some
to grouped collections of software in sections such as algorithmic composition, MIDI, analysis, multi-track recording, notation, synthesis and so on.
Put on your mortar board and pay it a visit.

Lucy Scale Developments
http://lehua.ilhawaii.net/~lucy/
'Promoting global harmony thru LucyTuning by setting tuning and harmonic standards for the next millennium, and having fun with them.' A
fascinating site for anyone interested in alternate tunings with audio samples and MIDI files to download so you can see – and hear! – what it's all
about.

Links

There are hundreds of URLs in this book. In the following few pages the
sites listed probably point to thousands of sites! Using Link pages is an
excellent way to surf around areas of interest.

Many sites include links and, if applicable, this has usually been mentioned in their description in the other sections of this chapter. Some sites
have a particularly excellent links section and, if applicable, they are mentioned here. The other sites here are made up almost solely of links. Get
ready to trawl.

AMP's MIDI sites
http://www.tiac.net/users/elements/amp/midi.html
Compiled by the Alternate Music Press. MIDI files, Mac and Windows
Utilities plus general music links.

The Anonymous Page
http://www.beotel.yu/~leon/index.html
A veritable plethora of links including over 600 – yes, 600! – on Techno-
related topics. There are also links to AWE sites of interest and virtual
synth sites.

Audio Architect links
http://www.audioarchitect.com/links.htm
Music resources, music magazines, synth sites and on-line music shops.

Audioworks list of Links
http://www.audioworks.com/links/linkindx.htm
Lots of links in lots of categories – hardware, instruments, music software, publications, organisations, bands list, MIDI resources, MIDI archives, guitar resources, records, CD's and Networking.

Lots of categories and lots of links at Audioworks.

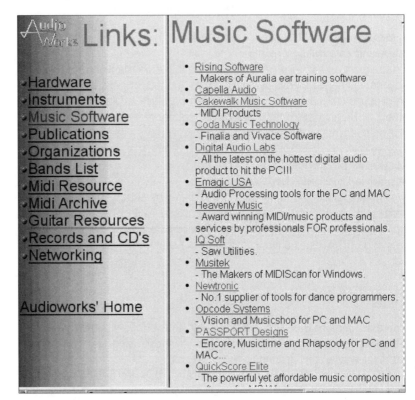

AWE Links
http://www.hyperreal.org/~trout/gear/awe/
Terrible cyan on a white background but if you're an AWE user it's worth squinting and bookmarking the links.

Cakewalk Links
http://www.cakewalk.com/Partners/links.html
Links to friends of Cakewalk. Music hardware and software companies, general computing companies, publications and Web browser software.

Computer Generated Music
http://www.prospernet.com/surfing/music/computergenerated.html
On Prosper Net. Covering all sort of music generated by computer. Fascinating stuff. Surf by one rainy afternoon.

Computer Music Programs for the Macintosh
http://shoko.calarts.edu/~tre/CompMusMac/
A collection of Tom Erbe's favourites with FTP links for downloading. Categories include Csound, Csound helpers, other music flavours (suck it and see), analysis/resynthesis, sound processors, sound generators, sound editors, plug-ins and utilities. See also Tom Erbe Links, page 230.

Cycling '74 Links
http://www.cycling74.com/support/links.html
Mainly Max and IRCAM-related links and a few eclectic ones.

DPS FX Links
http://www.dspfx.com/links.html
A varied collection of links covering all aspects of hi tech music. Check it out.

E-Music FTP Sites
http://sunsite.unc.edu/mcmahon/emusic-l/info-docs-FAQs/other-ftp-sites.html
An HTML version of Piet van Oostrum's monthly posting of e-music-related FTP sites.

E-Music on the Net
http://alt-www.uia.ac.be/u/esger/emusic/emusic.html
A massive collection of links to a wide range of electronic music sites. Categories include electronic and classical music, and there are lots of artist links, too.

Your route to loads of electronic music sites.

Welcome to the page that links you to the wonderfull world of electronic music.

Comments are welcome at esger@uia.ua.ac.be.

All clips are PkZip compressed au files 8 kHz, mono, 8 bit of 60 to 70 seconds

the Interview, Review and Event Calender sections are not empty anymore, check them out!

New links in the Other, buy, and artists(a-c mostly) section. More links coming up when I have time to massively surf the net again

Due to all the non-electronic music links that were added in the ADD URL section I change the adding scheme a bit. Links you add now will be mailed to me and I'll review them before adding them. Due to a lot of work I have to do for my job and for teaching class, it will take quite some time before I can add them

I'm using a stats site since 21/1/97 klik here to look at it

Ebi Ten's MIDI and Mod Links
http://www.tcp-ip.or.jp/~ebiten/
As it says, links to lots and lots of sites carrying MIDI files and Mods. Keep you busy for a while.

Emagic Links
http://www.emagic.de/english/links/
A collection of Emagic-friendly links to hardware and software developers, magazines, Emagic users' home pages and various Emagic support sites.

Entertainment – Music
http://www.ntgi.net/ntg/mall/music.htm
From the NTG Cyber Mall site. A vast collection of over 500 assorted links encompassing all kinds of music plus some hi tech links, too.

Fap7 Shareware/Freeware Links
http://www.realtime.com/~fap7/synthesis/synshare.htm
A collection of links to Mac and PC sites featuring browser plug-ins and audio applications.

FMJ Audio Links
http://hem.passagen.se/fmj/awlinks.html
Links to samples, software, soundcards and synthesisers.

Forrest Fang Links
http://pwp.value.net/ffcal/FFANG6.htm
Musicians, algorithmic music software and experimental music sources.

Fostex Links
http://www.fostex.com/links.html
An impressive collection of links covering Broadcast Media, concerts & events, magazines, music manufacturers, music retailers, musician's resources, nightclubs, publicity, record labels, sound industry, and studios & production.

Fractal Music Composition Software
http://members.aol.com/strohbeen/fmlsw.html
http://members.aol.com/strohbeen/links.html
The first page contains a variety of fractal music composition software and related utilities that you can download and use for exploring new musical ideas, or for composing novel original music. A good paragraph on each piece. Nice. The second URL points to a range of sites about fractal music and fractal music composers.

Tom Erbe Links
http://shoko.calarts.edu/~tre/links.html
A wealth of links ranging from the wild to the wonderful – from the Icelandic Music Page to Nixie Tubes. See also Computer Music Programs for the Macintosh (page 229).

Folk & Celtic
http://club.ib.be/claude.calteux/folk.html
Links to sites with a folk or Celtic connection with many bands and artists.

FX Rentals
http://www.fxrentals.co.uk/links.htm
A long list of links to manufacturers, dealers, various organisations and studios.

Handilinks
http://ahandyguide.com/index.html
Links to everything on the Net listed by subject including music.

Hinton Instrument Links
http://www.hinton.demon.co.uk/#links
A select list of links, synth and MIDI oriented.

Hyperreal Music machines
http://www.hyperreal.org/music/machines/links/
General music, MIDI and equipment sites, official manufacturer sites and unofficial machine sites, publications, retailers and dealers.

ICMA Computer Music Links
http://music.dartmouth.edu/~icma/links.html
Links from the International Computer Music Association, a little academic but covering a very wide range of subjects of relevance to most computer-based musicians. Bookmark and explore at your leisure.

Jamie's Links
http://www.channel1.com/users/jamieo/index.html
A very aesthetically pleasing site with links to MIDI, audio and composer sites.

Jump City Musical Links
http://users.aol.com/Jumpcity/more.html
A vast pot pourri of links from bands to music software.

Kalvos & Damian Music Resources
http://www.goddard.edu/wgdr/kalvos/musres.html
Sites for composers and sites by composers. A lot of links, many rated by K&D. Stop by.

Last Unicorn Links
http://www.lastunicorn.com/links/
Links generally to bands and music magazines.

Leeds University Music Department list
http://www.leeds.ac.uk/music/Menu/mus_depts.html
Links to Music Departments and Institutions in the UK and Ireland and all over the world.

MAZ Bookmarks
http://www.maz-sound.com/links.html
A selection of carefully-chosen links, each with a little comment.

The MIDI Archive
ftp://ftp.cs.ruu.nl/pub/MIDI/index.html
Some docs but mainly lists of links. Put the coffee on and browse.

MIDIBrainz links
http://www.midibrainz.com/extlinks.htm
A small but select offering with a few of off-the-wall links.

MIDI Home Page
http://www.eeb.ele.tue.nl:80/midi/
Some information about MIDI especially useful for beginners plus lots of links to a wide range of music sites and newsgroups.

MIDI Farm Links
http://www.midifarm.com/midifarm/software.asp
The Farm is a good site to bookmark. This link is to software developer sites.

MIDI Web Links
http://www.midiweb.com/links/index.shtml

Business sites, home pages, MIDI sites and personal favourites.

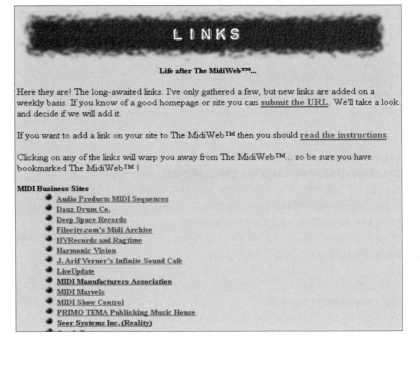

There's lots of browsing to be
had at MIDI Links.

MIDI LINKS

them...if you find a link that doesnt work, tell me

gremlins.mid

If you have Netscape2.0 and the [..............] (10K), you will be able to hear the background midi

The Locker Gnome's MIDI of the Month -Seinfield Theme

I CANNOT GUARANTEE THAT ALL THESE LINKS STILL WORK!!!!

Misc. MIDI files

- "Beat It"
- "Bohemian Rhapsody"
- "Born to be Wild"
- "E.T."
- "Charisma"
- "Do You Want to Know a Secret?"
- "Eine Kleine Nachtmusik"
- "Frankenheaven"
- "Sock Hop"
- "Staying For Blues"
- "Y O.L.S.Hair"

MIDI Links
http://www.wattyco.com/midi2.htm
A mega list of links to all sorts of music and MIDI file-related sites from Hole In The Wall. Definitely one to bookmark and browse through at off-peak hours.

MMF MIDI Links
http://www.geocities.com/~miditastic/midilink.html
Links to free MIDI sites, lyric sites, on-line music shops, MIDI directories and search engines.

Musica Y Technologia Links
http://www.musica-y-tecnologia.com/LINKS/LINKS.htm
A load of links from a Barcelona site but most are in English. Covers music information, magazines, guitars, manufacturers and the Internet.

Newsgroups
http://www.iqsoft.com/Links/NEWSGRPS.htm
Part of the IQS site, this contains newsgroups in the following categories – film and video production, music-related groups, radio, and computers and animation.

Noize Links
http://www.terzoid.com/nzlinks.html
Musical instrument company sites, software sites, MIDI sites, manufacturer contacts, price lists and newsgroups links.

Ocean Beach Great Sites
http://www.geocities.com/WestHollywood/9840/shareware.html
A page subtitled: 'Greatest sites for freeware, shareware and postcardware'. Not music-specific but so many links it'll make your mouse finger ache.

Passport Links
http://206.15.71.82/map/links_f.html
Links from the Passport company covering computer music, hardware & software, pro audio gear, interfaces and sound cards, digital audio tools, artist resources, copyright info, songwriting, lyrics, on-line publishing, legal assistance, agents, musician services, newsgroups, and music styles.

Quadratic Links
http://www.cycling74.com/support/links.html
Links to Mac-related sites. Not music-specific but they include software archives, Mac ezines, magazines, and shareware sites.

Quickscore Links
http://www.infoserve.net/quickscore/related.html
Lots of links from the Quickscore people – music Web sites, music newsgroups, music Listservs, music hardware, music software, and music software dealers.

Lorraine Quirke's Synthesiser and MIDI Links Page
http://www.interlog.com/~spinner/lbquirke/synthesis/links/
Divided into categories – general information FAQs, synthesisers, general MIDI info, do-it-yourself, vintage gear, specific models, corporate sites and info about recent keyboards, librarians and utilities for various machines and platforms, third-party synth products, MIDI files, music industry links, and sound related links.

Redshift Links
http://users.iafrica.com/r/re/redshift/links.htm
A select number of favourite sites covering synths, software, hardware, shops and so on.

Route 66 new Links
http://www.compulink.co.uk/~route66/newlinks.htm
Links which have not yet been incorporated into the Route 66 site. And there are generally a lot of them covering a wide range of topics. There are also links to other pages of links.

Softsynth's Music and Synthesis Links
http://www.softsynth.com/musiclinks.html
Lots and lots of links here. Categories include applications and applets, companies, DSP, editing & processing, information, link sites, MIDI, Net jamming, organisations, people, software synthesis, and standards.

Software Synthesis

http://www.xs4all.nl/~rexbo/pc_synth.htm

Everything you want to know about software synthesis. Almost. Categories include software synthesisers, hardware-accelerated synths, MIDI-to-digital-audio real-time generators, and MIDI-to-digital-audio non-real-time generators. There are links both to sites and to software.

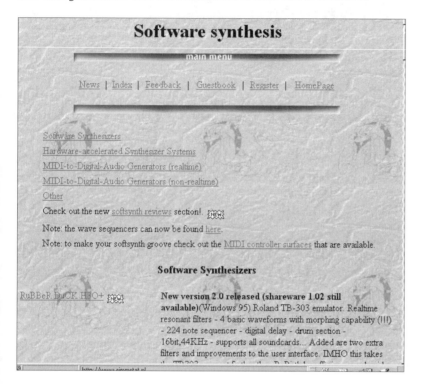

An essential bookmark for anyone interested in software synthesis

Soundcards

http://www.iqsoft.com/Links/soundcards.htm

Another part of the IQS site. Links to soundcard and MIDI interface manufacturers.

The Sound Machine Sound Music Makers Net Directory

http://alpha.science.unitn.it/~oss/sourcese.html

Lists created by the author after years of searching the Net. Divided into catgegories – documents and specifications, instruments, software samples, manufacturers, record companies, retailers and CD pressers

Standard MIDI Files on the Net

http://www.aitech.ac.jp/~ckelly/SMF.html

Lists and lists and lists of sites. You looking for some MIDI files? – start here! And try this:

http://www.cs.ruu.nl/pub/MIDI/MIRRORS/SMF/.

Synth Zone
http://www.synthzone.com/
Designed to ease the search for synth resources on the Net. Loads and loads of links to manufacturers' and user group sites.

Synth user's one-stop resource list.

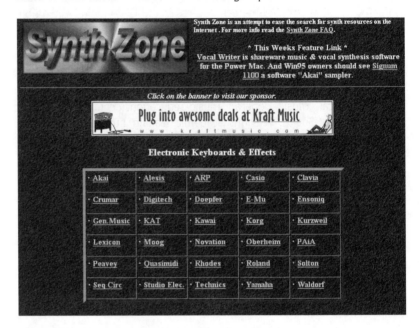

Techno Toys Links for Electronic Musicians
http://www.technotoys.com/links.htm
A great variety of links for computer-based musicians from virtual synths and music software to digital audio editors and plug-ins. Well worth a browse.

Tim Thompson Links
http://www.nosuch.com/tjt/links.html
Grouped under the heading of Interesting Musical Stuff, there are a lot of links here to composition software, electronic music sites and synth sites.

Tripon Music Links
http://members.tripod.com/~hoiyuen/MUSIC.html
Categories include chart/awards, karaoke, lyrics, MIDI, RealAudio, record companies, and Wave files.

Wave Links
http://www.waves.com/htmls/about/links.html
A list to sites of companies which support Waves software, MIDI links, and links to audio and multimedia magazines.

Worldwide Internet Music Resources
http://www.music.indiana.edu/music_resources/

Loads of links divided by category – individual musicians (all genres) and popular groups, ensembles, sites related to performance, composers and composition, genres and types of Music, research and study, and the commercial world of music, journals and magazines.

YAV's Music Links
http://www.yav.com/docs/MusicLinks.html

Computer music and MIDI, computer music studios, algorithmic computer music, classical music, opera, music education, composers, music resources and CSound. A slight academic leaning but many links that other sites miss. Well worth a visit.

YAV's interesting list of sites for a range of musical instruments.

Appendix
Acronyms and smileys

Acronyms

When communications used to take place on-line, users developed short-hand to save typing and to save time. Even though most email is now composed off-line, the practice has remained. Here are some of the more common – and printable – acronyms you may come across in email and newsgroups.

AFAIK	As far as I know
BTW	By the way
CUL	See you later
EOT	End of thread
FAQ	Frequently asked question
FWIW	For what it's worth
FYI	For your information
GAL	Get a life
IKWYM or IKWUM	I know what you mean
IMCO	In my considered opinion
IME	In my experience
IMHO	In my humble opinion
IMO	In my opinion
IOW	In other words
IYSWIM	If you see what I mean
LMK	Let me know
LOL	Laughs out loud
OTOH	On the other hand
PITA	Pain in the ass/arse (depending on which side of the Atlantic you sit)
POV	Point of view
ROFL	Rolls on floor laughing
RSN	Real soon now
RTFM	Read the !#%@$ manual
SIG	Special interest group
SO	Significant other
TIA	Thanks in advance
TTFN	Ta-ta for now
WYSIWYG	What you see is what you get
YABA	Yet another bloody acronym

Smileys

It's difficult to convey emotion in an email and the cyber community has developed a set of smileys or emoticons (emotion icons) for just that purpose. Don't underestimate their usefulness. You may say a remark in fun but if you don't let everyone know that it was a fun remark you may get flamed.

The most common and popular smiley is the smile which can be:

:-) with a nose

or

:) without a nose

You can pepper these liberally throughout any conversation, at the end of a humorous comment or after a remark which was said in jest but which could be taken the wrong way.

Other variations include:

:-> another smile

:-D said with a smile

(:-) full face

;-) wink

The other common one is the sad face:

:-(

(:-(

which can be used to mean unhappy, sorry, disappointed and other such feelings. Then there's the hug:

[ ]

This is usually put around someone's name:

[Julia]

and this:

[[[[Julia]]]]]

means a big hug.

There are lots, lots more but these are the main ones and most of the on-line community knows what they mean. Try to be too clever and not only will no one know what you mean but you'll be labelled a clever dick. Or some other, similar derogatory term in cyberspace parlance **(:-)**.

Index

Making music with digital audio

Direct to disk recording on the PC

Ian Waugh

£16.95 inc P&P

244 x 172 mm * 256 pp
ISBN 1870775 51 1

☆ How to assess your requirements
☆ How to cut through the tech spec jargon
☆ What hardware you 'really' need
☆ How to back up your digital data
☆ How to troubleshoot effectively

The future is digital. Computers have revolutionised the recording and music-making business. Digital audio gives you more flexibility, higher quality and more creative power than multi-track tape recorders. This leading-edge technology is available now to all PC users – and it need not cost the earth.

In this practical and clearly-written book, Ian Waugh explains all aspects of the subject from digital audio basics to putting together a system to suit your own music requirements.

Using the minimum of technical language, the book explains exactly what you need to know about:

☆ Sound and digital audio
☆ Basic digital recording principles
☆ Sample rates and resolutions
☆ Consumer sound cards and dedicated digital audio cards

On a practical level you will learn about, sample editing, digital multi-tracking, digital FX processing, integrating MIDI and digital audio, using sample CDs, mastering to DAT and direct to CD, digital audio and Multimedia

This book is for every musician who wants to be a part of the most important development in music since the invention of the gramophone. It's affordable, it's flexible, it's powerful and it's here now! It's digital and it's the future of music making.

PC Publishing

Tel 01732 770893 • Fax 01732 770268 • email info@pc-pubs.demon.co.uk
Website http://www.pc-pubs.demon.co.uk

Get up and running quickly

Fast Guide to Cubase

Simon Millward
144 pp • 244 x 172 mm
ISBN 1870775 49 X

★ For PC, Mac and Atari
★ Get up and running quickly
★ Covers all the essential elements
★ With hands on projects
★ Save hours searching though the manual
★ With 'Smart move' shortcuts

The Fast Guide to Cubase provides an easy way into the essentials of MIDI sequencing using Steinberg Cubase. The concise text, clear illustrations and no nonsense approach will save you hours of searching through the user manual and cut down on the 'bewilderment factor' felt by many users of music software.

The Fast Guide is the ideal handy companion for all Cubase users – beginners, home enthusiasts, songwriters and composers, recording studios, producers and sound engineers – even the most expert of users will find something of value here. It may be used as a quick reference, with its 'Smart Move' tables, short projects, comprehensive index and glossary, or it can form the basis of more in-depth exploration.

All the essential elements of Cubase are outlined, including the Arrange Window, The Inspector, Key, List and Drum Edit, Quantise, Synchronisation, The Master Track, the MIDI Effect Processor and special chapters on Score and Logical Edit.

The most important features of Cubase have, at last, been condensed into a handy sized book.

PC Publishing

Tel 01732 770893 • Fax 01732 770268 • email pcp@cix.compulink.co.uk
Website http://www.pc-pubs.demon.co.uk

Fast Guide to Emagic Logic

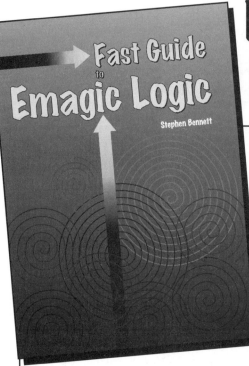

Stephen Bennett

1998 • 240 pp • 244 x 172 mm
ISBN 1870775 55 4

£16.95 inc P&P

★ For Atari, Macintosh and PC
★ Setting up the program
★ Achieve more musical results
★ User tips and tricks
★ Answers to commonly asked questions
★ Reference for most used functions

Making music is the raison d'etre of Emagic Logic, and this book helps you do just that. Logic is a completely flexible, totally user programmable, object orientated program and can be set up in many ways. This has led to its 'difficult' reputation, and It can appear daunting to the beginner, as well as to the more experienced user migrating from a more traditional sequencing package.

This book takes both types of user from the setting up of the program on Atari, Macintosh and PC platforms, right through to using Logic to make music.

This book describes Logic set-ups that will be useful to a typical user, while introducing some of Logic's more esoteric functions. It also serves as a handy reference to some of Logic's most used functions and contains some tips and tricks to help you with your music making.

Contents: Getting started with Logic, Using Logic, The Score editor, The Environment, The Arrange page, The Event list editor, The Matrix editor, The Transport bar, The Hyper editor, Key commands, Other useful Logic information, Logic menus, Preferences and song settings, Glossary, Logic and the Internet, Index

More information from

PC Publishing

Export House, 130 Vale Road, Tonbridge, Kent TN9 ISP, UK
Tel 01732 770893 • Fax 01732 770268 • e-mail info@pc-pubs.demon.co.uk
Website http://www.pc-pubs.demon.co.uk